Some Things

Make A Difference for Youth:

A Compendium of Evaluations of Youth Programs and Practices

American Youth Policy Forum

Institute for Educational Leadership

Table of Contents

Publisher's Foreword

Some things do make a difference for youth! That is the simple and inescapable finding of this unique Compendium of evaluation studies. Ranging over the past 15 years, and covering both government- and foundation-funded efforts to improve the lives of young people, the Compendium rebuts the mindless assertion that "nothing works!" and that investing in human capital is a waste of both public and private resources.

At the American Youth Policy Forum, a nonpartisan professional development organization serving the policy community in the fields of education, training for employment and youth development, we have often been struck by the stark disconnect between the gloomy perceptions of the media and many policymakers and our own vivid, often heart-warming, experiences in visiting actual programs in communities around the United States. The work we have seen of many thousands of talented and committed teachers, counselors, parents, employers, program developers and managers is often inspired. And the record of children and youth whose lives have been transformed is too striking to warrant the notion that society cannot improve the life chances of young people, including those most seriously at-risk of failure.

However, we don't expect the reader to take our word for it, or even the testimony of individual young people whose lives have been changed. We therefore undertook the preparation of this Compendium in order to:

- highlight research findings demonstrating what works—and why;
- share what is known about the specific ingredients of success underlying such programs; and
- provide a useful tool for policymakers and funders who must decide where and how, among a myriad of possibilities, to invest scarce resources.

This knowledge is ably summarized in the introductory essay by Thomas J. Smith, based on his careful reading of the evaluation summaries written by project leader Donna Walker James, assisted by Cheryl Donahue, and Tom's years of deep involvement in the evaluation of social programs.

To be sure, not all the evaluations are as strong and unequivocal as an investor in social programs would desire. Some programs didn't yield demonstrably good outcomes. Implementation of models was often spotty from site to site. Some programs are still too new for clear-cut results, but their designs, based on previous successes, seem most promising. In any case, they deserve inclusion here so that program planners and evaluators may have, in one convenient place, a fairly inclusive survey of the youth field.

Certainly, the science and art of program evaluations need further major refinements and more rigorous accountability. Yet, when all is said and done, the Compendium shows that quite a bit is now known about successful interventions in the lives of young people — whether those interventions take the form of schooling, preparation for employment, out-of-school supports or youth development programs generally.

The American Youth Policy Forum thanks the many scholars, evaluators and program directors who nominated particular studies for inclusion in this Compendium and who reviewed the summaries of their programs or evaluations for accuracy.

We would appreciate readers' referrals of other evaluations unknown to us with a view to publishing a second compendium as the state of knowledge about what works expands and deepens.

Special thanks are due to Kathryn Taaffe Young and The Commonwealth Fund of New York for encouragement and support of the development, production and dissemination of this Compendium, and to the following funders for their continuing support of the Forum's ongoing education mission — *To narrow the gaps between knowledge and policy, between policy and practice*: Pew Charitable Trusts, Charles S. Mott Foundation, Ford Foundation, John D. and Catherine T. MacArthur Foundation, W. K. Kellogg Foundation, Ciba Educational Foundation and General Electric Fund.

— Samuel Halperin
— Glenda Partee

Editor's Note

The 69 evaluation studies and reports of 49 programmatic interventions summarized in this Compendium were recommended for inclusion by a distinguished roster of academic researchers, professional evaluators and youth practitioners. Each of the initiatives evaluated are: published; supported by major legislation or foundation initiatives; nation-wide, multi-state or state-wide; and pilot or demonstration programs.

The briefs in this Compendium are summaries and readers are strongly encouraged to consult the original evaluations, especially for details on methodology. The evaluations were largely conducted by third-party researchers and well-known authors in the youth field and contain far greater detail than we were able to share in a three to four page synopsis. (The Bibliography contains full citations. Copies of the full studies can be obtained through the contacts listed in each summary.)

These Compendium summaries were designed to be readable, accessible, brief and of a consistent format for the purpose of sharing good news about youth, while at the same time not suppressing neutral, inconclusive or negative findings. To present as even-handed a report as possible, we did not include anecdotal information bordering on opinion or advocacy. We also omitted descriptions of the problems or pathologies the intervention was designed to address and the initiative and evaluation goals, assuming that these would be self-evident from the key components and data reported.

Each summary contains up to nine sections:

Overview of the program.

Population—a quick look at the population served, omitting definitions of at-risk youth which vary and may be found in each evaluation using this term.

Evidence of Effectiveness—primarily participant impacts for the full group and subgroups (especially on employment, earnings, academic achievement, further education), with referrals to the main study

for process information, impacts on other groups (teachers, service recipients), or impacts within the program (e.g., in-program attendance as opposed to school attendance), unless little or no participant impacts were reported, in which case process or related information is supplied. To the best of our knowledge, based on the information provided by the evaluators, data are "statistically significant," unless otherwise indicated. Cost/benefit data, where available, are reported in this section.

Key Components—a brief description of the intervention elements, if not covered in the Overview.

Contributing Factors—most subject to inconsistency, this section summarizes whatever information evaluators supplied regarding program results and their likely causes.

Study Methodology—indicates if evaluators used a randomized control group, a comparison group or other methods of evaluation.

Geographic Areas served.

Contact Information for both evaluators and program implementers.

Update—for those cases where program directors reported major program changes since the evaluation.

Each of the nearly 100 evaluators and program directors (listed in each summary under contact information) had an opportunity to review our summary of their work. Their comments and corrections have been incorporated.

As summaries were completed, they were sent to external reviewers: Stephen Hamilton, David Lah, Tom Smith and Julie Strawn. These reviewers were asked to comment on the format of the summaries, suggest corrections or edits, determine if the language was clear and balanced and recommend whether evaluations should be included in the Compendium, or not, based on possible criteria of having a control or comparison group, sufficient sample size, evaluation as an integral part of the project/program, quantifiable data and scientifically responsible third-party evaluators/third party funders of the evaluation. Reviewers' comments were carefully considered and their corrections, edits and recommendations for clearer language were incorporated.

Reviewers also provided, as requested, numerous thoughtful reasons why some studies might be excluded from the publication, including lack of: a control or comparison group, a large sample size, quantifiable participant impact data, third-party or arms-length evaluators, a focus on youth, an unbiased participant selection process, accessible and readable data. While taking into consideration the reviewers' concerns regarding inclusion of studies, the American Youth Policy Forum made a considered decision to include all the summaries and takes full responsibility for doing so. All summaries are included because they provide useful information on program design and principles, even when the findings are inconclusive, and they make a strong argument for further investment in high quality, comprehensive, long-term and controlled evaluation in the youth field.

The Forum will have opportunities to present the Compendium findings and may have follow-up publications to highlight additional evaluations. We trust our readers to judge for themselves the quality of each evaluation and the import of the findings, based on the summary information presented here and on the evaluation itself.

Special thanks are in order to Cheryl Donahue, who wrote the original drafts of half the summaries and filled her office with evaluations for many months. Thank you to each researcher, evaluator, youth policy expert and program director who recommended

studies for inclusion and commented on summary drafts! Thank you especially Margaret Terry Orr, Susan Curnan, Janet Quint and Jean Grossman for your extensive assistance! Thank you external reviewers: Steve, David, Tom and Julie! Thank you internal reviewers: Samuel Halperin, Glenda Partee, Vincent Spera and Lucille Easson! We also benefitted from the sound advice of several of our American Youth Policy Forum Resource Council members: Margaret Dunkle, Mary Gardner Clagett, Paul Barton, Patsy Matthews, Peter Joyce and Richard Murphy as well as from Kathryn Taaffe Young, Cliff Johnson, Marion Pines, Andrew Hahn, Robert Ivry, Shawn La France, Gary Walker, Joan Wills, Barbara Kaufmann, Alan Zuckerman, Edward DeJesus and Kate O'Sullivan. Thanks to each!

— Donna Walker James

Donna Walker James, the Senior Program Associate at the American Youth Policy Forum, has over ten years experience in youth employment, education and development. She was the first administrator of the West Philadelphia Improvement Corps (WEPIC), taught high school English and Social Studies, evaluated Philadelphia school reform, and helped develop the national School-to-Work legislation at the U.S. Department of Labor. In 1994, she started Going2Work, a consulting firm whose clients included the Council of Chief State School Officers, National School-to-Work Learning Center, Scholastic, Inc., Kids and the Power of Work (KAPOW), and Alexandria City Public Schools. She earned a Bachelor's degree in Urban Studies and a Master's in Education, both from the University of Pennsylvania.

Cheryl Donahue is a Washington, D.C. writer specializing in policy and political issues.

Introduction Thomas J. Smith

Researchers and practitioners in the youth field—the network of employment, education and supportive programs that help young people—believe they have now identified the basic principles that undergird effective programs for youth.

The principles involve:

- adult support, structure and expectations;
- creative forms of learning;
- a combination of guidance and rich connections to the workplace;
- support and follow up;
- youth as resources;
- and implementation quality.

The principles are discussed in the pages that follow. These principles emerge from 25 years experience of the youth field, from a careful reading of the evaluation research, both positive and not, and from a wide and consistent body of academic research, especially research about adolescent and youth development. Over time, these principles have been gleaned from and incorporated into numerous youth interventions. And a growing body of evaluations measures their efficacy with increasing precision, confidence and clarity.

The 49 evaluation briefs in this Compendium offer specific examples of programs that embody the basic principles and substantial evidence showing that careful application of the principles can lead to powerful results for youth.

This Introduction has two aims. First, it addresses the social and economic forces confronting youth and the reservations and concerns that currently surround the youth field. Second, it provides the reader an overview of the encouraging contents of this Compendium and their relevance to the formulation and implementation of youth policy.

The Compendium makes a strong argument that the youth field has grown in expertise and wisdom, through the inevitable process of trial and error that accompanies any large and complex undertaking in human affairs. The field holds promise in dealing with the difficult problems that face many of the nation's young people.

Why Doing Something Matters

There should be little disagreement about the urgency of these problems. While most young people navigate the passage from childhood to adulthood without falling prey to drugs, early pregnancy, poverty, crime, family breakup, abuse, violence and school dropout, far too many of our nation's future workers, parents and citizens are blighted by these rampant pathologies.

Young people today also face a far more challenging economic future than they did 20 years ago. Competition in the labor market is far more intense, the range of career paths that can be followed without pursuing some postsecondary education has narrowed, and the earnings prospects of young wage-earners, particularly young men, have eroded sharply.

Most observers agree that the skill requirements of the workplace have increased far faster than public education's capacity to respond to them. The "skills premium"—the value of having better education—and the capacity to apply it successfully in the workplace—is increasing. Indeed, the erosion in earning power experienced by young workers derives in good measure from the widening mismatch between their skill and education levels and the demands of a dynamic labor market.

Some statistics underscore the issue:[1]

- Over the period 1973-95, median inflation-adjusted weekly earnings of full-time employed young adult males under age 25 fell over 31 percent. (Female earnings also fell over 17 percent.)
- In March 1995, young adults, ages 17-24 not enrolled in school, were either unemployed (10 percent), unable to find more than a part-time job (7.2 percent), or working full-time but earning a wage below the family poverty

[1] Source: Professor Andrew Sum, Center for Labor Market Studies, Northeastern University, 1996.

line (26.6 percent earn under $300 a week). Altogether then, almost half of America's young people were experiencing severe problems in the labor market.

- Whereas young men, ages 16-24, earned 74 percent as much as men age 25 or older in 1967, by 1996 that ratio had fallen to only 51.2 percent. For young women, the decline was from 93.7 percent in 1967 to 64.2 percent in 1995.

Moreover, as the recent changes in national welfare policy move toward full implementation, the labor market standing of young people is likely to worsen as increasing numbers of adults compete for many of the same entry-level and low-skill jobs that now are the mainstays of young workers.

These problems, real and urgent enough, have until recently been mitigated by a demographic fact: the slow growth over the past decade in numbers of young labor market entrants. However, the demographic picture has now begun to shift quite radically. Over the decade of 1995 - 2005, America's 18-24 year-old population is expected to explode by 3.5 million, a rise of 14 percent. Some observers have suggested, alarmingly, that this bulge of young people presages sharp rises in the frequency and severity of violent youth crime, redoubling concerns about the social costs of idle and ill-prepared youth. What will be the response of public policy to the deteriorating economic and social situation of much of our youthful population?

Why the Hesitation?

The track record of the youth field contains both successes and disappointments. A focus on the dark cloud of the story, the "null effect" results, is construed by critics and ideologues as "proof" that "nothing works," particularly for at-risk and disadvantaged populations. This has contributed to a deep skepticism about the value and efficacy of publicly-funded investments in youth and to retrenchment in the availability of public funds for this vulnerable population. Indeed, public doubts about the value and limits of most kinds of governmental activity appear to be widening.

These circumstances recall a period 20 years ago when, faced with the influx of baby-boom youth into the labor market and sharply growing youth unemployment, the nation undertook a large-scale initiative to find ways to help youth—particularly the poorly skilled, inexperienced and disconnected youth whose numbers are burgeoning once again—find their way into the labor market and into successful adult roles. Youth programs were researched with considerable optimism and with scientific care. It seemed a fortuitous enterprise: the disciplines of social program evaluation were blossoming. Their findings would provide a firm base from which to proceed to refine social interventions.

What emerged from that knowledge development effort was a mixed picture. Recognizing that the science of human behavior is far more complex and diverse than are the physical sciences, and that the support and nurture of adolescent development is an experimental process requiring constant modification and repeated returns to the drawing board, the developers of social programs for youth still had much to learn. Operating in an highly charged and impatient political environment in which financial support was alternately offered and withdrawn, many program developers and implementers nevertheless stayed the course.

One strong, early lesson, reflected in the rigorous and positive 1982 Mathematica evaluation of Job Corps, was that most youth will not emerge from a short-term, three-to six-month education or employment training program well-equipped to find stable, long-term places in the labor market. On the contrary, the network of supports and handholds that young people need to make their way needs to be rich and multi-pathed, not quick and cheap. The Job Corps model, first begun in 1964 and subject to many refinements and improvements, established that, with proper and patient investment, striking results are possible.

Yet, even as the basic lesson of long-term intervention was documented, national policy turned in 1982 under the Job Training Partnership Act (JTPA) to strategies for young people that emphasized low costs and quickie interventions. Many of these strategies differ little from those used in programs designed for adults. It is unsurprising, therefore, that a study by Abt Associates (1993) found few positive effects for youth in its national evaluation of JTPA programs. These programs reflected much of what had been proven wrong, not right, about interventions on behalf of young people.

What Does Work?

The larger picture, as described by numerous entries in this Compendium, is far more promising. The youth field has grown substantially over the past decade and a half. Running through broad variations in the design of programs and in the quality, scope and extent of evaluations, there is now a quiet stream of good news in the form of research-validated studies that are both persuasive and encouraging. Notable among their solid findings are these:

- Well-conducted mentoring programs, widely available and at relatively modest cost, can significantly delay the onset of drug and alcohol usage among youngsters, and boost school retention and performance (for example, Big Brothers Big Sisters);

- A program that sticks tenaciously with youngsters from welfare families through the high school years can have strong positive effects on their graduation and college attendance rates (Quantum Opportunities Project);
- A 20-year-old training program in California that lifts employment and earnings for participants—many of them young mothers on welfare—through occupational training that incorporates basic skills instruction and an open-exit policy allowing participants to judge for themselves when they are ready to take a job (Center for Employment and Training).

Other entries in the compendium that are, in some cases, smaller-scale and less-well studied also provide mounting evidence for the proposition that Some Things *Do* Make a Difference for Youth.

What are the Guiding Principles?

The evaluations summarized in this Compendium are of programs which incorporate broad and fundamental principles, previously identified by researchers and practitioners in the youth field and intentionally worked into program design. These basic principles can be summed up as follows:

1. **Adult support, structure and expectations:** Effective youth initiatives connect young people with adults who care about them, who serve as role models for them, who advise, mentor, chide, sympathize, encourage and praise. The simplicity of this truth should in no way detract from its great importance. Adults who take time with young people, who advocate and broker on their behalf, who guide them, who connect them to the broader institutions of society, and who have the training and professional skills to help them develop and grow, are central to effective youth policies and programs.

The effectiveness of adults is enhanced by program settings that have coherence and structure, that offer challenging content, that give young people responsibility, and that establish rules and set practical limits for young people. Youth interventions must set clear and high expectations for young people while also carefully supporting each young person so that he or she can attain them. The balances between limits and freedom, expectations and support must be consistently demonstrated and maintained. Committed and skilled adults are essential to guide young people and help them to navigate the world on their own.

2. **Creative forms of learning:** The inculcation of basic and high level skills and knowledge, Secretary's Commission on Achieving Necessary Skills (SCANS) competencies and an on-going desire to learn should pervade initiatives serving

youth. Skills, and the capacity to learn more, are the gateway to success in the labor market and in life beyond the worksite.

Youth program settings need to make learning an ongoing challenge for young people. The joint tasks are to make learning engaging and relevant, with curricula and teaching strategies that are creative, substantive, and attuned to the interests of the learners; and to provide effective pathways for young people to finish high school and move successfully into college or other forms of postsecondary training.

Work-based learning strategies represent one cogent example of this principle. They build upon the incentive quality of work, make learning relevant and self-reinforcing, provide focus and content for teaching, and engage. These strategies, along with active and project-based learning and other innovative curricula and teaching methodologies highlighted in the Compendium, demonstrate how learning can be creative, effective and transforming. The high standards set by the best programs must be extended to the full range of youth interventions.

3. **A combination of guidance and rich connections to the workplace:** Young people want to work. To do so they need connections to jobs and employers, connections which many poor, inner city youth routinely lack. More than that, young people need encouragement, so they can learn to work, pursue part-time or full-time work options, grow as a result of their work experiences, succeed and sometimes (without excessive penalty) fail, and develop sound perspectives on work and careers.

Young people will frequently need support that extends beyond the initial job placement point. Supports include contacts in the employer community, job coaches, mentors, advocacy and structured opportunities (and incentives) to learn on the job, to appreciate the connections between academic, informal and work-based learning and

to become, over time, better and more effective workers.

Through Career Academies and School-to-Work strategies which effectively move youth quickly into authentic work and community service positions, such as those employed by the Center for Employment Training, YouthBuild, Youth Service and Conservation Corps and STRIVE, the youth field has begun to use work—not as a time-filler or an income support mechanism—but as a powerful lever for motivation, learning and growth. These are uses that need to be far more prominently emphasized in youth policy and programs.

4. **Support and follow up:** Young people, and particularly youth whose connections to social institutions may be weak (or adversarial), need time to develop trust and adult and peer relationships in any setting. Indeed, the development of trust may well be as important as the actual provision of service. Such interventions create a setting on which young people can depend and, in some small but important way, become part of. Quantum Opportunities Project currently provides an intervention in which youth graduate, but do not terminate. No phase of the QOP intervention is final. The young person knows he has friends and supports that he can return to as needed. Similarly, STRIVE highlights the importance of follow-up for two years or past a youth's first job, through the difficulties of the initial employer/supervisor relationship and into a second or third more career-oriented placement.

Supportive youth initiatives also make abundant connections to other services for young people, whether in tandem with their own activities or as next steps in a progression of coordinated activities and services (Career Beginnings, Youth Fair Chance). Many youth programs consciously operate as parts of a network. Each part provides a distinctive range of strengths, links to additional supports and services a youngster may need, and then hands off the young person to the next source of help and encouragement. Ideally, referrals are coupled with effective case management. Enlightened youth policy must stress both the quality of individual initiatives and the richness of the support network available for young people. However, referrals to services produced mixed results. In Project Redirection, in-house services, where youth knew the caring adults and had time to develop trust and relationships, worked better.

5. **Youth as resources**: Increasingly, the interventions and their evaluations are also telling us that young people respond positively when they are regarded by adults as resources, as contributors to their own growth and development, not merely passive receptacles requiring services. The encouraging findings from programs such as YouthBuild, Learn and Serve, School-to-Work, and Quantum Opportunities, among others, show us that young people can participate in the solution of many of

their own problems and act as solid contributors to the welfare of others in their communities.

6. **Implementation quality:** The quality of program implementation matters, as we know from experience in every social field. In the studies, especially in demonstration programs, it was usually the case that those sites that most faithfully executed the intended program design showed the best results. The inference is that less positive results are, therefore, not always due to design, but may be due to poor implementation. High quality implementation is thoughtful and well-managed, incorporating evaluation and continuous improvement into design, fostering communication within the program and among all partners and levels of government. It includes quality staff training, materials and the timely and effective use of sufficient resources. Initiatives require both flexibility to adapt to local needs and guidance and support to implement proven design characteristics.

What Follows

This Compendium demonstrates the results for youth of these basic principles when put into conscientious practice. The range and breadth of the youth programs reflect the possibilities and strategies being pursued from coast to coast. We have chosen to classify the 49 initiatives described here in three broad headings:

- **Extending Learning:** Initiatives that extend learning of high level academics and basic and occupational skills beyond traditional classroom-based, time-bound delivery through a combination of variations in: **place**— schools-within-schools, alternative settings (residential education, community and employer sites); **time**—short-term, long-term, extended class periods, summers; **focus**—career-based instruction, entrepreneurial activities, community service and leadership; and **delivery**—active and project-based learning, integration of academic and vocational education and of occupational training and theory, and team-oriented learning.

- **Building on the Community:** Initiatives with a focus on members of the community and their active roles in changing the learning environment for youth and in improving entire communities. Community partners offer fresh perspectives on careers, provide intensive mentoring, build trust and respect through guidance and reassurance and may even offer direct service in participants' homes. Students provide service to their communities while enhancing their academic, occupational and leadership skills.
- **Increasing Retention and Postsecondary Access:** Initiatives which work to retain students in middle schools, high schools and college and on making postsecondary education an option through life skills instruction, career awareness, intensive case management, counseling, financial aid, and referrals to a broad range of services.

Many individual programs, because they are multi-faceted, might be listed under more than one heading. Rather than exploring the cross-connections in depth, we have opted to keep the groupings simple and clear, and summarize each program in a consistent and accessible format.

All the programs we present have been researched. In a number of cases, there is positive and convincing evaluative evidence, not just that the programs embody the principles presented above, but that they work to improve young people s lives. In others, the evidence is less complete or clear-cut, but still indicative of programs that have measurable and salutary effects. Others, experiments that failed to achieve their aims, nonetheless provide touchstone knowledge that informs the thinking and further development of the youth field.

The Compendium depicts a field that continues to search for, and find, effective ways to move youth into responsible citizenship, labor market success and self-sufficiency. Its findings underscore the rich potential of investing in the future of our young people. In an era of pragmatism and limited resources, it illustrates the varied choices we now have available for making those investments more soundly than ever before.

Thomas J. Smith, a social policy consultant based in Philadelphia, has more than 20 years of experience in the human and social services, with special expertise in the area of youth development and the labor market. Over 16 years at Public/Private Ventures, he designed and managed both research and field demonstration projects, including P/PV's Summer Training and Education Program. Smith has also managed projects on national service, implementation of private industry councils, and school-based partnerships. He is the author of more than a dozen studies and articles on a broad array of issues regarding youth employment, education and development.

Section I
Extending Learning

*Initiatives that extend learning of high level academics and basic and occupational skills
beyond traditional classroom-based, time-bound delivery through a combination of variations in:*
place*— schools-within-schools, alternative settings
(residential education, community and employer sites);*
time*—short-term, long-term, extended class periods, summers;*
focus*—career-based instruction, entrepreneurial activities, community service and leadership; and*
delivery*—active and project-based learning, integration of academic and vocational education and
of occupational training and theory, and team-oriented learning.*

Academy of Finance

A Summary of:

An Evaluation of the Academy of Finance: Impact and Effectiveness

December 1987, Academy for Educational Development (New York, NY) by Margaret Terry Orr, Norm Fruchter, Earl Thomas and Lynne White

Employment and Educational Experiences of Academy of Finance Graduates: Final Report

November 1990, Academy for Educational Development (New York, NY)

(Both evaluations funded by American Express Foundation.)

Overview

Academies are schools-within-schools in which students take several classes together with the same group of teachers. Academies focus on a career theme, in this case financial services.

The National Academy Foundation (hereafter NAF) supports specialized career academies nation-wide, including 78 Academies of Travel and Tourism (see pp. 6–8), 114 Academies of Finance (hereafter AOF), and 10 Academies of Public Service. Each Academy follows the NAF model and uses NAF curriculum. Academies feature two to four years of course work focused on the Academy's career theme combined with a paid summer work experience.

> **POPULATION**
>
> Of the 196 AOF graduates interviewed by telephone in 1990, 49 percent were from minority groups (22 percent African American, seven percent Hispanic, and 20 percent Asian or "other"), 53 percent were female, all had participated in the full two-year AOF program and 84 percent had had an internship at a financial services firm or related company. Between 1984 and 1989, 747 students graduated from AOF programs in New York City.

Evidence of Effectiveness

Academy for Educational Development (hereafter AED) researchers reported the following 1990 educational and employment outcome data based on telephone interview of graduates of seven New York City Academy sites (in individual high schools). An analysis of the college degree completion and employment data on the numbers working, type of work and wages, should take into account the fact that the majority of AOF graduates were still in college at the time of the survey. Of AOF graduates:

- 95 percent pursued post-secondary education; 89 percent went on to a four-year college or university and 6 percent enrolled in a two-year college or other training program
- 33 percent (of those in two or four-year colleges) had completed a degree by the time of the interview
- 68 percent were employed, and, of those, about 50 percent were working in financial services or a related

field, 21 percent were looking for work, 10 percent were not working and were not looking for work
- 25 percent reported that they would like to have a job in the financial services field, but half of these were unable to find one and the rest had encountered difficulties, but were still seeking employment
- 77 percent of those working were in jobs paying $7.00 per hour or more (in 1990 dollars) and 39 percent were earning $10 per hour or more
- those from earlier graduating classes were more likely to be working full-time and earning over $10 per hour

Additional survey information included: (1) students' assessments of various components of the program and how much these components helped them with career and college decisions and, (2) work place supervisors' views of the program.

Key Components

AOF, started in 1982 in one New York City high school by Shearson-Lehman Brothers and the American Express Foundation, is a collaboration between school systems and the financial services industry to prepare high school youth for financial service careers. The major source of financial support for the development and expansion of this program currently comes from the Travelers Group. AOF operates through public high schools as a school-within-a-school offering an intensive two- to four-year instructional program in finance studies and a paid internship in a financial services firm. Students pursue regular academic courses in their school and also take AOF courses with other AOF students in the classes which are taught by NAF- and industry-trained teachers. The program provides:

- an interrelated series of required courses exploring the world of finance (i.e. Banking and Credit, Securities Operations, Accounting, Financial Planning, International Finance)
- a curriculum for each course, developed by NAF with the assistance of industry experts and revised to keep pace with the field (this curriculum is provided through a software program designed to manage the development and use of the curriculum)
- a series of special program events such as business tours and on-site workshops
- a paid summer internship developed by financial service firms working with the local program director
- training for teachers and program staff through NAF yearly conferences, internships at financial services companies, and college-level finance courses, usually provided tuition-free
- additional technical and financial support from a local business advisory board

"The Academy has successfully established a model for a productive school/business collaborative which motivates and prepares local youth for entry into the financial services."   AED

Contributing Factors

Employer Involvement

AED: "The Academy of Finance, both nationally and locally, does an excellent job of mobilizing formal and informal assistance from various finance-related sectors. The officials of the American Express Foundation and the American Express Corporation initiated much of the by-now substantial business support of the program." Travelers Group and its subsidiaries currently provide extensive support for activities of the AOF throughout the United States which includes designating key local Travelers affiliates to initiate other business involvement, and thereby spur the creation of formal advisory committees composed of representatives from local financial services companies (such as banks, brokerage firms, investment companies and insurance companies). These advisory committees, pledge and solicit internship slots, assist NAF staff with curriculum development efforts, provide staff development activities for central staff, and provide publicity and a series of linkages to local businesses and participants' parents.

Integrated Curriculum

AED: "All persons involved in the program—managers, coordinators, teachers, business sponsors and internship supervisors—generally thought the program did an excellent job in teaching financial concepts and introducing students to the world of finance and economics. Program alumni . . . indicated that their Academy of Finance courses were a good preparation for college. Program coordinators and managers agreed that the program was excellent preparation for entry-level financial service jobs and for college and other postsecondary education programs. Business sponsors all rated the interns' knowledge of the financial services industry as good . . . Program coordinators and managers indicated that the curriculum needs to be adapted to local financial service examples" and to be constantly updated and revised. Currently, NAF is able to deliver updated curriculum more rapidly as a result of changing its curriculum development methodology working with CTB/McGraw Hill (a publisher of assessment and curriculum materials).

Internship/Work

Seventy percent of graduates liked the internship best and 73 percent rated the internship as "somewhat" or "very helpful" in their career decisions. The best internship practices included weekly seminars, rotating interns though several departments, feedback from supervisors midway through the internship as well as at the end and required essays on the work experience. Work experience lasting more than six weeks and possibly extending into the school year have become common practice through the NAF Academy program.

Guidance/Support

AED: Substantial numbers of AOF seniors had career and/or college plans related to finance. However, "a few students and alumni noted that they would benefit from additional advice and guidance about their post-high school plans." Recommendations included incorporating career and college counseling into AOF and formal program support for following up graduates and organizing an AOF alumni organization. (NAF now puts a greater emphasis on career and college counseling and many local AOF alumni groups have been formed. A national effort to establish an alumni network is being developed.)

Study Methodology

The 1987 evaluation included interviews and surveys of selected staff and students from Fort Lauderdale, Minneapolis and New York City. The 1990 evaluation used phone interviews of 196 graduates from a randomly selected sample of 525 graduates (two sets of graduates were used as samples, as many students were difficult to reach) from the seven participating New York City programs.

Geographic Areas

AOF has expanded to 114 high schools in 64 cities. Over 7,000 students are enrolled.

Contact Information

Research Organization
Academy for Educational Development
100 Fifth Avenue
New York, NY 10011
(212) 243-1110, Fax (212) 627-0407

Evaluator for AED
Margaret Terry Orr, Associate Professor
Teachers College, Columbia University
525 W. 120th Street, Box 106
New York, New York 10027
(212) 678-3000/3728, Fax (212) 678-4048

Implementing Organization
John Dow, Jr., President
National Academy Foundation
235 Park Avenue South, 7th Floor
New York, NY 10003
(212) 420-8400, Fax (212) 475-7375

Academy of Travel & Tourism

A Summary of:

Academy of Travel and Tourism: 1993-1994 Evaluation Report

March 1995, Academy for Educational Development (New York, NY) by Margaret Terry Orr and Cheri Fanscali, with Carolyn Springer

(Evaluation funded by National Academy Foundation, through a grant from American Express Foundation.)

Overview

Academies are schools-within-schools in which students take several classes together with the same group of teachers. Academies focus on a career theme, in this case travel and tourism.

The National Academy Foundation (NAF) supports specialized career academies nation-wide, including 78 Academies of Travel and Tourism (hereafter AOTT), 114 Academies of Finance (see pp. 3-6), and 10 Academies of Public Service. Each Academy follows the NAF model and uses NAF curricula. Academies feature two to four years of course work focused on the Academy's career theme combined with a paid summer work experience.

POPULATION

There are 78 AOTTs nation-wide serving 4,700 students in 1997. The six schools evaluated served about 300 students recruited during their sophomore year. Eighty-seven percent were minority and 75 percent were female. About 25 percent spoke Spanish or another language exclusively at home. About 25 percent said that neither parent (or guardian) was working and three-fifths reported that neither parent had attended college. AOTT targets students who are not necessarily college-bound and who do not have clear career plans. Statistics indicate, however, that 90 percent of AOTT graduates do enter college after high school graduation.

Evidence of Effectiveness

"Most important, Academy of Travel and Tourism graduates are well prepared for pursuing postsecondary education and employment, as demonstrated by the success of these graduates within five years of program completion. Almost all graduates continue in postsecondary education, at least part-time, and most are employed, at least part-time." **AED**

The Academy for Educational Development's (hereafter AED) evaluation looked at education and employment outcomes for students in six AOTTs in two cities. Pre- and post-tests and survey information provided the following information:

- 90 percent of AOTT graduates enrolled in postsecondary education, 88 percent full-time
- 9 percent of AOTT graduates who enrolled in a postsecondary program attended two-year colleges, 49 percent attended four-year colleges, and 2 percent enrolled in other training programs
- 50 percent of AOTT students reported that they were working at least part-time with their internship employer right after graduation from high school and 32

percent were still working for these employers by mid-Fall of the following school year
- 40 percent of AOTT graduates worked in travel and tourism-related jobs after graduation
- nearly 66 percent of AOTT graduates reported that AOTT helped them in their careers a "great deal" or a "good amount"

One comparison with a group of students not in an AOTT was made:

- 70 percent of students in the AOTTs completed school vs. 46 percent of the non-AOTT group used for comparison

AED also interviewed worksite supervisors of AOTT interns, who reported that:

- 90 percent of the interns were the same or better than other entry-level employees on their ability to work with others, initiative, job-readiness, and self-discipline; 80 percent were the same or better in the areas of confidence, knowledge of the travel and tourism industry, and productivity; and over 66 percent were the same or better in problem-solving and academic skills
- 90 percent of the AOTT students had excellent or good personal characteristics such as character, relationships

with other employees, and attitude; and 78 to 82 percent rated highly on the quality and quantity of their work performance

AED also found that minorities and women, who have been under-represented in the management levels of the travel and tourism industry, were as likely as other students to pursue further education and employment in travel and tourism.

Key Components

AOTT students:

- take traditional academic classes (geography, math, English, science, and social studies) combined with career theme-related classes in travel, hospitality and tourism
- take college-level courses in travel and tourism, computing, or management in their senior year (taught by college faculty at the high school or at the college. AOTT pays for books and tuition is usually waived by the college.)
- have a paid, relevant work experience usually in the summer between their junior and senior years
- have structured field trips (e.g., to the International Hotel, Motel and Restaurant Show; the United Nations Plaza Hotel; walking tours of the city; "behind the scene" facilities tours of airports, cruise ships, hotels, etc.; trips to the State Capitol to learn about government's role in the industry)
- may attend annual AOTT student conferences in various cities

- may participate in travel clubs

In addition to the program model and curriculum, NAF provides oversight, technical assistance and quality control. Locally, AOTT is managed by a district-wide program director and funded by the local board of education and the travel and tourism industry. If implemented in several schools in one district, an Academy director receives release-time to assist with program implementation at the local sites. The national program and each local site is overseen by advisory boards consisting of senior executives in the travel and tourism industry (e.g., American Express, American Automobile Association, Marriott Hotels, Inc., American Society of Travel Agents, Alamo Rent-A-Car, American Hotel and Motel Association, Walt Disney Attractions).

Contributing Factors

Integrated Curriculum

A theme-based curriculum combined with relevant work experience challenged students and held their interest. About two-thirds of seniors who responded to the 1993 survey said their AOTT course work was more challenging than their other courses, and the materials and information more interesting. Almost 60 percent said they participated more in their AOTT classes.

Internship/Work

Paid internships gave students more confidence in their ability to actually work in the field and helped them improve their interaction with adults. They

also exposed students to career options of which they were previously unaware.

Workplace Mentors

In addition to the student internship supervisors, a program was developed to provide students with workplace mentors. To augment basic workplace skills and further the student/mentor relationship, a series of workplace problem-solving activities for mentors to do with students were developed. Both students and program officials believed the mentor component added greatly to the student's internship experience.

Staff Training and Support

In the summer before the AOTT program begins in a local site, teachers receive 2-3 weeks of staff development based on the NAF model. They visit local travel and tourism businesses, meet affiliated college staff, and learn how to use NAF's AOTT curriculum. NAF holds an Annual Institute for Staff Development for teachers from each school, local program directors and advisory board members. During the year, AOTT teachers meet informally several times a week with other AOTT teachers and the teacher coordinator. In communities with multiple AOTT sites, the coordinators meet with the program director monthly.

Study Methodology

AED administered various tests and surveys to AOTT participants and, where possible, to a comparison group of students. Evaluators also reviewed program records, visited school sites, observed program operations directly, and conducted interviews with program staff and internship supervisors.

Geographic Areas

NAF sponsors academies in 30 states, including 78 AOTTs. AED evaluated AOTT in six schools: five in New York, NY and one in Dade County, FL.

Contact Information

Research Organization
Academy for Educational Development
100 Fifth Avenue
New York, NY 10011
(212) 243-1110, Fax (212) 627-0407

Evaluator for AED:
Margaret Terry Orr, Associate Professor
Teachers College, Columbia University
525 W. 120th Street, Box 106
New York, New York 10027
(212) 678-3000/3728, Fax (212) 678-4048

Implementing Organization
John Dow, Jr., President
National Academy Foundation
235 Park Avenue South, 7th Floor
New York, NY 10003
(212) 420-8400, Fax (212) 475-7375

Alternative Schools

A Summary of:

Helping At-Risk Youths: Results from the Alternative Schools Demonstration Program

March 1997, Mathematica Policy Research, Inc. (Princeton, NJ) by Mark Dynarski and Robert Wood

(Evaluation funded by U.S. Department of Labor.)

Overview

In 1988, the U.S. Department of Labor (hereafter DOL) funded the establishment and evaluation of alternative high schools in seven urban school districts. Referred to as the Alternative Schools Demonstration Program (hereafter ASDP), it tested whether small high schools focusing on at-risk youths could raise high school graduation rates, improve basic skills, and increase the possibility that students continue on to college or to employment.

ASDP is one of three DOL initiatives to study ways to help at-risk youth using Job Training Partnership Act funds. The other two initiatives (pp. 48-50 and 73-76 of this report) are the Summer Training and Education Program (STEP)—for younger in-school youth—and JOBSTART—for older high school dropouts. While the other two initiatives involved collaborations with public schools, ASDP focused directly on improving education for at-risk youths who had been unsuccessful in regular high school settings, were about to or had recently dropped out and who wished to earn a regular high school diploma.

POPULATION

At all three ASDP evaluation sites, the average age was 17, roughly equal numbers of males and females were served, 9th grade was the highest average grade completed, and over half the students were dropouts (53 to 62 percent) when they applied to the schools. Other factors varied by site. At Stockton, students were: 45 percent Hispanic, 20 percent African American, 8 percent Asian, 8 percent "other"; 20 percent did not speak English at home; 14 percent had a child; and 54 percent were from families receiving welfare. At Wichita, students were: 9 percent Hispanic, 39 percent African American, 2 percent Asian, 5 percent "other"; 3 percent did not speak English at home; 15 percent had a child; and 39 percent were from families receiving welfare. At Cincinnati, students were: 82 percent African American, 16 percent Caucasian; 37 percent had a child; and 61 percent were from families receiving welfare.

Evidence of Effectiveness

"The evidence presented in this report shows that alternative schools can help youths stay in and complete high school . . . The evidence also shows that alternative schools will not necessarily have the desired effects."   **Mathematica**

Three schools were included in this evaluation. The Stockton, CA "Model Alternative High School" substantially increased the attendance, credits earned and graduation rates of its students. Compared to a control group, Stockton Alternative students:

- two years after admission, had attended school 54 more days and earned 1.5 more credits, an increase in attendance and credits earned of more than 60 percent

- four years after admission, graduated from high school at higher rates
- scored slightly better on basic reading and math tests, although the difference was not statistically significant

The Wichita, KS "Metro-Midtown Alternative High School" did not increase the attendance, credits earned or graduation rates of its students. Compared to a control group, students at Metro-Midtown:

- attended about the same number of days, earned about the same number of credits, and graduated at about the same rate
- scored almost a full grade level lower on basic reading and math tests

At both the Stockton and Wichita sites, rates of employment and college attendance were about equal (about 15 percent of students in the treatment and control groups reported having attended college three years after applying to the alternative schools) and no consistent effects were shown on arrest rates, drug use, pregnancies or welfare receipt. Twenty percent of Stockton students and 30 percent of Wichita students earned GED certificates.

The limited data available on the Cincinnati, OH site indicated that, relative to a control group two years after admission, students in the alternative school had somewhat higher attendance and graduation rates. Ten percent of Cincinnati students earned GED certificates.

As a whole, "dropout rates are in the range of 40 to 50 percent for ASDP alternative high school students." Dropout rates at the Cincinnati site were 83 percent for the treatment group and 88 percent for the control group.

Key Components

ASDP schools were modeled after "High School Redirection," an alternative high school in Brooklyn, NY that has been operating since the early 1970s, and were to include these key features:

- located separately from other high schools, in low-income areas
- an intensive remedial reading program for students with serious literacy problems
- operated autonomously from the school district's central office
- offered a regular high school diploma
- governed by local boards of education, and staffed by supervisors and teachers who met the district's normal standards

- on-site child care (two schools did not offer on-site child care, one of these provided buses to the child-care site)
- limited extra-curricular activities
- served 500 students (only the Stockton school had over 500 students, the others had 200 to 300)
- admitted students by referral and were not allowed to deny students based on past truancy or academic problems

High School Redirection, again the model for ASDP, emphasized basic skill development while promoting aspects of personal development through close student-teacher relationships with teachers acting as advisors and mentors and peer group support.

Contributing Factors

Alternative Educational Setting
An earlier impact study[1] indicated that "The positive climates of the schools may have been attractive to students who had not succeeded in comprehensive high schools."

Caring Adults/Peers
The schools tended to have small class sizes, high levels of attention for students from teachers and staff, and group meetings in which students talked with teachers and other students about personal and social problems.

Standard Curricula
The same early impact study also found that schools did not expose students to challenging curricula;

instead they used standard curricula, focused on basic skills, and allowed students to accumulate credits flexibly by dividing course work into small units and giving students credits as they moved through the units. Although at least one school increased attendance, credits earned and graduation rates of the students it served, skill levels were not improved beyond a basic level, if at all.

Length of Time to Complete Education
Three factors—low graduation rates (estimated at under 25 percent for the three sites evaluated), high dropout rates (40 to 50 percent at Stockton and Wichita, over 80 percent in Cincinnati) and high GED receipt (especially given the emphasis on the regular high school diploma)—are likely due to older

"[T]he standard curricular approaches may have frustrated those same students who had not succeeded in regular classrooms in the past. Specifically, the standard approaches typically did not allow students to accumulate credits quickly and make up time toward earning a diploma. . . . they may have needed to attend for three years or more . . . many may not have had the patience to remain in high school that long."   Mathematica students (on average over 17) being unwilling to spend substantial time to complete their education, especially when the school closely resembles the high schools they left originally.

Level of Disadvantage

The Cincinnati site had the highest dropout rates of the three sites in the evaluation for both the treatment and control groups (83 and 88 percent). Cincinnati students were also much more disadvantaged: they were older (17.5 vs. 16.8 and 16.9 years), farther behind in grade level (highest level completed 9.2 vs. 9.3 and 9.4), more likely to have already dropped out (62 vs. 55 and 53 percent), to be in families receiving welfare (61 vs. 54 and 39 percent) and to have their own children (37 vs. 14 and 15 percent).

Quality of Implementation

Implementation of the alternative school design recommended by DOL varied broadly across sites. Due to these variances, five of the seven schools could not be included in the full evaluation. Cincinnati was added late. The Los Angeles school did not follow the same model as the others. One site was not able to open. Recruiting sufficient students for random assignment was a difficulty at all except the Stockton school, which was also the only school with the requested 500 or more students. Two schools had enrollment so low they could not be evaluated through random assignment. Misunderstanding of the evaluation also led to contamination of some of the control groups by school personnel.

Study Methodology

This report focuses on academic, economic, and social outcomes for students at two of the seven sites in the demonstration (924 students in Stockton, CA and 358 students in Wichita, KS). A more limited analysis was conducted for the Cincinnati, OH site (912 students). Impacts were measured using random assignment, with applicants to the alternative schools assigned randomly to a treatment group, which was admitted to the ASDP-sponsored school, or to a control group, which was not. Data was collected through school records, surveys, and standardized basic skills tests. Due to extensive control group contamination (control group members admitted to the alternative schools) all impact analysis for Stockton is only for Cohort I students and may still be underestimated.

Geographic Areas

Los Angeles and Stockton, CA; Denver, CO; Wichita, KS; Cincinnati, OH; Newark, NJ; and Detroit; MI.

Contact Information

Research Organization
Mark Dynarski
Mathematica Policy Research, Inc.
P.O. Box 2393
Princeton, NJ 08543-2393
(609) 799-3535, Fax (609) 799-0005

Funding and Monitoring Organization
David Lah
Office of Planning and Research
Employment & Training Administration
U.S. Department of Labor, N-5637
200 Constitution Ave., NW
Washington, DC 20210
(202) 219-5472, Fax (202) 219-5455

---

[1] M. Rubinstein, _Giving Youth a Second Chance: The Evolution of the Alternative Schools Demonstration Program_, (Washington: Policy Studies Associates, 1995).

Career Academies

A Summary of:

Benefits and Costs of Dropout Prevention In A High School Program Combining Academic and Vocational Education: Third-Year Results from Replications of the California Peninsula Academies

Winter 1989, University of California, Berkeley by David Stern, Charles Dayton, Il-Woo Paik and Alan Weisberg (*Educational Evaluation and Policy Analysis*, Vol. 11, No. 4, pp. 405-416)

(Evaluation funded by William and Flora Hewlett Foundation to Policy Analysis for California Education (PACE).)

Career Academies: Partnerships for Reconstructing American High Schools

(Chapter Four—Evaluating the Academies), 1992, by David Stern, Marilyn Raby and Charles Dayton, Jossey-Bass Publishers

Career Academies: Early Implementation Lessons from a 10-site Evaluation

July 1996, Manpower Demonstration Research Corporation (New York, NY) by James J. Kemple and JoAnn Leah Rock

(Evaluation funded by a consortium of U.S. Departments of Education and Labor and 14 private foundations.[1])

Overview

Career Academies are "schools-within-schools" in which students (usually 30 to 60 per grade in grades 9-12 or 10-12) take several academic and career theme-related classes together. Academies prepare young people for postsecondary opportunities and for careers. The many Academies covered in these three sources have a variety of career themes and may place different emphases on dropout prevention, career preparation, and college preparation or pursue all three.

POPULATION

This summary includes studies covering a variety of Career Academies with varying student characteristics. The 10 sites selected for the MDRC evaluation were generally located in large school districts enrolling substantially higher percentages of African American and Hispanic students than the national average. Participating school districts also had higher dropout rates, unemployment rates, and percentages of low-income families than the national average. In general, Career Academies initially tended to target students at risk of dropping out, but have evolved over time to include a broad cross-section of students, including those doing well academically.

Evidence of Effectiveness

"The evaluations . . . suggest that it is possible to achieve the goals of dropout prevention and college preparation at the same time, in the same program."
Career Academies

Career Academies date back over 25 years. The MDRC report focuses on the early stages of its evaluation of 10 Career Academies and primarily provides qualitative descriptions of sites in the study and characteristics of students and teachers. It also includes the following information on patterns of student enrollment and maintenance in the program over a two-year period and early perceptions of academy and non-academy teachers:

- 84 percent of the students selected to participate in Career Academies actually enrolled; 73 percent of those who enrolled were still participating two years later
- Career Academy teachers placed a higher emphasis than did non-Academy teachers on personalized relationships with students (70 vs. 51 percent) and on responsibility and caring for students (67 vs. 55 percent)

Later stages of the MDRC evaluation will examine effects on student achievement, retention in school and success after graduation.

The 1989 "Benefits and Costs" paper reports evaluation results for 11 California academies. The study used a combination of performance measures—attendance, credits earned, grade point average, number of courses failed, and the probability that the student left high school during the given year—to indicate whether the performance of academy students was significantly better or worse than comparison students.

- Of 270 tests of combined performance measures, 61 show significantly better performance by academy students, while 11 show the comparison students did significantly better. Better performance by academy students is strongest in the first year of academy participation; performance remains better over subsequent years, but the difference in performance narrows.

The number of dropouts was estimated, along with the costs and economic benefits to society:

- at the eight academies for which graduation rates were available, 29 of the 327 students expected to graduate were estimated to be saved from dropping out

- the social _benefit_ of saving each dropout was estimated to be $86,000; the social _cost_ of saving each dropout over three years was estimated to be $41,000; the _net_ benefit to society was estimated to be $45,000 per dropout for a total estimated net benefit of $1.0 to $1.3 million

Career Academies by Stern, Raby and Dayton provides participant outcome information from quasi-experimental evaluations of several early Career Academies:

- Where dropout prevention was the primary goal, Career Academy students had lower dropout rates than students in the two original California Peninsula Academies (2 vs. 10 percent in 1982-83 and 4 vs. 11 percent in 1983-84).
- Some Academies placed more emphasis on college, while others placed more emphasis on career preparation. Results reported in this book on participants' likelihood to engage in postsecondary education are mixed. A 1987 evaluation of the original two California Peninsula academies found academy graduates' postsecondary enrollment considerably higher than a comparison group (62 vs. 47 percent). More than two years later, the educational objectives of academy graduates were still higher than the comparison group (55 vs. 22 percent expecting to complete at least a four-year degree), but these differences disappeared in 1989 and 1990 surveys. Relative to a comparison group, Philadelphia business academy students were more likely to work (64 vs. 42 percent) than to be in school (18 vs. 35 percent).
- In 1989 and 1990 surveys at California Peninsula Academy, former students reported working three more hours per week after graduation than a comparison group.
- In a 1986-87 evaluation of three business academies in South Philadelphia, graduates were as likely to be employed as graduates of other business programs, but "a significantly larger fraction of business academy graduates worked for companies that were official business academy sponsors." As those companies represented many of the "blue-chip employers in the city, this advantage is substantial."

Key Components

"A career academy curriculum combines academic and technical content. Both are essential, and the two are integrated, showing the relationship between academic skills and real-world jobs."
Career Academies

Career Academies each have:

- a career theme, such as health, business and finance or electronics, which is usually determined by local employment opportunities and evidence of growing demand for such expertise in the marketplace
- traditional academic classes (such as mathematics, English, science, and social studies) combined with career theme-related classes, innovative instructional methods and, often, project-based learning
- local employers from the career field who help plan and guide the program, serve as mentors and provide work experience for the students
- an advisory group including these local employers,

Career Academy representatives and school district officials
- clusters of teachers from academic and vocational disciplines who focus mainly on Academy students, who meet with each other regarding Academy curriculum, and who help shape Academy policy, curriculum content, and methods of instruction
- a lead teacher or director responsible for administrative tasks and communicating with the school principal, other administrators school- and district-wide, and employer partners
- career and college counseling
- financial or in-kind support from employers

Contributing Factors

"Even those planning to attend four-year colleges can benefit since they, too, are work-bound eventually and most of them will be employed while they attend college."   *Career Academies*

"Integrating the curriculum means coordinating courses so that a given topic is analyzed from different angles in more than one course."
Career Academies

Real-World Connections

Career Academies: "Courses in academic subjects include material specifically related to the academy's career theme, which makes them more interesting. Student's interest is further aroused by immediate connections between the program and the real world. Employer's representatives come to the school to speak and students take trips to workplaces. Adults working in the field serve as mentors for students, introducing them to settings in which they might work and helping them plan their careers. Students also have paid jobs, monitored by the school, in which they can practice and improve on what they have learned in the classroom."

Integrated Curriculum

Career Academies: "Simply identifying a strong occupational theme is not sufficient, however. Coordination between academic and vocational instruction is an essential part of the academy curriculum . . . traditionally these two categories of instruction have been taught separately . . .The very structure of the program encourages . . . the close alliance between the technical teacher and the academic ones in planning the program."

Inclusiveness/Rigor/Career Options

MDRC: Academies "include students with a wide range of demographic and educational characteristics. The appeal of the Academies has extended to students who may be at risk of failing academically or of

dropping out of high school, and to students who have done well in school." Academies have avoided tracking and broadened their base of appeal by ensuring that all their participants receive high level college preparation and are exposed to a wide range of occupations within any career field. The common focus provided by the Academy theme also motivates students to higher levels of achievement than they may have otherwise aspired to, thereby facilitating moves into a variety of career fields beyond the specific Academy focus.

Career Academies: "By including a sufficiently rigorous set of academic courses, the program also preserves students' options of attending college . . . The design of the academy makes it unnecessary to sort students into college-bound and non-college-bound tracks. This avoids demoralizing students who might otherwise be placed in a slow class. At the same time, the academy can improve students' academic achievement because it combines relevance with rigor."

Caring Adults

MDRC: "A central goal of the Career Academy is to create closer relationships between teachers and students and to personalize instruction . . . all of the Career Academies in this study emphasize and achieve closer relationships between teachers and students than do many other high school programs."

Career Academies: "Perhaps the most important motivating feature of academies is their family- like

"The resulting family-like atmosphere and the assignment of students to the same teachers for three years allows teachers to become familiar with each student's background. This gives responsibility for each student's educational development to teachers who can relate to each as an individual."   *Career Academies*

atmosphere. The school-within-a-school structure and smaller classes let students stay with the same classmates through four classes each day, so that they become a cohesive group . . . Teachers get to know their students well, a process that builds over the course of three years."

A Professional Learning Community

MDRC: "The primary difference between Academy teachers and their non-Academy colleagues in the same high schools were in their perceptions of their work environment . . . the Career Academies provide teachers with shared planning time . . . Career Academy teachers are more likely . . . to perceive their school environment as a professional learning community and to have developed closer relationships with students."

Career Academies: "The structure of the school-within-a-school allows the staff considerable freedom to develop the program, which leads to curriculum experimentation and program adjustment to meet student needs."

Quality of Implementation

MDRC: The Career Academy approach is essentially flexible and adaptable to local needs, capacities and circumstances, rather than rigid and prescriptive, demonstrating that the approach can work in a wide variety of school and community settings.

Career Academies: "[T]he most effective programs were those that had implemented the various features of the academy model most faithfully . . . individual academies vary greatly in their measured effectiveness."

Study Methodology

The MDRC report is the first report of their Career Academies Evaluation and focuses primarily on process measures for 10 high schools and the Career Academies that operate within them. MDRC randomly assigned 1,953 students to program and control groups for the full evaluation which will follow students through their high school careers and beyond. Data will be collected through student and staff questionnaires, student records, and site visits.

The 1989 "Benefits and Costs" paper reports 1987-88 results for 11 California academy programs from a matched comparison group study for each cohort of academy students at each site using a statistical regression model to test student performance.

Career Academies provides a summary chapter of many quasi-experimental evaluations conducted on a variety of academies. Methodologies vary.

Geographic Areas

There are Career Academies in more than 300 high schools. The ten Career Academies in the MDRC evaluation are in Pittsburgh, PA; Baltimore, MD; Washington, D.C.; Cocoa and Miami Beach, FL; Socorro, TX; Santa Ana and Watsonville, CA; and San Jose, CA (two). *Career Academies* shares evaluation results from the academies in Philadelphia, PA and California and from the Academy of Finance in New York, NY.

Contact Information

Research Organizations
Robert J. Ivry, Senior Vice President
Manpower Demonstration Research Corporation
Three Park Avenue
New York, New York 10016
(212) 532-3200, Fax (212) 684-0832

David Stern, Director
National Center for Research in Vocational Education
University of California at Berkeley
2150 Shattuck Avenue, Suite 1250
Berkeley, CA 94720-1674
(800) 762-4093, (510) 642-4004, Fax (510) 642-2124

[1] DeWitt Wallace-Reader's Digest Fund, The Commonwealth Fund, Pew Charitable Trusts and the Ford, William T. Grant, Rockefeller, George Gund, Grable, Richard King Mellon, American Express, Alcoa, Russell Sage, Westinghouse and Bristol-Myers Squibb Foundations.

Dropout [Recovery] Demonstration

A Summary of:

Evaluation of Projects Funded by the School Dropout Demonstration Assistance Program, Final Evaluation Report

March 1996, American Institutes for Research (Palo Alto, CA) by Robert J. Rossi

(Initiative and evaluation funded by U.S. Department of Education.)

Overview

In 1988, the U.S. Department of Education funded 89 projects under the School Dropout Demonstration Assistance Program (hereafter SDDAP) and funded an evaluation of 16 of these dropout prevention and recovery programs to assess their effectiveness. SDDAP provided funding for Local Education Agencies, Community-Based Organizations and education partnerships to establish these programs targeting dropouts and potential dropouts and to examine methods of early intervention for elementary and middle school students at risk of dropping out of school.

POPULATION

Of the 89 projects funded under SDDAP, 21 projects served students in K-8 only, 14 served students in grades 9-12 only and the remainder served both elementary and secondary students. Most projects served African American and Caucasian students, three projects served Native American youth exclusively and one provided assistance to Latino migrant youth. Over 75 percent of the projects used five or more criteria to recruit students. For younger students, teacher recommendation was used most frequently to identify students who might benefit from the program. For older students, poor attendance and the number of courses failed were used as indicators.

Evidence of Effectiveness

Findings from the three-year, intensive examination were mixed, with the most positive results at the high school level:

- At the high school level, three projects stood out—Des Moines, IA; Coleman, TX and Memphis, TN. Each showed positive outcomes, including a lower dropout rate. Other positive outcomes included higher grades (in Des Moines and Coleman), fewer absences (Memphis), a perception of more caring teachers and fairer discipline (Coleman), more frequent contact with counselors (Memphis) and more ambitious plans for high school completion (Memphis).

- At the middle school level, the Denver-Lake, CO program resulted in fewer absences, fewer suspensions, a perception of more caring teachers and a perception of fairer discipline in Year One. Subsequent years revealed no improvements, although researchers were limited in what they could measure due to incomplete data.
- A program in Portland, OR showed fewer absences, higher grades, more frequent incidents of counseling and greater frequency of parents attending school meetings in Year One. In Year Two, program students still had fewer absences compared to non-program students.

- The other two middle-school programs—in Broward County, FL and San Antonio, TX— had less positive outcomes, although the program group did have higher grades in Year One in the San Antonio project, as well as a lower dropout rate in Year Three.

- Some outcomes for program students improved in three out of four elementary school programs studied in Year One when measured against comparison groups. However, there were no significant improvements in Year Two.

Key Components

"In 1988, the U.S. Congress, recognizing the seriousness of the dropout problem in this country and the lack of rigorous information about effective dropout prevention programs, authorized demonstration programs . . . to encourage students to stay in school." American Institutes for Research

Although the 89 projects varied considerably, several similarities were observed:

- most operated through local school districts (76 of 89) and offered services within school or alternative-school settings
- the most frequent project goals were improving academic performance and increasing attendance; many

also tried to increase self-esteem and positive attitudes toward school, get parents involved, improve family coping skills and decrease discipline problems
- the majority offered academic skills instruction and counseling
- many offered supplemental services such as social support and, for older students, vocational/career counseling

Contributing Factors

"Early in their school careers, students at risk may especially need relationships on campus in which they feel they can speak their minds and talk about their worries and problems."
American Institutes for Research

Add Services Instead of Pulling Students Out

AIR: "In this in-depth evaluation, the dropout demonstration projects that utilized pull-out strategies achieved less convincing patterns of desired student outcomes than did other projects." There is sometimes a stigma attached to pull-out strategies, a student's sense of isolation from the school increases and teachers in regular classes often resent the disruption. Projects which were either integrated into the classroom (e.g., tutors were available for all students but paid particular attention to those most at-risk) or which were separate but coordinated with regular classes were the most successful.

Work/Incentives

The most successful projects incorporated some type of external incentive. For elementary school children, it was help in their homework; for middle school students, it was access to counseling; and for high school students, it was access to paid work. Paid work, as part of a program that prepares students for and monitors their job activities, was a "critical component" of keeping older students in school. Flexible class schedules—taking into account older students' work or personal commitments—were especially helpful in bringing students who had dropped out back to school.

Multiple, Coordinated Services

Students at risk for dropping out require a range of complementary and comprehensive services to meet their needs. Sites offering a greater number of services saw the most positive outcomes over the course of the study. SDDAP sites that coordinated services and resources among agencies and political entities were better able to increase the number of services available (this strategy requires time and effort in joint planning and review and may require increased funding).

Caring Adults

AIR: "Counseling services and adult advocacy for students are key elements of any . . . dropout prevention initiative." At the elementary school level, after-school tutoring and in-class adult friends seem to contribute to program success. At the middle school level, access to as-needed counseling services help students feel more affiliated with the school, while in high school "a network of supportive adults may increase young people's achievement, motivation and improve their awareness of educational and occupational opportunities . . . " The theme of "care, concern, and advocacy" was found in all the SDDAP projects that achieved positive student results.

Staff Training and Support

At the most successful sites, teachers motivated by and experienced in working with at-risk youth were recruited and actively supported by administrators. Successful projects "continue to provide skill-building opportunities, counseling, problem-solving sessions, and motivational aids to staff to maintain necessary focus on key goals and necessary interests and abilities in providing services." Sustaining programs over many years requires keeping staff committed and motivated. Programs did this "by creating a sense of team spirit among the work experience counselors and . . . teachers and by the development of teams that were able to work closely together and build a sense of 'family' with the students served."

Systemic Reform

SDDAP sites that initiated a large-scale reorganization or restructuring of the school or service environment—a complex process, requiring a great deal of time—were less likely to see short-term gains for students in the three years of the study.

Study Methodology

Researchers evaluated all sites through annual descriptive surveys, including information on funding, planning, implementation, organization, strategies, approaches, characteristics of participants and outcome measures. Researchers also studied 16 sites in-depth, conducting site visits, collecting extensive data via student surveys and school records, and using a comparison group to measure outcomes.

Geographic Areas

The program implemented 89 demonstration projects in 31 states and Washington, DC—some in major metropolitan areas, others in small towns and rural areas.

Contact Information

Research Organization

Robert J. Rossi, Principal Research Scientist
American Institutes for Research
P.O. Box 1113
Palo Alto, CA 94302
(415) 493-3550, Fax (415) 858-0958

Funding and Monitoring Organization

Audrey Pendleton
Office of The Under Secretary
U.S. Department of Education
600 Independence Avenue, SW
Room 4168, Federal Building 10
Washington, D.C. 20202
(202) 401-1026, Fax (202) 401-5943

A Summary of:

Strategies for Keeping Kids in School: Evaluation of Dropout Prevention and Re-entry Projects in Vocational Education, Final Report

June 1995, Research Triangle Institute (Research Triangle Park, NC) by Becky Jon Haywood and American Institutes for Research (Palo Alto, CA) by G. Kasten Tallmadge

(Initiative and evaluation funded by U.S. Department of Education.)

Overview

In 1989, the Office of Vocational and Adult Education (hereafter OVAE) in the U.S. Department of Education initiated a three-year project to demonstrate the effectiveness of vocational education components in 12 dropout prevention programs. OVAE awarded grants to school districts, universities and other organizations to replicate dropout prevention programs with a proven vocational education component.

POPULATION

The grants were targeted to communities with high dropout rates. All but one of the 12 projects evaluated served higher numbers of males than females (9 of the 12 had more than 60 percent males). The projects varied in racial/ethnic characteristics. Four of the 12 sites served Native American youth almost exclusively. Two sites served mostly white students and two sites served mostly African American students. Two of the sites served roughly equal percentages of African American, white and Latino students. The remaining two sites served a majority of white students and large percentages of African American and Native American youth. The evaluation provides no income data.

Evidence of Effectiveness

The Department of Education funded an evaluation of the grantees which found, of the 12 projects:

- 10 showed an increase in students' grade-point average
- 7 showed a reduction in the number of courses failed by the target students

- 7 showed an increase in students' perception that the school is safe
- 5 showed an increase in the number of credits earned
- 5 showed a reduction in the number of absences
- however, only 4 showed a reduction in the incidence of dropping out

Key Components

"The relatively modest student-related outcomes demonstrated by many of the projects over the course of the evaluation reflect the difficulty of overcoming the myriad political, logistical, and environmental factors that require attention as grantees attempt to implement even well-conceived and tested strategies for improving the educational experiences and outcomes of at-risk students . . . Even so, the demonstration included some successful projects, reflecting a variety of strategies for addressing the problems of their target population."   RTI/AIR

The dropout prevention projects represented a variety of strategies. However, seven of the 12 sites replicated the same project: Project COFFEE (Cooperative Federation for Educational Experience) featuring an abbreviated day alternative school integrating academic and vocational instruction. Project COFFEE components include:

- small class sizes
- a highly structured, nurturing environment
- a strong personal counseling component
- career awareness counseling
- student participation in entrepreneurial businesses

- physical education
- intense monitoring and evaluation of student progress

The following components at the 12 project sites were found by researchers to be the most critical to the success of a dropout prevention program:

- vocational education integrated with the academic curriculum and leading to a good entry-level job or postsecondary education
- counseling that includes attention to personal issues along with "career counseling, employability development, and life skills instruction"
- personal, supportive attention from adults

Contributing Factors

Caring Adults
Even where it had not been part of the original program design, all projects eventually implemented some type of formal counseling or mentoring support. Improvement in students' feelings of affiliation with the school appeared to be linked to this direct support from caring adults.

Systemic Reform
RTI/AIR: "Projects that changed the structure of the school, particularly those that created a smaller, more nurturing [and personal] environment, achieved positive effects on in-school performance and affiliation, though not in retention."

Integrated Curriculum
RTI/AIR: "Some level of integration, or at least coordination, of academic and vocational course

work appeared important in engaging students and leading to improvement in their overall performance," although participation in vocational education alone had a positive effect on student performance. There was such a wide variability in what the projects considered "vocational education" that it is difficult to draw definite conclusions about the effect of a vocational education component on dropout rates.

Services
Projects were more successful where the types of youth identified for services had been carefully analyzed, and the services provided were targeted appropriately. Also, service providers were more successful implementing project models with which they were already familiar.

Study Methodology

Researchers assessed student outcomes at 12 project sites that began services in 1989-90 (cohort I—1,062 students) and 1990-91 (cohort II—1,430 students) school years. Using either a random assignment (at nine sites) or comparison group method (at three sites), researchers also compared project students to "typical" students to see if/how the achievement gap was reduced. Staff visited the evaluation sites twice a year for two years and once at the end of the three-year demonstration to observe activities, collect information from records, and interview teachers, administrators, other staff and participants.

Geographic Areas

The 12 sites were: Woodside and Carlmont, CA; Cushing, OK; Oconee County, SC; Anne Arundel County, MD; Broward County, FL; Portland, OR; Detroit, MI; Turtle Mountain, Fort Totten, Fort Berthold and Fort Yates (Standing Rock), ND.

Contact Information

Research Organizations
Becky Jon Hayward
Research Triangle Institute
P.O. Box 12194
Research Triangle Park, NC 27709
(919) 541-6811, Fax (919) 541-5849

Donald H. McLaughlin
American Institutes for Research
P.O. Box 1113
Palo Alto, CA 94302
(415) 493-3550, Fax (415) 858-0958

Funding and Monitoring Organization
Ricky Takai, Director, Postsecondary, Adult and Vocational Education Planning
U.S. Department of Education
600 Independence Avenue, SW
Room 4103, Federal Building 10
Washington, D.C. 20202
(202) 401-3630, Fax (202) 401-5943

Gateway to Higher Education

A Summary of:

Make It Possible for Students to Succeed and They Will: An Evaluation of the Gateway to Higher Education Program

January 1997, Education Development Center (New York, NY) by Patricia B. Campbell, Ellen Wahl, Morton Slater, Elisabeth Iler, Babette Moeller, Harouna Ba and Daniel Light

(Evaluation funded by Aaron Diamond Foundation.)

Overview

Started in 1986, Gateway to Higher Education is a comprehensive four-year secondary school program administered through the City University of New York and operating in five New York City high schools. It aims to prepare students for higher education and for careers in science, medicine, and technology.

POPULATION

Gateway is aimed at students who are under-represented in mathematics, science and medical careers. To enter Gateway, students must be at the 50th percentile on New York City's Seventh Grade Math test and the Degrees of Reading Power test, have regular attendance, and generally have grades of 80 or better. Eighty-three percent of Gateway students are African American or Hispanic; about 60 percent are female. Through an analysis of students' zip codes and census data, researchers determined that the students come primarily from low- income or lower-middle income families. By the mid-1990s, Gateway was serving over 1,000 students per year in five high schools.

Evidence of Effectiveness

The evaluation compares the success of Gateway to national data regarding the participation of minorities in math and science studies. For example, the proportions of African Americans, Hispanics and Native Americans of the entire population who participate in the following are very low: undergraduate science and engineering degree recipients (11 percent), medical school entrants (14 percent), and medical degree recipients (11 percent).

Similarly low are the proportions of African Americans and Hispanics among high school graduates (21 percent), bachelor degrees in science and engineering (10 percent), and doctorates in science and engineering (five percent). African American and Hispanic high school graduates are less likely than whites to earn high school credits in science and mathematics courses, less likely than whites to score at the proficient level on the National

"On the one hand, these results should not be surprising, given that Regents course-taking and exam-taking are a required part of the Gateway program. On the other hand, it is noteworthy that students accepted this requirement, succeeded in these courses, and stayed on the college track while their control group counterparts, with ostensibly equal potential, exhibited a very different course-taking pattern and path toward post-secondary education."   **EDC**

Assessment of Educational Progress (NAEP) science and mathematics tests (when they are 13 to 17 years old), and score lower than white and Asian American students on both the verbal and math portions of the SAT and on science and math achievement tests.

Gateway evaluation data is reported in terms of course-taking, test-taking, standardized test scores and grades, graduation and postsecondary attendance and retention compared to the overall high school population, a comparison group of New York City students, and to subgroups.

Course-taking (in 1992):

* Gateway students were much more likely to take advanced math and science courses than were high school graduates in general (98 vs. 52 percent took "Math III").
* Gateway students were much more likely than all 1992 high school graduates to have taken chemistry (97 vs. 56 percent) and physics (83 vs. 25 percent).
* African American Gateway students were much more likely than all 1992 African American high school graduates to have taken chemistry (95 vs. 46 percent) and physics (90 vs. 18 percent).

Test-taking

* Gateway students took the state-wide Regents exam at a much higher rate than other New York City high school students (e.g., 96 vs. 24 percent took the Chemistry Regents Exam; 76 vs. 14 percent took the Physics Regents Exam).
* Gateway students were more apt to take the SAT test (93 vs. 15 percent of the comparison group took the SAT at least once).
* Sixty-two percent of Gateway students took the SAT II Biology Achievement Test and 54 percent took the SAT II Chemistry Achievement Test.
* In the 1994-95 school year, 37 percent of the eligible Gateway students took the Advanced Placement (AP) Biology Exam; and ten percent took the AP Chemistry Exam.

Standardized test scores:

* Gateway students had relatively high scores on Regents Exams (from a low of 70 in Physics to a high of 81 in Math I).

* Gateway students' SAT scores exceeded the national average. SAT: Mathematics 486 vs. 423 and SAT: Verbal 444 vs. 413; higher average mathematics and verbal combined scores (930 vs. 836).
* Gateway student scores were nearly 200 points higher than the mean 1993 SAT scores for African American students (SAT: 741, SAT M: 388, SAT V: 353) and the mean 1993 scores for Puerto Rican students (SAT: 762, SAT M: 409, SAT V: 353).
* Gateway students scored lower on the SAT Achievement Tests (a mean score of 496 vs. 558 for all, 491 for African American students and 518 for Puerto Rican students on the Biology test and a mean score of 467 vs. 582 for all, 514 for African American students and 523 for Puerto Rican students on the Chemistry test). [EDC: It is not clear why Achievement Test and Chemistry AP exam scores (below) were low. The data offered no clues, and the program directors had no definitive explanations to offer; they will use these findings to inform further program development and evaluation.]
* Gateway students' mean Biology AP score was 3.29, which was higher than the 1993 mean score of 2.98 for all Biology AP students, and higher than the mean score of 2.11 for African American students and 2.62 for Puerto Rican students.
* Gateway students' mean AP Chemistry score was 2, lower than the national mean of 2.86 and the mean score for Puerto Rican students (2.3), but at the same level as the mean AP Chemistry exam score for African Americans (2.02).

Grades, Graduation and Postsecondary Attendance and Retention:

* Gateway students maintained relatively high course grades (between 83 and 85).
* Gateway students who entered in 1989 were more apt to graduate from high school relative to the matched comparison group (93 vs. 73 percent).
* Ninety-two percent of Gateway graduates went to college (eight percent to Ivy League schools; four percent to competitive technical schools; 39 percent to other private, four-year institutions). Of 177 former Gateway students who graduated in 1990 and 1991 and responded to a survey, 94 percent either graduated from college or are continuing toward a degree and 52 percent remain in the math, science, or engineering/technology fields.

- Of the 1,753 students who entered Gateway since its inception in 1986, 18 percent have dropped out of the program.

Interviewers of Gateway students found them motivated, confident and competent. They also tend to be very engaged in their communities, taking on leadership roles.

Gateway costs $1,600 more per student per year than the mean New York City per pupil expenditure (mean not given in report).

Key Components

"Gateway requires students to engage in rigorous academic content and to avail themselves of ancillary opportunities such as internships, tutoring, and college visits. It provides guidance and resources (such as paying for the SAT) so that students stay on track to higher education." EDC

Each Gateway school has a coordinator and a team of teachers who stay with the students throughout their four years. The program is based on a strong belief that high expectations for all students, a demanding curriculum and a strong support system can lead to student success. Gateway features:

- an extended school day, including a double period of mathematics or science with a laboratory component and after-school tutorials
- an extended school year (11 months), including a month-long summer program for students entering the ninth grade and academic summer programs for juniors and seniors at high-level universities and research institutes

- classes composed solely of Gateway students, especially in mathematics and science, with a maximum enrollment of 25 students
- four years of regents-level science, mathematics, social science, foreign language courses and an average of three Advanced Placement courses for all Gateway students
- the expectation that all Gateway students will take the SAT
- information about college, beginning in the ninth grade, including an annual college fair and seminars for parents
- other enriching activities: exposure to professionals in science; field trips to museums, the theater, opera and symphonies; and after-school experiential internships

Contributing Factors

Systemic Reform
EDC: "While high expectations for all students have been part of the rhetoric for several decades, until recently, responsibility for success was still laid mainly on the student and barely on the system. Gateway was developed based on the assumption that responsibility for success needs to be equally shared by the student and the system . . ."

Staff Qualifications
Teachers for Gateway are carefully selected, based on their qualification to teach the assigned course, their teaching experience, their willingness to put in the time and effort required to push Gateway students, and their ultimate belief that the students can succeed.

Focusing Limited Resources
EDC: Program developers "viewed the Gateway approach as a necessary step along the way to more major change, and they put their energy into strategies they believed were likely to produce

immediate results for the current population of students." Once these results were gained (and they were gained the very first year of the program), it was much easier to engage teachers in continuing development.

Caring Adults
EDC: "Gateway students, teachers, and directors talked about the sense of connectedness they enjoy as part of a small entity within a large institution, how teachers know what is going on with all their students and make sure they don't get lost or off the track, the commitment above and beyond their contract that Gateway teachers invest, and the opportunity that teachers have to talk with each other and be part of a team of educators."

Other Factors
Other factors contributing to Gateway's success are high expectations, a peer culture supportive of achievement, appropriate equipment in laboratories, and information about college admission.

Study Methodology

Researchers compared outcomes for Gateway students to those of a comparison group of non-Gateway students matched according to gender, race/ethnicity, and math and reading scores. Each of the comparison students met the academic criteria for eligibility for Gateway. Researchers also analyzed an existing database, conducted a series of interviews and focus groups with program participants and graduates, visited the five Gateway high schools, interviewed college admissions staff, and administered a survey to 1990 and 1991 Gateway graduates. They also compared SAT and Achievement test scores of Gateway students with national averages.

Geographic Areas

Gateway operates in five New York City public high schools.

Contact Information

Research Organization
Ellen Wahl
Education Development Center, Inc.
96 Morton Street
New York, NY 10014
(212) 807-4229, Fax (212) 633-8804

Implementing Organization
Morton Slater and Elisabeth Iler, Directors
Gateway to Higher Education
94-50 159th Street
Science Building, Room 112
Jamaica, NY 11451
(718) 523-6301, (212) 241-4428, Fax (718) 523-6307

High Schools That Work

A Summary of:

Making High Schools Work: Through Integration of Academic and Vocational Education

1992, by Gene Bottoms, Alice Presson and Mary Johnson

"Seven Most Improved *High Schools That Work* Sites Raise Achievement in Reading, Mathematics, and Science"

1995, by Gene Bottoms and Pat Mikos, (High Schools That Work, A Report on Improving Student Learning)

Both reports by Southern Regional Education Board (Atlanta, GA).

Overview

The High Schools That Work (hereafter HSTW) initiative was launched by the Southern Regional Education Board (hereafter SREB) in 1987 to ensure that all students in participating schools and school districts, including those who do not plan to pursue a 4-year college degree, are prepared to enter the competitive workforce. HSTW is a full-school reform initiative that changes what children are taught, how they are taught, and what schools expect of them, including improving how academic and vocational teachers relate to each other and to their students. HSTW is especially designed to raise the achievement levels of career-bound high school students.

POPULATION

HSTW is aimed at making sure the "forgotten half" of students learn and achieve at the same levels as those planning for college. SREB defines career-bound high school students as the 60 to 70 percent of students who plan to work after high school, attend a two-year college or enter the military. These students do not *plan* to attend college, but may make a decision to attend a four-year college at a future time. At SREB schools, in 1993, 31 percent of students were minorities. SREB collected data on parental education of parents: 23 percent had college degrees, 23 percent had more than a high school education, 39 percent had a high school diploma and 13 percent had less than a high school education.

Evidence of Effectiveness

All 650 HSTW sites (both schools and school districts) in 21 states commit to "closing the gap" between achievement levels of career-bound young people and college-preparatory students and agree to participate in a common assessment process which includes pre- and post-scores on tests similar to those used by the National Assessment of Educational Progress (hereafter NAEP) and student and faculty surveys. Site data is broadly shared among sites and sites are compared against themselves and against NAEP data to measure success at meeting HSTW goals. SREB chose to report data showing

"The vocational curriculum's potential for advancing the academic achievement of career-bound youth is often underrated. Vocational teachers who concentrate on vocational skills only, while expecting others to teach academic skills, are short-changing their students." **SREB**

improvement over time (from 1990 to 1993) in student outcomes from seven HSTW schools which improved the most. These schools:

- increased scores by 65 percent in reading, 36 percent in math and 70 percent in science
- increased the percentage of students taking four or more full-year courses in mathematics (32 to 40 percent) and increased student mathematics scores even as students took more challenging courses (294.1 to 299.132 on NAEP-like tests)
- increased the vocational credits of career-bound students from 6.0 to 6.6 credits
- increased the percentage of students who completed four credits in a planned career major from 63 to 67 percent
- increased the average total credits earned from 23.6 to 24.5 credits
- made vocational courses more challenging and placed greater emphasis on getting students to use academic content and skills in vocational studies. [From 1990 to 1993, students at these schools reported that their vocational teachers more often stressed reading (46 vs. 55 percent), mathematics (54 vs. 64 percent) and science (26 vs. 39 percent).]
- reported increases in the percentage of students receiving extra help from family (48 to 58 percent),

mathematics teachers (60 to 73 percent), vocational teachers (21 to 37 percent), resource teachers (3 to 11 percent), tutors (8 to 17 percent)

SREB also compared practices at high achieving HSTW schools with practices at low achieving HSTW schools (often those newly on board) with the expectation that these practices contributed to the better schools' higher levels of achievement. Students at the most-improved schools, compared to students at the newest HSTW sites, reported:

- vocational teachers stressed reading (55 vs. 42 percent), mathematics (50 vs. 39 percent) and science (39 vs. 23 percent)
- academic teachers related academic content to real-world applications (75 vs. 67 percent); used mathematics to solve work-related problems more than twice a year (51 vs. 43 percent); related science to the real world weekly (78 vs. 70 percent)
- courses were challenging and exciting (70 vs. 54 percent), they were encouraged to take mathematics and science (67 vs. 46 percent), they took mathematics in their senior year (50 vs. 40 percent) and science in their senior year (37 vs. 30 percent)

Key Components

Each HSTW site has, or aims to have, the following characteristics:

- high expectations of students in both academic and vocational classes
- vocational courses emphasizing students' communication, math, and science competencies
- academic courses teaching concepts from the college preparatory curriculum through functional and applied strategies
- elimination of the general track
- all students complete a challenging program of study, including three courses in math and three in science

(with a least two credits in each course equivalent in content to courses offered in the college preparatory program) and are actively engaged in the learning process
- a structured system of work-based learning
- vocational and academic teachers working together to integrate academic and vocational curriculum and instruction and receiving staff development, materials, and time to work together
- guidance and counseling services, including parent involvement
- a structured system of extra help to enable career-bound students to complete an accelerated program of study

that includes high-level academic content and a career major

- student assessment and program evaluation (using data to continuously link school and instructional practices to improved student learning)

The seven most-improved sites vary in location, size, student characteristics and types of programs offered. One school belongs to the nation's 10th largest school district, four schools have fewer than 1,000 students, two have between 1,000 and 1,500, and one has over

1,500. Five of the seven sites are ethnically diverse, enrolling a minority student population of 24 to 56 percent. Five are comprehensive high schools, one is a technical high school, and the seventh is a high school working with an area vocational center. All seven most-improved schools use applied learning materials developed by the Center for Occupational Research and Development (CORD) in Waco, Texas, as stand-alone courses or as part of regular college preparatory mathematics and science courses.

> "Students in general and vocational programs of study deserve a better deal than they are getting. They are entitled to just as much encouragement, rigorous coursework, faculty guidance, planning, and evaluation as students preparing for a four-year college or university. They are not just the majority in high school; they represent the majority in the work force as well."   SREB

Contributing Factors

> "Schools making the most progress in High Schools That Work motivate students by establishing higher standards and getting students to work harder and longer to meet them. At most American high schools, time is fixed and standards are flexible. HSTW's most-improved schools reverse the process by setting high standards and providing extra time and help for students to meet them."   SREB

Quality of Implementation

Implementing the key practices identified by SREB for HSTW sites—high expectations; increasingly challenging and integrated academic and vocational studies; a structured system of work-based learning; vocational and academic teachers have time, materials and encouragement to work together; advising system including parents; extra help; student assessment and program evaluation—led to the most improvement on achievement levels in reading, mathematics and science.

High Expectations

SREB: "Students achieve at a higher level if they are required to simulate and use information, manipulate abstract concepts, perform complex calculations, and solve practical problems. Students also make more gains if they use technology in their studies." At the most-improved schools "English teachers . . . required [students] to make oral presentations, state and defend opinions, compare ideas, write research papers, and read books outside of class."

Integrated Curriculum

More students in high achieving schools read technical materials, solved mathematics problems related to their vocational studies, and completed projects assigned jointly by their vocational and academic teachers.

Academic teachers at the most-improved schools used applied learning strategies to teach mathematics, science and English to career-bound students.

Eliminate the General Education Track

SREB: "Schools that have made the most progress in raising expectations have replaced general mathematics, general science, and low-level English with courses that contain rigor and relevance to work and further study."

Guidance/Support

SREB: "Sites that made the most improvement . . . offer a guidance and advisement system to help students plan and pursue a challenging program of study. Teachers and parents participate actively in the process by helping students choose courses and understand the importance of a demanding program."

Extra Help and Time

SREB: "Schools that make gains in student achievement do more than enroll students in college preparatory courses, hold them to high standards, and get them to work harder and longer. They give students extra help and time to meet more demanding requirements." Extra help comes from mathematics, vocational and resource teachers, tutors and family.

Study Methodology

For analysis, SREB uses data from student and faculty surveys designed to capture perceptions about high school and a one-year follow-up survey of high school graduates; NAEP-type test data on student achievement in reading, mathematics and science; an analysis of transcripts to link student achievement to the number and types of courses taken in high school; and site-visits.

Geographic Areas

Established in 1987 at 28 sites in 13 states, HSTW has now grown to over 650 sites in 21 states: AL, AR, DE, FL, GA, HI, IN, KS, KY, LA, MD, MA, MS, NC, OK, PA, SC, TN, TX, VA and WV.

Contact Information

Research and Implementing Organization
Gene Bottoms, Director
The Southern Regional Education Board
Vocational Education Consortium
592 Tenth Street, N.W.
Atlanta, Georgia 30318-5790
(404) 875-9211, Fax (404) 872-1477

Manufacturing Technology

A Summary of:

An Evaluation of the Manufacturing Technology Partnership Program

February 1996, The W.E. Upjohn Institute for
Employment Research (Kalamazoo, MI)
by Kevin Hollenbeck

(Evaluation funded by Charles Stewart Mott Foundation.)

Overview

The Manufacturing Technology Partnership (hereafter MTP) originated as a way to ensure a supply of skilled workers for the General Motors (hereafter GM) Truck and Bus Flint Metal Fabricating Division (hereafter the Truck and Bus Plant) after a quality study revealed the plant faced a skilled worker shortage. In addition to working with GM, MTP committed to expand the program to six small-to-medium manufacturers and three large manufacturers. Beginning in high school, students took courses at the Genesee Area Skill Center (an area vocational school) and worked at the Truck and Bus Plant and other worksites after school.

POPULATION

The MTP program, implemented in Genesee County, MI, was aimed at high school students with at least a C average, including a B in 9th grade algebra; a 9th grade reading level; a good attendance record and an interest in manufacturing as a career. Students also, for the most part, had to be JTPA eligible. Interested students took an aptitude test and were interviewed by a panel of four or five adults. All students in the first MTP class (50 students—24 seniors and 26 juniors) were minority or female. The second class (55 juniors) included some non-minority males. Over one-third of MTP's graduates have been women. In 1997, about half of MTP participants are from minority groups and half are female.

Evidence of Effectiveness

The Upjohn Institute's evaluation of the first two MTP classes (comprised of students who entered the program in Fall 1992 and Fall 1993) followed program participants and a comparison group of students for each MTP class through October 1995. Results showed that, relative to the comparison groups, MTP students:

- were more likely to be employed at higher average wages [Cohort One: 80 vs. 70 percent were employed two and a half years after graduation from high school, $10.69 vs. $5.92 average hourly wages, Cohort Two (including many MTP graduates who were enrolled in postsecondary education): $5.81 vs. $5.20 average hourly wages, 31.2 vs. 25.2 hours worked per week.]
- had higher average GPAs and similar or higher class ranks (Cohort One: GPA 2.97 vs. 2.66, class rank in the 21st vs. 42nd percentile; Cohort Two: GPA 3.13 vs. 2.87, and similar class ranks)
- had considerably higher levels of vocational credits and more math and science credits
- had higher (but not statistically significant) average postsecondary education attendance rates

MTP did not calculate the cost per student. The program was developed with the idea of

For Cohorts One and Two combined: "The wage advantage is almost 75 percent—$9.79 per hour compared to $5.59." Upjohn Institute

institutionalization and sustaining resources after outside grants ended, and therefore primarily used pre-existing funding sources and in-kind assistance. Outside funding was provided by the Mott Foundation and the U.S. Department of Labor, but these funds did not cover all program costs and did not continue after the third year. Curriculum development, instruction and transportation for students were funded out of the Skill Center. GM/UAW employees donated their time to help

develop the curriculum. Mott Community College provided mentor training. Job Training Partnership Act (hereafter JTPA) funds were used to pay student wages and mentors' salaries were paid by GM. [The Mathematica evaluation "Facing the Challenge of Change: Experiences and Lessons of the School-to-Work/Youth Apprenticeship Demonstration, Final Report", August 1996, cites MTP as costing 30 percent more per apprentice than the regular per pupil expenditure (pp. 181).]

Key Components

MTP is one of 18 programs recognized as exemplary by the Promising and Effective Practices Network (PEPNet) in 1996. (PEPNet, a program of the National Youth Employment Coalition, is a nationwide network of youth employment development initiatives that demonstrate high standards in the areas of quality management, youth development, workforce development, and evidence of success. PEPNet offers organizations tools to analyze and evaluate their practices against identified effective principles and practices. STRIVE, pp. 88-90, is also a recognized exemplary PEPNet program.)

MTP prepares high school students for GM's rigorous apprenticeship program. It was originally designed and run by a partnership among the Truck and Bus Plant, Baker College, Mott Community College and JOBS Central [the local service delivery agency for JTPA]. The Truck and Bus Plant is one of 14 GM facilities in Flint employing approximately 3,500 workers who are members of the United Auto Workers (UAW). MTP worked early on to expand the partnership to other employers, including small-to-medium manufacturers and additional large manufacturers.

"... the program's originators had two objectives: to develop a reserve of well-trained students/workers who could fill skilled trades slots and to attract minority and women apprentices." Upjohn Institute

The first MTP class was comprised of 50 11th or 12th grade students from four high schools; the second class had 55 students from 16 different high schools. Students were transported to the Genesee Area Skill Center from their home schools for a two- or three-hour block class each day. In 11th grade, students

were divided into three groups and rotated through three 12-week classes — principles of manufacturing, electronic circuitry, and machining. In 12th grade, students were divided into two groups and rotated between computer-assisted design (CAD) and manufacturing. Instruction was primarily delivered through hands-on practice with students grouped in teams.

The MTP program became a separate department within the Skill Center with its own director, assistant director and teachers (from other programs within the Skill Center). In Year One, three full-time Skill Center teachers were assigned half-time to MTP and half-time to other departments. Three academic teachers were also on staff to integrate mathematics, language arts and physics into the Skills Center curricula.

MTP provided a paid work component after school and during the summer. In Year One, after their Skill Center course, and in the summer, MTP students worked at the Truck and Bus Plant. Worksite training occurred in a special facility in the plant that was converted for the purpose. Four employer worksites were added in Year Two and eight in Year Three. The Truck and Bus Plant created full-time mentor positions for seven competitively selected employees. Mentors were trained by Mott Community College.

MTP originally intended to cover tuition for an Associate's degree in Manufacturing Science (or a related field) at a two-year college if students passed the apprentice test above the national average or at the higher level required to qualify for an apprenticeship as an "outsider." However, there was confusion over who would actually pay tuition costs: the business partners, Jobs Central, the MTP program or the postsecondary institutions. Eventually students entering MTP were told there was no tuition guarantee, unless they were accepted into an apprenticeship.

Contributing Factors

"It strikes us that the flexibility and adaptability that the MTP program has demonstrated fits well the milieu within which the program's employer partners operate. It is quite appropriate that a program that strives to provide students with world-class manufacturing skills should itself have the flexibility and adaptability that are hallmarks of today's manufacturers."   Upjohn Institute

Integrated Curriculum

MTP integrated academic and vocational curricula from the very beginning. Truck and Bus Plant staff, Skill Center staff and postsecondary teachers assisted in curriculum design. As GM's apprenticeship exam strongly emphasized basic math and reading skills, academic teachers also participated in curriculum development.

Teachers from Industry; Appropriate Equipment

MTP teachers who had years of applied experience in the field and in machining and electronics courses taught in the advanced Skill Center labs. Design and drafting courses were taught in a classroom equipped with computers and Computer Aided Design (CAD) software. The lab in which "principles of manufacturing" was taught also received a large investment in equipment.

Employers Involvement

Employers felt a close tie with and commitment to MTP, because it was linked so closely to their own identified needs and because they were essential partners on the planning and design team.

Eligibility Criteria Strengthened

In the first year of MTP, 10 students were dismissed due to inadequate skill levels. Program staff tightened their acceptance criteria to ensure that students accepted into MTP had the necessary baseline skills to successfully complete the program. Staff also changed the curriculum in response to employer comments.

Work

Students were paid $6.25 per hour at the worksite, well above the minimum wage that a typical high school student would be earning. Since students could not participate in the work component of the program without attending classes, they had a strong incentive to attend.

Update

The MTP Coordinator provided the following updated information on MTP as of 1997:

Enrollment

Over 100 students are enrolled and approximately 60 new students are selected to begin the program each year.

Curriculum and Assessment

Curriculum development is now overseen by the advisory committee which includes employers and postsecondary representatives. MTP infuses reading, writing, algebra and physics into manufacturing areas such as welding, drafting, machining or electronics. The senior year is entirely project based and is team taught by two teachers. Benchmark testing is used periodically to measure the progress of students.

Employer Involvement

The cooperative venture now involves 22 Genesee County manufacturing employers from a wide range of sectors plus two additional GM facilities and prepares students for manufacturing careers in the skilled trades, manufacturing management, manufacturing design, drafting, CAD/CAM, electronics, engineering or first-line supervision. Employer involvement is expanding in the area of donations, guest speakers, and providing college financial support.

Postsecondary Connections

The majority of MTP students (90+ percent) enter postsecondary education and/or continue on with their employers. One reason for the high attendance rate is that Baker College and Mott Community College now offer scholarships to MTP graduates.

Study Methodology

Upjohn Institute researchers developed comparison groups of students similar to the first two classes of MTP students and compared high school experiences, postsecondary attendance, and labor market outcomes. The comparison group for the '92 class consisted of students who applied to MTP and were interviewed, but did not enroll. The comparison group for the '93 class was difficult to create and involved two sets of students who volunteered to be in the comparison group and additional students who applied to MTP, but did not enroll.

Researchers interviewed students, teachers, administrators, employers, postsecondary administrators and representatives of school districts and other organizations involved with MTP to analyze how the program was implemented. The evaluation reflects the structure and operation of the program between Fall 1992 and Fall 1994.

Geographic Area

Genesee County, MI.

Contact Information

Research Organization
Kevin Hollenbeck
The W.E. Upjohn Institute for
 Employment Research
300 S. Westnedge Avenue
Kalamazoo, MI 49007
(616) 343-5541, Fax (616) 343-3308

Implementing Organization
Patrick Leaveck, MTP Coordinator
GASC Technology Center
G-5081 Torrey Road
Flint, Michigan 48507
(810) 760-1444, Ext. 163, Fax (810) 760-7759

ProTech

A Summary of:

The Evolution of a Youth Apprenticeship Model: A Second Year Evaluation of Boston's ProTech

March 1994 Jobs for the Future (Boston, MA) by Hilary Kopp, Susan Goldberger and Dionisia Morales

(Evaluation funded by Boston Foundation.)

ProTech Health Care: An Assessment by Partners of Current Status and Future Priorities, Final Report

January 1997, Jobs for the Future (Boston, MA) by Anthony Alongi and Victoria Nelson

Overview

ProTech Health Care (hereafter ProTech) started as a youth apprenticeship program in allied health careers. Youth apprenticeship is a school-to-career initiative using an educational approach linking school, work and postsecondary education. ProTech has also expanded into four other career clusters — Finance, Utilities & Telecommunications, Environmental Services, and Business Services— not covered in this report.

POPULATION

ProTech "targets students who are unlikely to complete college-level training without a supported pathway." Participants in the 1994 study were primarily minorities (Year One: 45 percent African American, 31 percent Latino, 6 percent Asian/Pacific Islander; Year Two: 64 percent African American, 24 percent Latino, 4 percent Asian/Pacific Islander), largely female (Year One: 68 percent, Year Two: 60 percent) and included a significant proportion of bilingual students (Year One: 27 percent, Year Two: 23 percent). Although better academic records and attendance were required of Year Two entrants, they still were educationally disadvantaged: 29 percent had failed to earn a C average in the 10th grade; only 41 percent were enrolled in the college-preparatory program. Of students entering in Year Two, 60 percent had thought about pursuing a health career before joining.

Evidence of Effectiveness

The 1994 and 1997 Jobs for the Future (hereafter JFF) reports focus primarily on operational issues. However, each also provides participant data as follows:

- Retention of students in the program (measured as the proportion of ProTech juniors who graduate from high school as ProTech students) increased even as program size increased at a rate of 70 students per year. Retention increased from 41 percent (1991 Junior class) to 68 percent (1994 Junior class) to 80 percent (1995 Junior class, on track to graduate in the Spring of 1997).

"Students make the transition from 'net cost' to 'net benefit' in anywhere from one week to six months, with 'one to two months' being the most frequent estimate by employers."   **Jobs for the Future**

- All of the 38 ProTech seniors who graduated in 1993 enrolled in a postsecondary program (almost equally divided between two and four-year programs). These students also received significant financial aid from the postsecondary institutions to which they applied.
- As of 1997, 81 percent of students who had graduated high school as part of ProTech since 1995 were enrolled in postsecondary programs, and 7 percent of students had completed a technical certificate or Associate's degree, 82 percent of these students were employed (79 percent of employed students were working for ProTech employers).
- ProTech students are encouraged to take more rigorous college-preparatory courses than they otherwise would have. Of those 11th grade students who passed geometry in the 10th grade, a higher percentage of ProTech students than a comparison group (students in the school's health career pathway who do not receive

the same structured worksite and classroom experiences) chose to continue on a college preparatory track in math (100 vs. 81 percent). Of students enrolled in a science class in the 1991-92 school year, more ProTech than comparison group students chose to continue to study science in the 11th grade (96 vs. 67 percent).
- Grades improved for the first cohort of ProTech students by their senior year, but grades of non-ProTech seniors also improved. In part due to the more rigorous course load, 34 percent of the second cohort ProTech students were unable to maintain a C average in their first year.

The 1994 report indicates ProTech cost $3,500 per student in the 1st and 2nd years and $2,000 per student in the third year (in 1992, 1993 and 1994 dollars). The 1997 report provides PIC estimates of per-student cost at $4,200 in 1991 to $2,600 within three years to a 1997 figure of $740. For the 1996-1997 school year, the eleven employers in ProTech provided an estimated $1,000,000 in wages, scholarships, and in-kind time.

Key Components

In 1991, the Boston Private Industry Council and its partners (city hospitals, medical centers and the Boston public schools) launched Project ProTech. ProTech's youth apprenticeship model combines classroom learning, clinical internships, and paid work experience. Approximately 25 juniors from each of three Boston public high schools enroll in ProTech each year. In 1992-1993, 121 students participated.

School-Based Learning:

- ProTech juniors and seniors are grouped together for 2 or 3 courses in which only other ProTech students are enrolled. Some schools include a ProTech seminar on work readiness preparation, career exploration, and additional science instruction.
- Students study a modified curricula which reinforces the concepts and skills learned at hospital worksites and are challenged to pursue more rigorous math and science classes.
- Students can take some college courses during their senior year in high school.

"ProTech is an outgrowth of the Boston Compact, a landmark agreement between the business community, political leaders, and the schools to improve the quality of education in the city and connect young people with jobs."
                    Jobs for the Future

Work-Based Learning:

- ProTech juniors complete 16 three-hour clinical rotations in different hospital departments.
- Second-semester juniors are placed in part-time hospital jobs (12-15 hours per week).
- Seniors continue a part-time job with hospital staff mentors to develop workplace skills and further target their occupational interests.
- In their first and second years of postsecondary education, students work in hospital positions closely aligned to their occupational interests and areas of post-secondary study. Students rotate to different work stations within departments. Training plans address position-specific responsibilities and knowledge including hospital organization, medical terminology, ethics, etc..
- In the summer, students hold full-time paid hospital jobs.
- As of 1997, ProTech shifted from work-based learning that was occupation specific to instruction based on broadly-transferable skills embodied in 11 broad competencies, which allow for a parallel process within the classroom, where teachers can identify related curriculum activities.

"When Project ProTech enrolled its first students in the Fall of 1991, there were few school-to-work transition initiatives anywhere in the country. As a pioneering program in an emerging field, its implementation experiences and program modifications provide important lessons for local and state officials who are just starting to design their own initiatives."   **Jobs for the Future**

Connecting Activities:

- Project coordinators, each assigned full-time to a high school, work closely with students as case managers preparing them for work-based activities, monitoring their performance at both school and work, addressing any barriers students may have to successful participation and getting them through the college and financial aid application process. They work closely with participating teachers to integrate school and work

experiences and help to coordinate work-based activities.
- A hospital coordinator at each hospital arranges rotations, identifies work placements, orients and supports supervisors, troubleshoots, and interfaces with project coordinators. Students also have individual worksite mentors.

Contributing Factors

"At the time of ProTech's development, Boston- area hospitals, like others around the country, were unable to find a reliable local supply of skilled, qualified workers for many technical and professional positions . . . ProTech offered hospitals an opportunity to contribute to the community while training potential workers to help alleviate the shortage of highly-skilled technicians."
          Jobs for the Future

Improved Retention Efforts

Over time, ProTech has made changes aimed at increasing retention in the program, including: a stricter recruitment and selection process (higher level academic and attendance requirements for program entry), the assignment of a full-time project coordinator at each school, quality job placements for all students, academic supports such as tutoring, a flexible program structure to reduce the number of hospital rotations, delaying the start of jobs (students must achieve academically before being placed on the job [the opposite of the approach taken by CET — see JOBSTART, pp. 73-76]), and allowing students time to participate in sports and other extra-curricular activities.

Work/Quality Positions

In 1993: "One significant predictor of student retention was the quality of the student's job placement. The difference in the quality of first-year job placements between terminated students and retained students is striking. Sixty-three percent of students terminated from the program were employed in service positions such as dietary aide or equipment transporter, while only a third were employed in more challenging and engaging clerical, technical, or patient care jobs. In contrast, 81 percent of students retained in the program were employed in clerical, technical, or patient care positions."[1] In 1994, JFF reported substantial program changes: "ProTech has made significant progress in securing quality placements for all students . . . students are being assigned tasks which require high levels of

responsibility . . . In many cases, students are assigned much of the same responsibilities as regular entry level staff."

Caring Adults

JFF: "ProTech students received support from project coordinators, hospital coordinators, job supervisors and coaches, and PIC staff hired to provide career counseling and assistance with postsecondary planning and college transition . . . Through greater class clustering and an increase in the number of 'ProTech teachers,' students are more likely to have some of the same teachers in their junior and senior years and/or the same teacher for both homeroom and a class. As students and teachers are together more, stronger relationships develop and the importance of the teachers' roles in students' lives increases . . . students also reported that they get a great deal of support and encouragement from their hospital supervisors and department co-workers." In 1997, the rising numbers of ProTech students, while resulting in a lower cost per student, are putting pressure on key personnel and have increased the student/coordinator ratio.

Systemic Reform

JFF: "[I]t was hoped that participation in high-quality, paid learning experiences would motivate students to study harder and achieve more, even without major changes in the schools. This hope has not been realized. Despite extraordinarily rich worksite learning opportunities, a solid network of supportive adults, and the promise of a high-paying

"[S]tudents interviewed about the program spoke with joy about friendships they had made and encouragement they had received from hospital and program staff."   Jobs for the Future

career upon completion of the four-year program, ProTech continues to have little effect on students' academic performance . . . Unfortunately, it appears that many ProTech students are not acquiring the academic skills they will need to succeed in these programs . . . It would appear that high quality work-based learning experiences cannot substitute for—but

must go hand-in-hand with needed reforms in the schools." Recommendations for school change include beginning intervention earlier, developing stronger school-within-school structures, and involving teachers more in curriculum reform. Some of these recommendations are being implemented.

Study Methodology

The 1994 evaluation included data collected from school records (on both ProTech and non-ProTech students at the participating high schools), program records (student termination, employment, and worksite clinical experience), surveys (of all incoming students), interviews (with ProTech staff, students, school and hospital personnel), and site visits.

The 1997 evaluation used interviews of ProTech, PIC and JFF staff; participation in Task Force meetings; and interviews with health employers, school personnel and a PIC-selected group of students.

Geographic Areas

ProTech operates in three of Boston's 16 public high schools.

Contact Information

Research Organization
Susan Goldberger
Jobs for the Future
One Bowdoin Square
Boston, MA 02114
(617) 742-5995, Fax (617) 742-5767

Implementing Organization
Keith Westrich, ProTech Director
Boston Private Industry Council
Two Oliver Street, 7th Floor
Boston, MA 02109
(617) 423-3755, Fax (617) 423-1041

[1] Susan Goldberger, *Creating an American-style Youth Apprenticeship Program: a Formative Evaluation of Project ProTech*, (Boston: Jobs for the Future, 1993).

Rural Entrepreneurship

A Summary of:

An External Evaluation Of REAL: *Rural Entrepreneurship through Action Learning*

April 1996, Center for Human Resources, Heller Graduate School, Brandeis University (Waltham, MA) by Andrew Hahn, Paul Aaron and Roblyn Anderson

(Evaluation funded by Pew Charitable Trusts.)

Overview

Rural Entrepreneurship through Action Learning (hereafter REAL) is a high school and college-based entrepreneurship program combining experiential learning and community partnership-building to encourage students in rural areas to develop entrepreneurial skills and start their own businesses. REAL's secondary aim is to revitalize rural communities through home-grown businesses providing income and jobs.

REAL sees itself as a national model for fostering entrepreneurial thinking and action on the part of young people and adults. At the high school level, REAL is integrated into the regular schedule through a class that students take for credit (over one or two semesters) with teachers already employed at the school. In community colleges or business centers, REAL is sometimes a regular for-credit course counting 60 - 90 hours of instruction typically toward a college degree and sometimes a non-credit continuing education offering.

POPULATION

REAL serves all types of students in any participating community. REAL students have a mix of incomes and academic levels. They are not, as a whole, highly disadvantaged or from desperate rural poverty backgrounds and relatively few receive public assistance. While only 40 percent of REAL students from 1991 to 1995 pursued a "college preparatory" curriculum, 80 percent self-reported their intentions to continue their education after high school once they became involved in REAL. Participants are primarily from rural areas, but REAL does include a few inner-city sites. Many students had considerable family experience in small business or self-employment before REAL and about ¾ wanted to start their own businesses.

Evidence of Effectiveness

Brandeis evaluators used pre- and post- test scores to assess the impact of REAL on student acquisition of business and communication skills. Evaluators found:

- On pre- and post- test scores both high school and college-level REAL students showed an improvement in business skills between program enrollment and

program completion, but no meaningful changes in communication skills.

To collect information on the establishment of entrepreneurial ventures, average monthly sales and hiring rates, REAL conducted interviews of REAL graduates in North Carolina (where the program started) believed to be engaged in starting or expanding businesses.

- Among 30 graduates who had started businesses, the average monthly sales were $3,622. Twenty-three percent of the 30 graduates were drawing more than half their personal income from the new business.
- Of the 12 entrepreneurs surveyed who already had businesses when they entered the REAL program, and

who were able to provide data, average monthly sales were $17,608. These 12 firms employed 41 full-time and 25 part-time workers.

- At Edgecombe Community College, the site of a REAL program, about half of the students enrolled in REAL graduated from REAL, and 60 percent started or expanded businesses between 1992 and 1996 (31 businesses).

Key Components

"REAL aimed to stem the economic decline of rural communities by equipping young people with the skills they needed to create their own employment."   Brandeis

Key features of REAL are:

- REAL classes, where students: keep journals; formally assess their personal strengths and weaknesses; analyze the local community, including an inventory of existing businesses and an assessment of local needs for products and services; and research and write a business plan that includes cash flow projections, and a comprehensive strategy for operating and marketing the business
- an emphasis on: business concepts; business and management skills; self-management and organizational

skills; intellectual independence, critical thinking, and analytical and planning skills
- loans to participants for business start-ups
- community Support Teams of local business and community leaders who act as advisors to the program and individual students
- professional development program and on-going support for instructors
- an experiential activity-based curriculum with an integrated technology component

Contributing Factors

REAL is not just a source of training but "the nexus of a sustained, supportive relationship. . . . Graduates who became entrepreneurs can count on REAL to serve as a friend, sounding board and management consultant."   Brandeis

Role of the Business Plan

Creating a business plan means regular collaboration among students and community members. Students learn practical skills, such as planning, problem-solving, and tracking down and using data (e.g. liability insurance, interest rates) and they make contacts in the local business community. Community members feel they are making an investment in the future health of the local economy and get drawn into the workings and the goals of REAL.

Expansive Vision of Entrepreneurship

Approximately 10 percent of REAL high school students open and operate their own enterprises after high school. While starting an actual business is a program goal, it is not the highest priority for high school students—developing critical thinking and life skills, and exploring entrepreneurship as a career come first. For postsecondary students, starting a business is a higher priority. REAL provides a protective environment (a) to start a business, including access to a revolving loan fund for new

enterprises and (b) to experience business failure—a valuable learning experience. In North Carolina, program operators found that when students were exposed to REAL, they often changed their career plans and decided to attend college. While this meant that many were not starting businesses immediately, both they and the community were still benefiting from a wider vision of entrepreneurship—one that focused as much on independent thinking as on starting a business.

Community Support Team

The most successful REAL programs enlisted extensive outside help from respected, visible business and political leaders in the community. Brandeis: "One site's team joins together strategically selected community stakeholders: bankers; accountants; businessmen; public sector executives; board members of the community college. This multi-sector and multi-ethnic coalition has become an important example in a community still prone to racial fissures . . . As a conduit for institutional prestige and political legitimacy, the support team serves an indispensable anointing function. As a source of personalized, hands-on business consultancy with REAL students, the support team in theory plays the part both of mentor as well as of intermediary between the classroom and the world of work."

Staff Qualifications

At each site where REAL was most successful, the project sprung from a committed "visionary" and was implemented by carefully chosen and trained staff. REAL's national director noted that people attracted to REAL "tend to be people who themselves are entrepreneurial, who thrive on challenge and who are attracted by the opportunity to start something from scratch." Complementing their inherent talents, REAL teachers also receive eight days of training in REAL's Summer Institute. A key feature of the

Institute is the use of mentor instructors, or teachers who have already been through the Institute, to reinforce the program's focus on experiential learning. "The REAL Institute has a large impact on the knowledge and comfort level of the REAL teachers they are training . . .[resulting in] vast improvements in the percentage of teachers who say they feel they are comfortable with the concept involved in experiential learning."

Quality of Implementation

Over time, REAL has worked to serve as an intermediary for its many sites and to centralize some aspects of implementation—a move also recommended by the evaluators. At start-up, REAL tried to be very adaptive to local circumstances and therefore looked somewhat different across sites.

Study Methodology

Brandeis researchers used a number of methods to evaluate the REAL program: case studies, development of an assessment system for all REAL sites to capture data, pre- and post- tests and analysis of data. Researchers also set up a pilot, quasi-experimental study in two sites to compare the outcomes of REAL program graduates to those who had not gone through the program. Finally, Brandeis researchers reviewed program data that had not been thoroughly analyzed previously.

Geographic Areas

REAL operates in 23 states: CA, GA, ID, MA, ME, MT, NE, NM, NY, NC, OH, OK, PA, SC, SD, TN, TX, VT, VA, WA, WV, WY and WI. Programs are in 160 schools — approximately 100 high schools, 40 community colleges, a few universities and several community-based organizations. The quasi-experimental sites were Riverside, WA and Swainsboro, GA.

Contact Information

Research Organization
Andrew Hahn
Center for Human Resources
Heller Graduate School, Brandeis University
Waltham, MA 02254-9110
(617) 736-3770, Fax (617) 736-3773

Implementing Organization
Richard S. Larson, National Director
REAL Enterprises
115 Market Street, Suite 320
Durham, North Carolina 27701-3221
(919) 688-7325, Fax (919) 682-7621

A Summary of:

Promising Practices: A Study of Ten School-To-Career Programs

Jobs for the Future (JFF), (Boston, MA) by Hilary Kopp and Richard Kazis, with Andrew Churchill

(Study funded by Pew Charitable Trusts, DeWitt Wallace-Reader's Digest Fund, Lilly Endowment, Charles Stewart Mott Foundation, Ford Foundation, and an anonymous donor.)

Experiences And Lessons of the School-To-Work/ Youth Apprenticeship Demonstration

August 1996, Mathematica Policy Research (Princeton, NJ) by Marsha Silverberg, with Jeanette Bergeron, Joshua Haimson and Charles Nagatoshi

(Evaluation funded by U.S. Department of Labor.)

Overview

In 1990, JFF launched its National Youth Apprenticeship Initiative (hereafter NYAI) and the U.S. Department of Labor (hereafter DOL) funded a demonstration project on School-to-Work (hereafter STW) with grants to six organizations. In 1992, DOL sponsored an additional 10 organizations with a specific focus on the youth apprenticeship model. At that time, DOL provided extended funding to five of the initial grantees contingent upon their revising the school-to-work programs toward the youth apprenticeship model. JFF's NYAI focused on ten programs around the country that could serve as models for future initiatives. Although these sites varied, key components across the sites were:

School-Based:

- career counseling and guidance
- integration of academic and vocational instruction
- applied learning; hands-on curriculum
- maintenance of high academic standards, with an aim toward postsecondary education

Work-Based:

- job shadowing (brief visits to a workplace to see what various jobs entail)
- "formal, structured, progressive skills development integrated with school-site learning"
- job rotation to learn the different occupations within an industry

POPULATION

The target population across the programs varied, especially with regard to previous academic achievement and expectations. Some programs targeted mid-level students and encouraged them toward four-year colleges; others targeted students at-risk for dropping out, hoping to get them into any postsecondary college or training opportunity. The racial composition of the program students tended to reflect that of the surrounding population. Overall, the programs served an economically disadvantaged population. Mathematica researchers noted that some programs had a very high percentage of students who spoke a language at home other than English. Both Mathematica and JFF noted that despite attempts to recruit male and female students into nontraditional training, most manufacturing programs were largely male, while programs focused on areas such as health were largely female.

- paid work experience, with earnings increasing in accordance with an increase in skills and experience
- workplace mentors
- instruction in general workplace competencies

Postsecondary Links:

- include postsecondary study as part of the program (i.e., two years of high school and at least two years of college)
- agreements with postsecondary institutions allowing

credit for academic and worksite learning done in high school
- arrange for seniors to take college-level courses and possibly obtain certification

Evidence of Effectiveness

JFF and Mathematica conducted evaluations of STW programs across the country. The Mathematica report focused on DOL programs (funded in 1990 and 1992) with a youth apprenticeship orientation. (See pp. 45-47 for a summary of Mathematica's first report on a five-year evaluation of STW under the National School-to-Work Opportunities Act of 1994.) Mathematica's evaluation was designed to present broad, qualitative findings since youth apprenticeship programs were still in their initial stages. The JFF study focused on 10 model sites, all funded in 1990, and was also qualitative. Neither study used comparison groups. Evaluators found:

- STW students enroll in postsecondary education and training at high rates; in the three programs in JFF's study that track students post-graduation, Cornell reported 77 percent, Boston Protech 84 percent, and Kalamazoo 80 percent of their students over two years enrolled in postsecondary education. In JFF's survey of seniors in eight programs, 90 percent planned to enroll

in a two- or four-year college.
- Programs have expanded over time in number of students served, the type of student served (more minority, female, college-bound, and at-risk students), and the number of industries participating.
- Programs have formed strong relationships with a core group of employers and have sustained those relationships over time. Executives involved in designing and implementing the program in their worksites have become vocal advocates for STW programs, both locally and nationally.
- Students, program directors and parents expressed positive feelings about STW. Students especially liked project-based learning. Others felt the higher standards required by the program (with respect to attendance or grades) inspired them to work harder. Students also felt that work-based components gave them needed skills and contacts for the future. Program directors and parents saw positive changes in student behavior and achievement. As the programs progressed, they became more focused on systemic school reform.

Contributing Factors

"Through experimentation, the projects have provided important lessons to policymakers and practitioners about the benefits and challenges of implementing these types of programs."
Mathematica

Common Student and Employer Interests Improves Program Success

If students are not really interested in the occupation featured in their worksite experience, they tend to drop out of the program after high school. This is frustrating to employers who commit training resources to the program. Screening for interest up front leads to stronger relations with employers. Employers become more willing to have students in the workplace and give them more demanding and meaningful work, once they see that students can work well, and perceive the potential future payoffs in terms of a more skilled workforce. Employer commitments to maintaining a student at the worksite, helping pay for postsecondary education,

and granting priority in hiring to youth apprenticeship students are strong factors in student decisions both to enroll in STW programs and to complete postsecondary education or training.

Using Business Organizations and Other Employers to Recruit Employers

Groups such as the chamber of commerce, private industry councils, and trade associations have the contacts and the resources to bring employers into STW initiatives. As large, well-known employers buy-in to the program, other employers are likely to follow. Schools can minimize the problem of putting too many demands on local employers (particularly as the initiative expands) if the business community is the prime organizer for employer participation.

"... integration of programs into more systemic planning for districts, regions, and even states, as in the case of Pennsylvania, was evident several years ago, when JFF first began studying and working with programs. However, these connections are much more explicit and well-articulated today. They indicate the potential of the school-to-career movement to have exactly the effect the federal government has wanted—to be the catalyst for system-building at the local and state levels."

Jobs for the Future

The fact that the programs expanded their industry contacts over time means that "demand for these efforts is strong, that evidence of success in one industry can have a positive spill-over effect, and that the initiatives have sufficient credibility to attract and engage new partners."

Caring Adults

In JFF's survey of seniors, more than 75 percent said the program had allowed them to develop special relationships with adults, generally a worksite mentor or supervisor. Worksite mentors who have some training in adolescent behavior can more effectively guide students in the workplace than those without training. The mentoring experience often has the effect of making the mentor more enthusiastic and positive about his or her own job.

Systemic Reform/Integrated Curriculum

Clustering students in key courses makes the integration of school- and work-based experiences much easier. New curricula that emphasize hands-on learning are crucial for increasing student interest in learning and developing basic skills. Students said that "working in teams, solving problems in groups, and hands-on lab or building activities were some of their more enjoyable and interesting school-based exercises." STW initiatives are very focused on

finding worksite placements for their students, possibly at the expense of curriculum development. Mathematica: "Because the availability of intensive workplace experiences may be limited in a broader school-to-work system, curriculum reform efforts are likely to benefit more students in the long run than is involvement in specific work-site activities."

Flexibility

Both students and teachers need a flexible schedule. Teachers need time for training and to plan and coordinate STW initiatives. Students need the freedom for more intensive classroom experiences as well as worksite time, which is hindered by the current Carnegie Unit graduation requirements. Entrance requirements to four-year colleges and universities need to be more flexible to accommodate work-based experience.

The Federal Government Has a Role to Play in STW Efforts

Local STW programs expressed a need for federal leadership in developing a common vision and common performance measures, providing information about "best practices," giving information and access to specific tools developed by other districts, and reducing the development time and the cost of skill standards.

Study Methodology

Mathematica's evaluation was designed to present broad, qualitative findings since youth apprenticeship programs were still in their initial stages. Evaluators collected data through: (1) executive interviews, (2) focus groups, (3) site visits/observation of program activities, (4) examination of project records and materials and (5) review and abstracting of student records. See pp. 45-47 for Mathematica's first report on a five-year evaluation of STW under the National School-to-Work Opportunities Act of 1994.

JFF evaluators used written materials provided by each of the ten sites, supplemented by follow-up questionnaires, phone interviews, surveys, focus groups and site visits.

Geographic Areas

Sites evaluated by JFF and Mathematica: Oakland, Los Angeles, San Diego and Pasadena, CA; Seminole County, FL; Gwinnett, Houston, Bibb and Dodge Counties, GA; DuPage County, Chicago and Rockford, IL; Baltimore, MD; Boston and Cambridge, MA; Kalamazoo County and Flint, MI; Broome County, NY; Toledo, OH; Tulsa, OK; Portland, OR; Lycoming, Philadelphia, Pittsburgh, Williamsport and York, PA; and Easley, SC.

Contact Information

Research Organizations
Hilary Kopp and Richard Kazis
Jobs for the Future
One Bowdoin Square
Boston, MA 02114
(617) 742-5995, Fax (617) 742-5767

Marsha Silverberg
Mathematica Policy Research, Inc.
P.O. Box 2393
Princeton, NJ 08543-2393
(609) 799-3535, Fax (609) 799-0005

Funding and Monitoring Organization
Eileen Pederson
Office of Policy and Research
Employment and Training Administration
U.S. Department of Labor
200 Constitution Avenue, NW, Room N-5637
Washington, D.C. 20210
(202) 219-5472, Fax (202) 219-5455

School-to-Work

A Summary of:

Partners In Progress: Early Steps In Creating School-to-Work Systems

April 1997, Mathematica Policy Research, Inc. (Princeton, NJ) by Alan Hershey, Paula Hudis, Marsha Silverberg, and Joshua Haimson

(Evaluation funded by U.S. Departments of Education and Labor.)

Overview

The School-to-Work Opportunities Act of 1994 (hereafter STWOA) authorizes five-year federal grants as "seed money" to help states implement school-to-work (hereafter STW) systems which include work-based learning, school-based learning and connecting activities.

POPULATION

This evaluation surveyed a representative sample of all 1996 high school seniors in STW partnerships in eight in-depth study states to determine the level and quality of their participation in STW activities. This report focuses on students of high school age. The effect of STW reforms on elementary and middle school students, participants in postsecondary education and training, and out-of-school youth will be given greater attention in later reports from this evaluation.

Descriptive Findings

"There is wide participation in some STW components, but few students . . . so far participate in a full range of STW activities . . . Student involvement in defined programs of study that integrate academic and vocational curriculum was relatively uncommon for the 1996 baseline cohort."
Mathematica

This evaluation report includes: (1) estimates derived from student surveys of student participation in STW activities and (2) qualitative findings based on in-depth site visits to eight states. Of a representative sample of 1996 seniors in STW partnerships in the in-depth study states:

- about 63 percent had a comprehensive set of career development activities in that they met four of the following five criteria: (1) talking to school staff about career plans (87 percent); (2) completing an interest inventory (80 percent); (3) attending talks by employers at their school; (4) taking a workplace readiness class; and (5) going on a worksite visit (over 50 percent) or a job shadow organized by their school (25 percent)
- about 16 percent had participated in what could be described as a "linked workplace activity" by ever having:

- (1) held a paid job obtained through school (15 percent); or at some point in high school (88 percent); or held an unpaid internship or volunteer work obtained through school (17 percent) or at some point in high school (42 percent);
- (2) completed an assignment in an academic class using information or skills acquired during that work-based activity (17 percent of seniors had taken an English, mathematics, or science course specifically designed for students with their career interest; 12 percent had had an assignment in such a class concerning the career area they had chosen); or
- (3) had their performance in that work-based activity count toward a grade at school (58 percent reported that school staff received an assessment of their worksite performance, but only 25 percent reported that school and employer staff ever spoke to each other about their performance)

- two percent of 12th graders in the in-depth study states' STW partnerships engaged in all three primary STW components: (1) a comprehensive set of career development activities (63 percent); (2) something like a career major—choosing a career focus for their high school studies, being grouped with other students who have similar career interests, and having classroom assignments related to that career interest (12 percent); and (3) a linked workplace activity (16 percent)

The following qualitative findings were reported:

- Of the eight states studied, all have begun building a system infrastructure by implementing key STW components: three by creating employer incentives, six by promoting career development models, two by facilitating college enrollment and five by defining target career clusters. However, only one state has done *all* of these.
- STW concepts have become a central element of broader education reform in two of the eight states. In other states, STW priorities are still peripheral to other education reforms.

- The most widely available aspect of STW is those activities designed to improve students' career awareness. However, few schools yet deliver a coherent career development sequence.
- Changes in school curriculum (such as career majors and integrating academic and vocational instruction) are, so far, a lower priority than career development or workplace activities. Two states set goals for student participation in career-focused programs of study, whereas four states have established goals for participation in work-based learning.
- Many local partnerships are concentrating early efforts on promoting workplace activity. However, expanding the scale of workplace activities and linking these activities to the school curriculum have presented obstacles.
- A widespread set of local partnerships has been created, most of which have taken the first steps toward creating common policies and practices, spanning multiple school districts and employers.

"Educators and employers alike in large numbers are excited about the prospects for linking school and workplace learning to prepare students better for successful careers."   Mathematica

Key Components

The STWOA provides states with 5-year grants as "seed money" to help implement STW systems involving a broad collaboration among employers, organized labor, educators, and public agencies responsible for economic and workforce development, education and human services. By late 1996, federal funding totaling $643 million had been provided to: eight states in 1994, 19 in 1995 and 10 more in late 1996. By July 1996, there were 875 local partnerships in the first 27 states that had received either substate or direct federal implementation grants. Federal grants had also been made to an additional 30 local partnerships in other states, and to a total of 26 organizations serving Native Americans

or youth in urban and rural high-poverty areas. The STW systems funded were to include the following core components:

- **Work-based learning**: providing students with workplace mentoring and a planned program of work experience linked to schooling;
- **School-based learning**: including a coherent multi-year sequence of integrated academic and vocational instruction tied to occupational skill standards and challenging academic standards; and
- **Connecting activities**: ensuring coordination of work and school-based learning components by involving employers, improving secondary-postsecondary linkages, and providing technical assistance.

Contributing Factors

State Governance

The choice by states of a primary focus on workplace activity or on changing schools "reflects choices about where administrative responsibility for STW implementation is placed." In some states, STW administration is in agencies with responsibility for workforce development which have set goals for

getting large fractions of high school students into some form of workplace activity, ranging from brief job shadowing visits to extensive internships or apprenticeships. Other states rely more on their state departments of education or have independent STW offices, outside of any existing agency.

"Over the longer term, we will assess progress towards creation of a STW system by the *consistency* between state STW policy and other education and workforce policies, the *continuity* achieved in innovative program features, the *connectedness* of activities available to students, the *breadth and diversity* of student participation, and the *sustainability* of the institutional relationships forged by STW partnerships."   Mathematica

NOTE: A forthcoming book by Lynn Olson (Senior Editor of *Education Week*), *The School-to-Work Revolution* (Addison-Wesley, 1997), offers the following observations based upon Olson's coast-to-coast school and worksite visits. School-to-Work can:

- engage and motivate students;
- lower dropout rates, improve school attendance and increase academic course-taking; and
- increase students' participation in postsecondary education.

However, it is still too early to assess whether STW can significantly raise academic achievement.

Early Focus on Carer Awareness

A focus on career awareness is facilitated as it is often an expansion of earlier efforts. Career awareness was also widely implemented because it "can help students select their high school courses, choose a career major where that option exists, and decide what workplace activity to pursue . . . [P]arents generally see career development activities as useful for all students, rather than a form of 'tracking.'"

Work/Quality of Positions

Evaluators found that workplace opportunities that students get through school are of higher quality than opportunities they find on their own, including being in more diverse industries and occupations, working in areas related to their expressed career interests, spending more time learning and practicing skills as opposed to doing regular production work and providing training in a structured classroom or workshop setting.

Guidance/Support

Mathematica: Making career awareness activities "a systemic part of students' experiences requires overcoming shortages of counseling personnel and expanding the role of counselors beyond the traditional focus on helping students get into college

. . . To multiply the effect of their work, counselors are becoming consultants to other school staff, organizing and overseeing career development services and activities rather than doing all the work themselves. Counselors are more commonly managing career centers where students do self-directed interest assessments and research on careers, using new software products. Teachers in some sites have been enlisted and trained as auxiliary advisors to students. Career awareness units commonly are incorporated into English or social studies classes taught by academic teachers."

A Low Rate of Participation in Multiple STW Components

STW is still a new venture and this report only provides baseline information. However, evaluators interpret the low rate of participation in multiple STW components as a reflection of the fact that states have set priorities on certain components rather than seeking to expand all at once. Moreover partnerships and schools have limited capacity, so far, to involve large numbers of students in career majors or intensive workplace activities linked to their school.

Study Methodology

This first report of the five-year evaluation effort of STW under the STWOA presents baseline information from in-depth site visits to eight states and 39 communities and a survey of a random sample representing all 1996 high school seniors from STW partnership schools in these states. Future reports will include follow-up surveys of students and local partnerships and information on academic course-taking and postsecondary education, training and employment.

Geographic Areas

Eight states (FL, OH, MA, MI, WI, OR, KY, and MD) and 39 communities.

Contact Information

Research Organization
Alan Hershey and Marsha Silverberg
Mathematica Policy Research, Inc.
P.O. Box 2393
Princeton, NJ 08543-2393
(609) 799-3535, Fax (609) 799-0005

Funding and Monitoring Organization
David Goodwin
Planning and Evaluation Service
U.S. Department of Education
Office of the Under Secretary
600 Independence Avenue, SW, Room 4131
Washington, D.C. 20202-8240
(202) 401-0263, Fax (202) 401-5943

A Summary of:

Summer Training and Education Program (STEP): Report on Long-term Impacts

Anatomy of a Demonstration: The Summer Training and Education Program (STEP) from Pilot Through Replication and Postprogram Impacts

Winter 1992, Public/Private Ventures (P/PV), (Philadelphia, PA) by Jean Baldwin Grossman and Cynthia L. Sipe

Winter 1992, Public/Private Ventures (P/PV), (Philadelphia, PA) by Gary Walker and Frances Vilella-Velez

Overview

The Summer Training and Education Program (hereafter STEP) was designed to stem summer learning loss of youth at-risk of dropping out of school by providing paid summer work and remedial education. Economically and educationally disadvantaged youth, ages 14 or 15, were eligible to receive two summers and an intervening school year of services.

POPULATION

The program was targeted at low-income youth performing below grade level. Most were in the 8th or 9th grade, but their average reading level was 6th grade, and their math level was 7th grade. Almost ⅓ had been held back in school at least one grade. Almost ½ lived in single-parent households. Forty to forty-five percent of STEP participants were sexually active and 2/3 of that group reported that they did not use contraceptives. The racial makeup of the sample group was roughly 45 percent African American, 20 percent Asian, 20 percent Hispanic, and 20 percent "other."

Evidence of Effectiveness

Short-term and long-term findings for STEP varied considerably.

Short-Term

Compared to a randomized control group, STEP treatment group members:

- tested a ½ grade higher in math and reading at the end of each summer

- who enrolled in the program in Year One of the pilot reported less consumption of alcohol than the control group (46.5 vs. 52 percent)
- significantly increased their knowledge of birth control methods and availability after the first summer and sustained these gains over the 15 month program
- who came to STEP not having had sex, may have been more likely to use contraception in the future, but the results were not consistent across participant cohorts

Long-Term

At 42 months post-enrollment:

- among STEP girls who had enrolled in Year One (mostly 18 or 19 at post-program interview time), about 45 percent had been pregnant. These rates were comparable to those in the control group, and somewhat higher than national rates
- nearly one-third of the girls who had enrolled in STEP in Year Two (and who were mostly 17 and 18 when interviewed) had had at least one pregnancy

- STEP participants did not differ substantially from the control group in terms of (1) educational measures (dropping out, graduating, going on to further education, standardized test scores), (2) being employed, or (3) the percentages of self-reported drug use in the post-program interview (Year One: 14.4 vs. 17.2 percent reported marijuana use; 1.9 vs. 2.3 percent reported cocaine use. Year Two: 17.1 vs. 16.2 percent reported marijuana use; 1.5 vs. 1.4 percent reported cocaine use)

Key Components

STEP was designed to decrease or reverse summer learning-losses of at-risk youth by targeting the risk factors of a break in academic instruction over the summer months, low basic skills, and teenage parenthood. It addressed these risk factors by combining summer work between the 8th and 9th grades with remedial education programs and "life skills" training emphasizing social and sexual responsibility. The national demonstration of STEP began in the summer of 1985.

The STEP program encompassed four key components:

- Remediation. STEP youth had a minimum of 90 hours of group and individually-paced remedial reading and math instruction over the course of the summer (4 half-days per week). The remedial program was designed to address two problems: (1) a lack of basic skills; and (2) "a lack of control over the learning process."
- Life Skills and Opportunities (LSO). This component of the STEP program (1 half-day per week) stressed responsible social and sexual decisions. Instructors

emphasized the relationship between sexual decisions and personal development (by demonstrating the "economic, health and social implications of early childbearing") and provided information on the availability and proper use of contraceptives.
- Work experience. STEP youth worked half-time (5 half-days per week) in minimum-wage jobs.
- School-year support. STEP initiated periodic group activities and individual counseling/advocacy throughout the school year. Program staff also tried to enlist parental support with informational mailings and meetings held at the beginning of the school year.

Additional factors that distinguish STEP from other youth programs:

- targeted at in-school youth (14-15 year olds)
- lasted for 15 months (two summers, plus some contact during the school year)
- offered pay for summer class hours as well as for work hours
- directly addressed the interactions between teenage parenting and high school graduation

Contributing Factors

"The STEP experience offers a complex set of lessons . . . They challenge our public leaders to approach the lives of an increasing number of American youth with the resourcefulness, hardheadedness, commitment and money that investment in change requires."

Public/Private Ventures

A Business-like Approach

P/PV: "STEP's designers and funders were willing to invest the resources necessary to produce innovative education approaches and materials that learning theory indicated would generate improvements." The project required a development investment of about half a million dollars, installation costs of about $15,000 per site, and ongoing support of between $10,000-$15,000 per site. "These kinds of costs are familiar to business, but are often not

adequately considered or taken into account in dealing with social issues."

Targeting Critical "Gap Periods" for At-risk Youth Can Have Positive Results

The STEP program was aimed at the summer gap—when youth are without the structure and focus of school—because research had shown that at-risk youth lose much ground during the summer. Given the positive short-term results of the program, it appears that it may be useful to target other gap periods—such as after-school and weekends—to give needed structure and support to vulnerable youth.

Short-term Programs Can Have Only Limited Effects on the Lives of At-risk Youth

P/PV: "STEP's strength was its highly organized, intensive and controlled involvement in each youth's life during the summer. But once that involvement ended, there was no vehicle to reinforce and continue STEP's positive impacts. Thus, those impacts were not carried forward, and dissipated. STEP's major lesson for policymakers and leaders is that short-term interventions . . . do fill critical gaps in the lives of disadvantaged young people, and do provide youth with much-needed boosts and experiences, but cannot alone produce long-term change."

Successful Components of STEP Not Replicated in Students' Everyday School Experience

The STEP program produced learning gains in a short period of time. Key features of STEP are intensive adult contact and paid work in the summers. These generally are not features of a typical public school environment.

Study Methodology

The evaluation used a random assignment method to develop a treatment group and a control group (offered a summer job only). Researchers gathered data on program outcomes from post-program interviews with both groups and from school transcripts.

Geographic Areas

STEP was implemented in five cities beginning in the summer of 1985: Boston, MA; Fresno and San Diego, CA; Portland, OR and Seattle, WA.

Contact Information

Research and Implementing Organization
Maxine Sherman, Communications Manager
Public/Private Ventures, Inc.
2005 Market Street, Suite 900
Philadelphia, Pennsylvania 19103
(215) 592-4400, Fax (215) 557-4469

A Summary of:

The 1993 Summer Youth Employment and Training Program: Study of the JTPA Title IIB Program During the Summer of 1993, Final Report

Westat, Inc. (Rockville, MD)

(Evaluation funded by U.S. Department of Labor.)

Overview

The Summer Youth Employment and Training Program (hereafter SYETP) has been operated by the U.S. Department of Labor (hereafter DOL) and funded by Title IIB of the Job Training Partnership Act (hereafter JTPA) since 1981. It provides disadvantaged young people with supervised and meaningful summer work experience and short-term financial assistance. Remedial educational services began to be required, as needed, only in 1986.

POPULATION

The 1993 SYETP served over 600,000 youth. The 50 sites included in the evaluation served 168,000 youth of whom 42 percent were 14-to-15-years-old; 36 percent were 16-to-17-years-old; and 21 percent were 18-to-21-years-old; 70 percent African American; 12 percent Hispanic; 13 percent white and 5 percent "other"; about 44 percent were from families receiving welfare; 86 percent were enrolled in school; 10 percent high school graduates; 4 percent high school dropouts; 3 percent limited English proficient; 7 percent disabled; 44 percent from families receiving welfare; 6 percent were parents.

Descriptive Findings

"[A] positive picture emerges from this study of the SYETP for 1993. We found that youth received substantive work assignments and they showed a strong desire to work. Participants were generally well supervised, learned about the culture of work, and acquired work-related skills. Further, most SDAs are making a serious effort to incorporate academic components into their summer programs."   **Westat**

This evaluation describes summer 1993 programs and practices, assesses the work and academic components, and provides recommendations. It showed:

Work
- youth were almost always engaged in real work, not make-work
- youth wanted to work
- youth were generally well-supervised by competent and motivated worksite supervisors

- youth rated their supervisors highly in the majority of sites
- youth acquired or strengthened general work skills

Academic Component
- just over 40 percent of youth nationally participated in an SYETP academic component
- these academic programs varied broadly
- most of the academic programs incorporated important aspects that were unlike regular school offerings
- youth's opinions of the academic programs were generally favorable (of 450 youth who filled out a

confidential questionnaire, 56 percent said that the summer academic program was more useful than regular school), but they preferred to work

- there was little substantive coordination between the work and academic components or between the summer academic program and the public school system

SYETP cost $1,362 per youth per year.

Key Components

Started as part of the War on Poverty in the 1960s, SYETP was re-authorized under JTPA in 1981. Each summer program is managed by Service Delivery Areas (hereafter SDAs) defined under JTPA. It began as a work experience program designed to provide short-term financial assistance to economically disadvantaged youth in exchange for work of benefit to their communities. In response to 1986 JTPA amendments and through subsequent policy guidance, DOL has reoriented the IIB program to incorporate educational remediation as a major program component. In the Summer of 1993, SYETP participants received varying amounts of work experience and academics: 59 percent[1] were in work experience only, 28 percent had both work and academics, and 13 percent had academics only. Youth participating in the program earned an average of $810 over the summer.

Work experience was roughly split among:

- "working with paper"- office or clerical work
- "working with property"—building maintenance, landscaping, or conservation work
- "working with people"—recreation facilities, schools or hospitals

Academic components included:

- reading, mathematics and writing
- some included more advanced academics, SAT preparation, vocational exploration, specialized vocational training, "pre-employment work maturity" instruction, fine arts, and life skills training (see pp. 70-73 for a more complete description and evaluation of the educational components of the Summer 1994 SYETP)

Instructional settings included:

- traditional school classrooms and non-traditional settings, such as computer labs at vocational-technical schools and community colleges, university campuses, libraries, JTPA worksites and individual tutoring arrangements

Contributing Factors

Employers Not Difficult to Identify
Westat: "SDAs did not encounter serious barriers to securing worksites for the program. When asked what worked best about the worksite development process, the largest number of SDAs responded that it was their ability to return to a core of employers demonstrating the capacity and interest in providing quality work assignments to program participants."

Worksite Supervisors Are Critical
Westat: "Good supervisors combined knowledge of the job with empathy for and genuine interest in the youngsters enrolled in the program." Westat recommends careful recruitment, orientation and ongoing support for worksite supervisors, including at least weekly on-site visits.

Participant Expectations and Requirements
Westat: "While some SDAs were more flexible and accommodating than others, there was broad agreement that clearly defining the program's rules and procedures at the outset and holding youth accountable for attendance and behavior during the course of the summer helped make the program an important 'world of work' learning experience. Rules and procedures should be spelled out in mandatory orientation sessions, preferably supplemented with written materials."

Youth Need Not Be "Job Ready" in Order to Benefit from the Work Experience Program
Westat: "While it is desirable to hold youth to reasonable standards of attendance and behavior, it is

"Worksite supervisors need to be selected who have the ingenuity to achieve the goals of the program by balancing the special problems of disadvantaged youth with the importance of learning the basic skills and discipline of the workplace."   Westat

"When SDAs decide to couple work experience with academic remediation, they may need to depart from conventional methods of instruction and familiar service providers in order to successfully overcome youth's resistance to 'school as usual' in the summer months."   Westat

also important to view the summer program as a learning experience for youth as well as a period of productive employment. In many of the SDAs visited, youth were not considered to be job ready in terms of either work discipline or job skills, but good worksite supervision succeeded in closing this gap during the program."

Unlike Regular School

Westat: "Youth's receptiveness to the academic component of the summer program appears to be greater to the extent that the academic component is unlike regular school." Smaller classes (average student/teacher ratios of 11:1), individualized attention, use of computers, and non-traditional curricula "particularly appealed to participants."

Time and Attention

Westat: "Students repeatedly remarked .. that the smaller class size allowed them to get needed individual attention from their teachers. The teachers also frequently stated that these disadvantaged youth needed teacher personal time and attention, and they were much more able to give the time and attention in the summer program than would be possible in regular school."

Flexibility

Westat: "Flexibility and creativity in making the optimum use of the resources available to SDAs in administering the summer program [are important to program quality]. . . . Flexibility in staffing and creative linkages with other resources can maximize the limited funds available under IIB."

Study Methodology

Researchers conducted in-depth observations on site (3-5 day case studies) at 50 SDAs. Approximately 1,000 youth, 200 worksite supervisors, 200 teachers and tutors, hundreds of program managers, academic coordinators and community leaders were interviewed. In addition, researchers analyzed responses to a mail survey of all 631 SDAs.

Geographic Areas

Sites located across the U.S..

Contact Information

Research Organization
Ellen Tenenbaum, Senior Study Director
Westat, Inc.
1650 Research Blvd.
Rockville, MD 20850
(301) 738-3617, Fax (301) 294-4475

Funding and Monitoring Organization
David Lah
Office of Planning and Research
Employment & Training Administration
U.S. Department of Labor, N-5637
200 Constitution Ave., NW
Washington, DC 20210
(202) 219-5472, Fax (202) 219-5455

[1] Based on survey responses from sites with 542,000 of the 600,000 youth in the 1993 SYETP.

Summer Youth Employment, 1994

A Summary of:

Evaluation Of The Educational Component Of The Summer Youth Employment And Training Program: Interim Report

December 1995, Social Policy Research Associates (Menlo Park, CA) by Ronald D'Amico, Katherine Dickinson, Deborah Kogan, Maria Remboulis and Hanh Cao Yo Center for Human Resources, Heller Graduate School, Brandeis University (Waltham, MA) by Susan P. Curnan, Christopher Kingsley and Jennifer Nahas

(Evaluation funded by U.S. Department of Labor.)

Overview

(Please see Summer Youth Employment, 1993, pp. 51-53.)

POPULATION

In the Summer of 1994, SYETP programs served 620,000 economically disadvantaged youth aged 14 to 21. This evaluation included 1,700 youth in 83 programs most of whom were performing below grade level in English and mathematics (75 percent) and many of whom performed four grades below level.

Evidence of Effectiveness

"Given that summer learning loss is common among disadvantaged youth during the summer months, the ability of these students to maintain their skills levels let alone increase them must be viewed very favorably."   **SPR/Brandeis**

This evaluation examined the effect of the "educational components" of the U.S. Department of Labor (hereafter DOL) -funded Summer Youth Employment and Training Program (hereafter SYETP) during the Summer of 1994. Researchers found (at statistically significant levels) that of participants in the evaluation:

- there was an average change in test scores from pre-test to post-test of 1.2 grade levels in reading and 1.3 grade levels in mathematics
- over 65 percent improved their test scores over the course of the summer

- about 15 percent maintained their skill levels over the course of the summer

Comparing across the three primary forms of instruction identified by researchers—traditional classroom training, classroom training using a real-life focus, and project-based learning— the study found that:

- students who participated in project- based learning realized the largest gains in reading and math, compared to students in either of the other methods. The traditional classroom approach was second in effectiveness.

"We found that learning gains were greatest in programs: providing project-based approaches to instruction, using active learning methods, having well-specified and individualized objectives for instruction, providing high-quality educational content taught in a functional context, and using high-quality instruction methods. Additionally, learning gains were greatest in programs that were of longer duration and intensity and that had smaller class sizes."   SPR/Brandeis

Comparing other instructional delivery styles, researchers determined that:

- students who participated in active learning realized larger gains in reading and math, than students receiving just lecture and exercises or just computer aided instruction
- students in high quality programs with high quality content and instruction realized large gains in reading and math

- students in programs with instructional methods supporting practice of skills identified by the Secretary's Commission on Achieving Necessary Skills (SCANS) realized gains in reading and math
- more hours of educational training and low youth-to-instructor ratios contributed to small gains in reading and math

Key Components

In Summer 1994, DOL funded a variety of summer youth employment and training programs under SYETP. These were intended to stem summer learning loss for disadvantaged youth, most of whom already had very low academic skill levels. Funds went to service delivery areas (SDAs) which engaged "service providers" to run the programs. Service providers included schools, community-based organizations, non-profits, local governments and some private businesses. All students:

- were assessed for possible placement in an educational component, for which they usually received close to the minimum wage for class time [41 percent of youth received some "academic component," 13 percent received academics only (no work experience)]
- if in classrooms, had small classes and individual attention

Other services which varied from site to site included:

- summer jobs at minimum wage
- pre-employment and work-maturity skills
- life skills instruction
- supplementary activities, such as recreation, guest speakers and field trips
- child care, transportation and other support services

In traditional classroom training programs (39 programs[1]), instruction revolved around the academic content of the course. These programs used three primary forms of instruction to deliver remedial basic skills instruction: 1) lectures and workbook exercises, 2) computer assisted instruction, and 3) active, student-focused, interactive team learning.

Programs providing classroom training teaching academics using a real-life focus (32 programs), looked very similar to the traditional classroom training programs in delivery, but organized academic instruction around a primary focus on world-of-work or life skills. Academic skills were focused on secondarily, if at all. When academic skills were covered the instruction was short and of low intensity. Some programs achieved some success when they incorporated group discussions, role playing and mini-projects.

In programs using project-based teaching (26 programs), participants develop and are offered multiple opportunities to regularly use, practice, master and verbalize an array of important and integrated skills, including basic skills, thinking and problem solving skills, interpersonal skills, work maturity skills and vocational skills as they plan and produce a tangible product or service. Project-based learning is an educational approach that requires teachers to become facilitators and students to take charge of their own learning through the planning, implementation and evaluation of an authentic project. Through this process, young people apply and refine their skills to complete a project.

The quality and amount of project-based learning differed broadly at these sites. All project-based learning sites included active learning and the practice of SCANS skills (and some CAI and lecture).

Active learning in educational components was part of a second set of measures used to analyze instruction. Active learning methods were described as including group discussions, peer-to-peer teaching or team teaching. These methods could have been used in "traditional classroom", teaching academics with a real-life focus or project-based classrooms, but more often coincided with project-based instruction..

Contributing Factors

"Through planning and completing their projects young people are offered multiple opportunities to regularly use, practice, master and verbalize an array of important and integrated skills, including basic skills . . . , thinking and problem solving skills . . . , and interpersonal skills . . . , as well as work maturity skills and vocational skills." SPR/Brandeis

Project-Based Learning

SPR/Brandeis: Project-based approaches "hold great merit in fully integrating work and learning and can be very effective in imparting substantial learning gains."

Careful Implementation Coupled with Technical Assistance

The higher quality programs had superior implementation characterized by clear communication of goals and objectives and strong leadership from the federal and SDA levels to the service providers. SPR/Brandeis considered the following factors when looking at successful implementation: proper training of staff in innovative instructional methods and working with at-risk youth, appropriate placement of youth into educational services (not based solely on logistics, age, or prior skill level), effective case management (in tune with the personal issues of youth and not just the paperwork), small classes and longer duration of services, including connections back to the regular school year. In many cases, programs were aided in implementation by an experienced technical assistance provider.

Opportunities to Learn and Time on Task

For high quality instruction, participants need sufficient opportunities to learn, instruction of sufficient duration and intensity to prevent summer learning loss and, ideally, improve participants' skills. It also requires that youth spend substantial time on task, learning and practicing skills.

Personal Attention and Caring Adults

Providing personal attention to each participant is another way to increase their opportunity to learn. "[T]he instructors need to be _caring adults_ who approach their tasks as "coaches" or mentors rather than "directors" of participants' activities."

Study Methodology

Evaluators interviewed staff in 30 SDAs, went on in-depth site visits and conducted focus groups at each of the 83 service projects managed by these SDAs. At each site, detailed case histories were established for two young people, one-third of whom received follow-up calls a year later. Pre- and post- scores on basic skills tests and data on client characteristics were collected for 1,700 youth in 27 programs in 13 SDAs.

Geographic Areas

SDAs included in the evaluation were in AL, AZ, CA, FL, IL, IN, IO, KY, MA, MD, MI, MN, MT, NC, NJ, NY, OK, PA, RI, TX, VA and WA. CA, FL, PA, TX, and WA had more than one SDA involved.

Contact Information

Research Organizations
Ronald D'Amico
Social Policy Research Associates
200 Middlefield Road, Suite 100
Menlo Park, CA 94025
(415) 617-8625, Fax (415) 617-8630

Susan Curnan, Executive Director
Center for Human Resources
Heller Graduate School, Brandeis University
Waltham, MA 02254-9110
(617) 736-3770, Fax (617) 736-3851

Funding & Monitoring Organization
Greg Knorr, Statistician
Office of Planning and Research
Employment & Training Administration
U.S. Department of Labor, N-5637
200 Constitution Ave., NW
Washington, D.C. 20001
(202) 219-5472, Ext. 120, Fax (202) 219-5455

[1] Some educational programs had multiple components, in which case they might have been classified in more than one of the categories identified above. Youth received a combination of services, but only those considered part of the "educational component" were evaluated.

Talent Development

A Summary of:

The Talent Development High School: Essential Components

September 1996, by Velma LaPoint, Will Jordan, James M. McPartland and Donna Penn Towns

The Talent Development High School: Early Evidence of Impact on School Climate, Attendance, and Student Promotion

September 1996, by James M. McPartland, Nettie Legters, Will Jordan and Edward L. McDill
Both evaluations by Center for Research on the Education of Students Placed At Risk (CRESPAR) Johns Hopkins University, Baltimore, MD and Howard University, Washington, D.C.

(Both evaluations funded by Office of Educational Research and Improvement, U.S. Department of Education.)

Overview

The Center for Research on the Education of Students Placed At Risk (hereafter CRESPAR), a collaborative between Johns Hopkins and Howard Universities, created a model of educational reform called "Talent Development" (hereafter TD) which features a multiple "school-within-a-school" career academy structure. Each academy is organized around a demanding curriculum, high expectations for student achievement, and an environment conducive to learning. In a partnership with CRESPAR, Patterson High School in Baltimore, Maryland— slated for reconstitution due to poor performance—was the first site to implement the TD Model.

POPULATION

About 2000 students attend the TD high school studied, Patterson High School. Sixty percent of the students are African American; 30 percent are white (mostly ethnic, working class); and 10 percent are American Indian, Asian or Hispanic. In 1994, Patterson was designated by the state of Maryland as one of the two worst high schools in the state because of its chaotic environment, poor attendance, excessive student tardiness, student failure (in 1993-94, over 80 percent failed the 9th grade), and poor test performance (only about ¼ of Patterson 9th grade students could pass a state math competency test that is supposed to be taken in 7th or 8th grade).

Evidence of Effectiveness

CRESPAR conducted an evaluation on TD at Patterson High School which compared school records of the high school students (all of whom were "participants" in this full-school reform initiative) from the 1994-95 school year to the 1995-96 school year and found:

* 9th grade attendance improved by 9.4 percentage points (from 65.6 to 75 percent)
* attendance school-wide went up 6.1 percentage points (from 71.6 to 77.7 percent)
* compared with eight other non-selective Baltimore high schools, Patterson moved from second worst in attendance to second best
* 9th grade promotion went from 47.3 to an expected 69.1 percent (based on first semester course grades)
* teachers' perceptions of the school changed dramatically
   — the percent of 9th grade and upper grade teachers who thought the school environment was not conducive to student achievement went down (80 and 86.7 percent respectively in 1994-1995 to 27.5 and 4.5 percent in 1995-1996)
   — the percent of 9th grade and upper grade teachers who thought absenteeism was a major problem went down (96 and 97.8 percent respectively in 1994-1995 to 45.5 and 19 percent in 1995-1996)
   — the percent of 9th grade and upper grade teachers who thought the school "seemed like a big family" went up (13 and 13.7 percent respectively in 1994-95 to 45.5 and 54.5 percent in 1995-1996)

The cost of restructuring the school was approximately $25.00 per student or between one and two percent of the previous year's total costs. This will vary up or down at other sites depending upon needs to redesign the building and for planning time and professional development.

Key Components

"The Talent Development Model provides a comprehensive package of specific high school changes for students placed at risk. It is based upon research on student motivation and teacher commitment. It can be reliably implemented with adaptations to meet local circumstances."
                                              CRESPAR

The first TD site, Patterson High School, was completely restructured both physically and socially and reorganized into five academies—one freshman development academy and four upperclass career-oriented academies—focused on fostering individual student talents. The major TD components at Patterson were:

* establishing a general preparatory academy in the 9th grade featuring interdisciplinary teacher teams responsible for a maximum of 150-180 students
* setting up career academies in the 10th-12th grades to provide a relevant focus for studies
* maintaining the same homeroom class and teacher grades 10-12
* revising the homeroom teacher role to include advising and counseling
* making each academy physically separate to create a smaller learning community (separate entrances and stairways; a maximum of 300-350 students in the upper grade career academies)
* establishing a common core with all courses at the college-preparatory level (separate program tracks for College Prep, General Studies, or Vocational-Business were eliminated)
* holding students to demanding standards to pass courses
* setting up a four-period day (instead of seven) so classes are more in-depth and students have fewer teachers
* bringing in employer advisory boards to help design relevant curriculum and provide internship opportunities

Contributing Factors

Caring Adults
The school-within-a-school framework meant that teachers could more easily get to know their students and form stronger relationships with them. Having four class periods in a day instead of seven reduced the number of teachers with whom a student interacted daily and fostered stronger relationships. The teacher's role was changed from evaluator to coach, with examinations based on departmental standards, thus relieving teachers from student pressure to alter tests or grades. Finally, homeroom teachers took on counseling and advisory roles, helping students with both their academic and non-academic problems.

"These early results indicate that one of the worst high schools in an urban district, designated for reconstitution by the state, is well on its way to becoming a very good school in its first year as a Talent Development High School. The teachers and administrators of Patterson High School have been able to turn their school around in terms of the climate for learning. They have also significantly improved student attendance and the probabilities of student promotions and graduations."

CRESPAR

School-within-a-School Framework

The separate Ninth Grade Success Academy and four upper grade Career Academies (Arts and Humanities, Business and Finance, Sports Studies and Health/Wellness, and Transportation and Engineering Technology) were housed in their own parts of the building, with separate entrances and stairways. While the 9th grade academy was the largest, students within the academy were divided into teams of no more than 150-170 students. The career academies were no larger than 300-350 students. This physical restructuring helped foster a more family-like feeling in school.

Emphasis on Attendance

When Patterson studied the causes behind its low student promotion rate, it found that poor attendance was the strongest predictor of course failure. To combat student absenteeism, teachers under the new system made a determined effort to monitor attendance problems at the start, making calls directly to the student whenever she or he did not attend class. Researchers noted that improvements to the overall school climate also increased attendance, as students felt safer and more nurtured. They expect continuing improvement in attendance as new teaching methods are implemented (use of technology, project-based learning, cooperative learning) to more fully engage students in learning.

Recovery

Students who fail in terms of attendance, grades, or promotion have an opportunity to come back. Students with five or more absences per quarter automatically receive a failing grade, but if they have perfect attendance for five days in a row they can erase an earlier absence from the record. Students also have the opportunity to retake a failed course at Summer School, "Saturday School," or "Credit School" (an hour after the end of the regular school day). If students are not promoted, they can gain a mid-year promotion by earning the missing credits during the first 18-week term of the next year.

Modified Assessment Tools

Patterson's assessment tools recognized both achievement against standardized criteria and improvement against a student's own starting point. Achievement and improvement grades are combined (with achievement weighted twice as much as improvement) to arrive at a final grade.

Additional Services to Address a Range of Student Needs

The Patterson TD school incorporated a number of services: coaching classes, peer tutoring, and extra computer drill and practice. The school took note of students who were falling behind and placed them in smaller classes, or classes with longer periods. For the most demanding courses, students were scheduled in double periods. The school also provided help with personal problems through school social workers and mental health professionals. A full-time "professional health suite" was set up, and school staff regularly discussed health issues with the students. Finally, students with severe disciplinary problems were placed in the "Twilight School," which featured a smaller student/teacher ratio (10:1) and instruction in life coping skills so these students could eventually return to the regular school.

Study Methodology

Researchers compared outcomes at Patterson High School from the 1994-1995 school year with the 1995-1996 school year. To gauge outcomes, they used faculty surveys, student attendance rates, report card grades and course credits earned.

Geographic Areas

Patterson High School in Baltimore was the initial TD model. The TD model is in various stages of implementation in four other Baltimore schools and in Washington, D.C. Replication is planned in Baltimore, Chicago, Los Angeles, Washington, DC, and six southern states.

Contact Information

Research Organization

Center for Research on the Education of Students Placed At Risk (CRESPAR):

James McPartland, CRESPAR Co-Director
Johns Hopkins University
Center for Social Organization of Schools
3505 North Charles Street
Baltimore, MD 21218
(410) 516-8800, Fax (410) 516-8890

Velma LaPoint, CRESPAR Co-director
Howard University
2900 Van Ness Street, NW
Washington, D.C. 20008
(202) 806-8484, Fax (202) 806-8498

Transitional Environment

A Summary of:

The School Transitional Environment Program

by Robert D. Felner and Angela M. Adan, in *14 Ounces of Prevention: A Casebook for Practitioners* 1989, American Psychological Association, (editors by Richard H. Price, Emory L. Cowen, Raymond P. Lorion and Julia Ramos-McKay)

Overview

The *School Transitional Environment Program* (hereafter STEP) is a primary prevention program designed to identify students at-risk for potential problems at predictable school transition times (e.g., from elementary school to junior high, or junior high to high school) and help them through those transitions. STEP redesigns the high school environment to make school transitions less threatening for students.

POPULATION

STEP targets students who are entering large schools which receive students from multiple feeder schools. The program also targets students with other risk factors, such as low socioeconomic status, minority group membership, simultaneous life transitions or stressors, entering puberty and low levels of coping ability or family support.

Evidence of Effectiveness

Researchers conducted a pilot project of STEP in a large urban high school and assessed the academic performance, absenteeism, self-concept and dropout rate of STEP students compared to a matched group of other students within the high school (the comparison group) after the first year and over a four year period. As one would expect of students undergoing difficult transitions between schools without outside support, comparison group students showed decreased academic performance, increased absenteeism, decreased self-confidence and an increased dropout rate. In contrast to the comparison group, STEP students:

- not only showed no significant decreases in academic performance, they had significantly higher grades and fewer absences in the first and second years of high school (By the third and fourth year of high school, STEP students did not have higher grades and fewer absences than the comparison group.)
- showed no significant increases in absenteeism
- dropped out of school at a lower rate (21 vs. 43 percent)
- showed no significant decrease in their self-concept scores
- perceived the school environment as more stable, understandable, well-organized and supportive

Teachers reported they had more informal and individual meetings about students (in addition to the formal team meetings) than they did before STEP was implemented, and were more satisfied with their jobs due to their involvement with STEP.

Key Components

"... recent research has shown that the transition to high school is often followed by significant decreases in academic perfor-mances and by increases in absenteeism, marked declines in psychological well-being, and increased potential for substance abuse, delinquency, and other behavioral or social problems."   Felner and Adan

There are two major components to STEP:

(1) reducing the degree of flux and complexity in the new school situation; and (2) restructuring the roles of homeroom teachers and guidance personnel.

- STEP usually consists of subgroups of 65-100 students
- STEP students take all primary classes (English, math, social studies, science and homeroom) together, reducing the need to cope with constantly shifting peer groups
- STEP classrooms are located near each other within the school building

- homeroom teachers serve as primary links between students, their parents and the rest of the school, and also take on guidance and counseling roles (help choose classes, follow-up on absences, etc.)
- each student receives a 15 to 20 minute homeroom counseling session, roughly once a month
- STEP teachers meet with each other once or twice a week to identify students who may need additional help

Contributing Factors

"STEP projects and their evaluations underscore the potential for developing inexpensive but effective prevention programs based on informed modification of school environments and practices."
Felner and Adan

Close Community

Both students and teachers felt more comfortable in the school environment through their participation in STEP and the small community it creates within the larger high school. Students felt more supported and teachers had higher job satisfaction and reported more informal interaction with their peers.

Teacher Training

Before the start of the school year, STEP teachers receive two days of training to build knowledge and skills on adolescent developmental and emotional issues, strategies to handle those issues and team-building. School guidance or mental health personnel deliver the training. If they are not available, outside experts can deliver the training and consult throughout the school year. During the school year, STEP team members meet frequently to discuss issues and special student problems.

Academic Impacts Smaller in Later Years Because of Differential Dropout Rate

Significantly more comparison group members performed poorly in their first and second years than STEP students. In many cases, these poor performers then dropped out, thereby increasing the overall performance measurement of the group. This explains why the performance gap between STEP

and comparison students narrows in the third and fourth years of high school.

Long-term Effects are Due to Program Intervention in Year One Only

The STEP program assists new high school students only in their first year. The long-term effects on dropout rates, academic performance and absenteeism are due only to this initial intervention.

Assistance with Difficult Transitions

Large high schools with several feeder schools, high schools with less academically successful or low-income students, and even schools with challenging academic programs may benefit most from STEP as each characteristic creates a difficult transition from one school to the next for students.

Non-Disruptive and Inexpensive

The researchers find that many interventions take much-needed time away from basic academic instruction for at-risk youth. STEP aims to restructure the physical school and class arrangements, not instruction content or classroom time. STEP also does not engage schools in full-school reform or changes in instructional methods. This makes STEP a less expensive, but still effective, form of intervention.

Study Methodology

Sixty-five STEP students were matched with a comparison group of 120 students. Researchers assessed program effects after the first year of high school and also gauged longer-term impacts (dropout rate, subsequent academic performance) through school records.

Geographic Area

The initial experiment of the STEP program was conducted in a large, urban high school.

Contact Information

Research Organization
Robert D. Felner and Angela M. Adan
Center for Research and Development
University of Illinois
IGPA 1002 West Nevada
Urbana, IL 61801-3813
(217) 333-6699, Fax (217) 244-0214

A Summary of:

Wisconsin Youth Apprenticeship Program In Printing: Evaluation 1993-1995, Findings in Brief and Executive Summary

1995, Jobs for the Future (JFF), Boston, MA
by Margaret Terry Orr, Teachers College,
Columbia University

(Evaluation funded by U.S. Department of Education.)

Overview

Wisconsin's Youth Apprenticeship Program in Printing (hereafter YAP) combines two years of classroom instruction in printing technologies with part-time paid, structured work-based training and experience. Students also earn at least one semester of college-level credit.

POPULATION

The YAP class of 1995 was 73 percent male and 97 percent white. As sophomores, they had slightly below average grades, few absences, and almost no disciplinary problems. Students were recruited in their sophomore years often from the graphic arts or print technology classes.

Evidence of Effectiveness

"For the most part, young people who successfully complete the program don't flounder after high school. They have a clear vision and direction about their careers and educational plans and have substantive choices available. These circumstances are less clearly evident for their peers, particularly those who had only classroom instruction in printing."   **Jobs for the Future**

Researchers evaluated employment, educational, and social outcomes for YAP graduates at five sites in Wisconsin. Compared to non-participants, YAP graduates:

- were more likely to be working and to have jobs in the printing industry (94 percent, compared with 60 percent of the co-op graduates and 13 percent of those who took printing classes only)
- were more likely to be working for their youth apprenticeship employer 6-8 months after graduation (75 vs. 20 percent of co-op graduates)
- had better jobs, gauged by hourly earnings, skills required and full-time status

- had a strong interest in the industry and solid, long-term career plans
- while less likely to be enrolled in a college program 6-8 months after graduation (45 vs. 63 percent of their peers), they were more likely to be majoring in printing (71 percent of those enrolled in college)
- were more likely than their peers to have long-term educational plans (at least a four-year degree)
- maintained low absenteeism rates while in school
- felt that they were well-prepared and had a strong direction and focus for postsecondary education, training and employment

Key Components

YAP was designed by the Wisconsin Department of Public Instruction, the Wisconsin Department of Industry, Labor, and Human Resources, and representatives of the printing industry, labor unions, professional associations and local school districts. It features two years of classroom instruction in printing combined with paid work experience and an opportunity to earn college credit. Although conceived as an alternative for non-college bound youth, YAP serves students who have college plans and facilitates postsecondary enrollment through its college credit accumulation. The main features of YAP are:

- competency-based curriculum and assessment systems

- two-year, part-time training and work experience at one or more printing companies
- work-based mentoring
- technical college instruction in printing technology, with some academic courses
- integrated academic and vocational instruction
- collaborative school and industry oversight

Most sites used an advisory committee to plan the program, solve problems as they arose and conduct everyday operations. These committees were formed with representatives of employers, school districts, postsecondary institutions and business associations. The printing companies used contracts for each student to formalize the training process.

Contributing Factors

Employer Involvement

Employers provided lengthy, paid work experience, supported extensive staff time for training and coordination, and followed the rigorous competency-based curriculum and assessment system. In return, employers received well-trained entry level employees, saw their own employees benefit from their mentor role and gained community recognition.

Adult Role Models

JFF: "Most YAP students thought that program participation helped them to learn to interact with others and made them feel better about themselves . . . they formed close attachments with adult role models through the program, as evidenced by the majority of YAP graduates' continued contact with program staff and worksite employees following graduation."

Integrated Curriculum

JFF: "The Wisconsin YAP used a competency-based curriculum structure to organize the school-based and work-based instruction. Through this structure, training is synchronized, students apply in their printing courses what they learn at the worksite and apply their printing course skills and knowledge to their worksite experiences . . . Students are most likely to be clustered for their printing technology

courses, so the instructors, who often supervise students' worksite training, could coordinate and integrate their learning . . . most students rate their printing course as being mor challenging and having more interesting materials and information than in other academic courses. Their attendance was better in their printing courses . . . These reactions seem to be attributable to the contextualized and integrated instruction, suggesting that the students find this approach to be more worthwhile educationally."

Competency-based Assessment Process

JFF: "The competency-based curriculum and assessment process is well-used by the school staff and worksite mentors and trainers. The quarterly (and later semester-based) review and assessment of student performance according to these competencies is jointly done by the school and worksite staff. This reinforces the expectation that student progress will be measured by the competency system. Unlike the traditional assessment system, the YAP assessment structure determines the proficiency level that all students are to attain. The students must keep practicing and relearning the competencies until they demonstrate that they can perform them with moderate to little supervision. Because of their participation in this assessment process and the competency and proficiency standards used, employers in turn recognize and value highly the training and certification YAP students have."

Easily Replicable

JFF: YAP's "core components proved to be easily replicable and adaptable to local resources and conditions in their implementation in five sites, without threatening program fidelity. The model offers considerable flexibility in sequencing the competency areas, scheduling training and classroom learning, using multiple employers for each student's training, and adapting to youth apprenticeship by an individual school or a regional consortium of schools . . . The competency-based curriculum seems to have been key to structuring and integrating both the worksite training and the printing classes training in each site. The collaborative oversight helps to integrate programs further, emphasize quality, and address operational challenges."

Study Methodology

Researchers compared YAP students who graduated from the five sites with other students in less intensive printing preparation or general studies programs. Data was collected through interviews and surveys of seniors, six-month follow-up interviews, interviews of employers, principals, and programs coordinators, and school and employer records on student performance.

Geographic Areas

Operated in five sites in Wisconsin: the Cooperative Education Service Agency (CESA) #2, CESA #7, Fox Valley, Milwaukee, and West Bend.

Contact Information

Research Organization
Jobs for the Future
One Bowdoin Square
Boston, MA 02114
(617) 742-5995, Fax (617) 742-5767

Evaluator for JFF:
Margaret Terry Orr, Associate Professor
Teachers College, Columbia University
525 W. 120th Street, Box 106
New York, New York 10027
(212) 678-3000/3728, Fax (212) 678-4048

California Conservation Corps

A Summary of:

The California Conservation Corps: An Analysis of Short-term Impacts on Participants

June 1987, Public/Private Ventures (Philadelphia)
by Wendy C. Wolf, Sally Leiderman and Richard Voith

(Evaluation funded by William and Flora Hewlett Foundation, Charles Stewart Mott Foundation, State of California and Ford Foundation.)

Overview

The California Conservation Corps (hereafter CCC) involves California youth in improving their lives while benefiting the State of California through conservation work.

CCC is a state-funded program with dual aims: conducting useful conservation work and improving the employability of youth. It is one of a class of youth programs, including the original Civilian Conservation Corps of the 1930s, the successor federal Youth Conservation Corps, Young Adult Conservation Corps and what has become a nationwide network of year-round state and local conservation and service corps. CCC requires work that is paid, physically demanding, production-oriented, resulting in high quality conservation products, completed by "crews" closely supervised by crew leaders, and meaningful and valued by the community.

POPULATION

The CCC accepts 18- to 23-year-old California residents for up to one year. Though the CCC imposes no economic, educational or employment-related conditions on enrollment, it serves a high proportion of educationally or economically disadvantaged youth. Of Corpsmembers who enrolled during the study year (1983-1984) about 70 percent were at-risk in the labor market based on their economic or educational status and nearly half had neither a high school diploma nor GED.

Evidence of Effectiveness

Participant impacts of CCC differed for youth by income, length of stay and racial and gender subgroups. Relative to a comparison group, in the first post-program year, residential youth corps members:

- who were poor (measured by whether they were JTPA-eligible) earned $678 more annually (all dollar figures in 1984-85 dollars)—the positive earnings effect was strongest in months 7-12 ($147/month more)
- who stayed in CCC more than 4 months, earned $726

more annually. In post-program months 4-6, the difference in earnings was $106/month more

- who were dropouts earned $492 more annually (not statistically significant)
- who were black (male and female) earned $51 more per month
- who were Hispanic females earned $58 less per month
- who were Hispanic males and stayed in CCC longer than four months earned $1,205 less annually
- effects for both white males and females were slightly positive (not statistically significant)

"The program pays for itself, just in the value of the work and the corpsmember earnings it produces."
Public/Private Ventures

- who had been residential corpsmembers, worked 138 more hours than a comparison group, but had slightly lower wages (not statistically significant)

The CCC met its work goals to enhance California's environmental resources through the work of young people and to accomplish useful public works. The CCC "accomplishes a large volume of work of substantial monetary value . . . The financial benefits in terms of the work accomplished and economic benefits for youth approximate the State of California's costs to run the CCC program."

In 1984-85, the CCC cost $4,468 per participant, not including wages (in 1984-85 dollars).[1]

Key Components

CCC *"significantly improves the post-program income of its economically disadvantaged participants and improves certain attitudes and behaviors that are part of the constellation of values central to effective citizenship."*
Public/Private Ventures

The CCC is run through the California Resources Agency and 11 service districts (18 regional centers at the time of the study) that recruit participants and run projects statewide.

Services and requirements of centers include:

- residential and nonresidential facilities
- a training academy designed to prepare youth for the CCC experience (there is no longer a training academy as training is now decentralized)
- educational experiences scheduled around the required work, for Corpmembers:

  - with no high school diploma, mandatory GED preparation
  - reading below the 6th grade level, remedial reading
  - not proficient in English, English as a Second Language
  - with high school diplomas, advanced eudcation, including enrollment in local community college classes
- employability development, primarily derived from the work itself, rather than from formal employment training

Contributing Factors

The Power of Work

P/PV: The continued positive post-program results for disadvantaged youth occur because "the CCC may be an unusual opportunity to improve work habits, establish a positive work record and gain a credential to offer employers in the future. Furthermore, a stint in the CCC may 'certify' these youth as job-ready to employers who might otherwise be unlikely to hire them because of their lack of a high school diploma or work experience."

The Power of Service

Participating young people showed improved attitudes, relative to comparison group members, towards recycling, littering, awareness of environmental problems, donating blood and spending time in service work. The physical aspects of the service work were particularly important. Participants gained in physical self-esteem and had positive attitudes toward nontraditional work for women because hard physical work was required of both male and female members. However, some attitudes were not affected: overall tolerance, measures of non-physical self-esteem, attitudes on alcohol consumption and promoting the protection of natural areas.

Relative Benefit of Corps Services

Participation in CCC had greater benefits for youth whose opportunities outside the Corps would have been most limited. Disadvantaged youth earned higher wages than their comparison group counterparts, but less disadvantaged youth did not.

Update

Since Public/Private Ventures studied it in 1983-1984, CCC has continued to grow. It is one of the oldest and definitely the largest conservation corps program in the world, with more than 65,000 former participants since 1976. There are now 11 residential centers and more than 20 nonresidential "satellite" centers.

Study Methodology

The evaluation covers a four-year period ending in 1987. Baseline and follow-up interviews (at 6 or 9 months after leaving the program) were held with 943 participants and 1,083 comparison group members to assess economic and non-economic (behaviors and attitudes) effects of CCC. In addition, a simple cost-benefit analysis looked at program costs and the value of CCC work.

Geographic Areas

At the time of the study, CCC included 18 residential centers and 20 nonresidential "satellites" in California.

Contact Information

Research Organization
Maxine Sherman, Communications Manager
Public/Private Ventures
One Commerce Square
2005 Market Street, Suite 900
Philadelphia, PA 19103
(215) 557-4400, Fax (215) 557-4469

Implementing Organization
Suzanne Levitsky
Public Information Office
California Conservation Corps
1719 24th Street
Sacramento, CA 95816
(916) 341-3145, Fax (916) 323-1125

[1] See also Alvia Branch, Sally Liederman, and Thomas J. Smith, *Youth Conservation and Service Corps: Findings from a National Assessment*, (Philadelphia: Public/Private Ventures, 1987).

Job Corps

A Summary of:

Evaluation Of The Economic Impact Of The Job Corps Program: Third Follow-Up Report

September 1982, Mathematica Policy Research, Inc. (Princeton, NJ) by Charles Mallar, Stuart Kerachsky, Craig Thornton and David Long

(Evaluation funded by Office of Research and Evaluation, Employment and Training Administration, U.S. Department of Labor.)

Job Corps Annual Report: Program Year 1995

(July 1, 1995-June 30, 1996), Job Corps, Employment and Training Administration, U.S. Department of Labor

Overview

Job Corps is a 33-year-old national training and employment program administered by the U.S. Department of Labor (hereafter DOL) and delivered primarily through residential settings to economically disadvantaged young people 16-to-24-years old.

Enrollment in Job Corps is voluntary, and programs are open-entry, open-exit and self-paced. The average length of stay in 1977 was 6 months and nearly 7½ months from 1991 to 1995. Eighty-two Job Corps centers are managed by major corporations and nonprofit organizations under contract to DOL. Another 29 centers are operated by the U.S. Departments of Agriculture and Interior under interagency agreements with DOL.

POPULATION

In 1977, there were approximately 22,000 Job Corps slots (increasing to 41,000 by 1982). Seventy percent of Corpsmembers were male, over 75 percent were minorities (59 percent African American, 11 percent Hispanic, 5 percent American Indian, and less than 1 percent Asian or Pacific Islander), nearly 90 percent of new entrants had not completed high school, over one-third had never held at least a 20-hour per week job and over 90 percent had incomes below the poverty line or were receiving welfare.

In Program Year 1995, 60,757 students "terminated" (a DOL term for leaving) from Job Corps centers. Sixty percent of these participants were male, reading on average at the 8th grade level, 29 percent were white and 71 percent were minorities (49 percent African American, 16 percent Hispanic, 4 percent Native American and 2 percent Asian-Pacific Islanders), 78 percent were high school dropouts, only 36 percent had ever held a full-time job and 40 percent of their families were receiving public assistance.

Evidence of Effectiveness

"Job Corps is an economically efficient use of public resources in the sense that the program provides greater value to society than the value of the resources it uses up."   Mathematica

The 1982 evaluation showed that, relative to a comparison group, Job Corps participants experienced the following *annual* gains, averaged over a four-year post-program observation period:

- three weeks more employment per year
- $655 more earnings (over a 15 percent annual increase in then current dollars)
- five times greater probability of earning a high school diploma or GED (25 vs. 5 percent)
- nearly one week more college attendance (nearly double that of comparison group members)
- one less week of serious health problems
- two fewer weeks of welfare receipt (a 50 percent reduction)
- nearly one week less of Unemployment Insurance receipt (a 50 percent reduction)
- a significant shift in criminal activity to committing less serious crimes (a reduced incidence of felonies, less theft and more traffic violations)

Gains were directly related to the program. Participants who stayed in the program longer had higher gains than participants who stayed for shorter periods. Relative to similar comparison group members:

- Completers had the highest gains, far above the program average, partial completers had some gains and early dropouts experienced little or no gains.

Outcomes were also different for men, women with children and women without children. Relative to similar comparison group members:

- Women who had children before or after Job Corps participation showed little gain.

- Women without children tended to have larger gains in earnings, education and health, and reduction in welfare.
- Men were more likely to join the military and have a reduction in unemployment benefits.

These effects persisted throughout the four years of post-program observation. Researchers estimated that the benefits to society from the Job Corps program were about 45 percent greater than program costs. Benefits exceeded program cost by over $2,300 per corpsmember in 1977 ($3,500 in 1982 dollars). The economic benefits included the increased value of output from corps members, reduced government assistance, increased earnings and decreased criminal activity.

The Job Corps Annual Report for Program Year (PY) 1995 reported the following outcomes for Job Corps participants:

- 75 percent found jobs or returned to higher education after leaving Job Corps
- for those placed in employment, average hourly wages were $5.98 and 46 percent found jobs which matched the training received in Job Corps
- placement rates were significantly higher for GED recipients and vocational training completers than for those participants who did not obtain a GED or complete vocational training
- Job Corps had an early dropout rate of 31.4 percent from PY '91-94, as a result of implementing the Zero Tolerance for Violence and Drugs policy in 1994, the dropout rate rose to 37.7 percent

Key Components

"Our analysis has shown that Job Corps had a larger impact on earnings than did other training programs available to our sample, and that it was an efficient social investment."   Mathematica

Job Corps was designed to address the multiple barriers to employment faced by disadvantaged youth throughout the United States through a comprehensive mix of services delivered in an integrated and coordinated manner in one facility. The array of services provided by Job Corps, as of 1995, included:

- entry diagnostic testing of reading and math levels

- occupational exploration programs and world of work training
- a comprehensive basic education program, including reading, math, GED, health education, parenting, introduction to computers and driver education
- competency-based vocational education
- zero tolerance for violence and drugs
- intergroup relations/cultural awareness programs
- social skills training
- counseling and related support services

- regular student progress reviews
- student government and leadership programs
- community service through volunteer and vocational skills training programs
- work experience programs
- health care

- recreation programs and avocational activities
- meals, lodging and clothing
- incentive-based allowances
- child care support
- post-program placement and support

Contributing Factors

Comprehensive Services

Job Corps programs provide intensive, comprehensive services encompassing all aspects of a participant's life. Researchers found that the more services received, the more positive impacts were recorded over the duration of the study.

Residential Living

Residential living provides an opportunity to address and correct a range of problems experienced by disadvantaged youth in a structured setting that they generally lack in their own homes and neighborhoods. Participants receive supervision, work on bonding and relationships with adults and peers, are given responsibility for activities that benefit the group as a whole and have leadership opportunities. This 24-hour a day reinforcement of positive social values contributes greatly to the long-term positive impact of Job Corps.

Investments in Human Capital

Because Job Corps programs do not provide one-time only benefits, but rather contribute to an individual's overall level of human capital, the effects persist over time. Investments in education, job training, health and employment history become part of an individual's permanent store of assets.

Study Methodology

Baseline interviews of 5,200 Job Corps participants and comparison group members in 1977 detailed demographic, socio-economic, work history and related activities. Follow-up interviews at 9, 24 and 54 months focused on work history. DOL implemented a new longitudinal study in PY 1994 which will follow-up and compare the experiences of a sample of Job Corps students with a randomly selected control group over a four-year period following enrollment. Preliminary results will be available in Program Year 1997 and impact results in 1999.

Geographic Areas

Job Corps is nationwide. Funding is allocated according to regional data on the incidence of poverty and unemployment among youths. In Program Year 1996, there were 111 Job Corps centers.

Contact Information

Research Organization
John Burghardt
Mathematica Policy Research, Inc.
P.O. Box 2393
Princeton, New Jersey 08540
(609) 799-3535, Fax (609) 799-0005

Funding and Monitoring Organization
Mary Silva, Director
Office of Job Corps, N-4510
Employment and Training Administration
U.S. Department of Labor
Washington, D.C. 20210
(202) 219-5556, Fax (202) 219-5183

JOBSTART

A Summary of:

JOBSTART: Final Report on a Program for School Dropouts

October 1993, Manpower Demonstration Research Corporation (New York, NY) by George Cave, Hans Bos, Fred Doolittle and Cyril Toussaint

(Initiative and evaluation funded by U.S. Department of Labor, National Commission for Employment Policy, Exxon Corporation, Chase Manhattan Bank, N.A., and the Rockefeller, Ford, Charles Stewart Mott, William and Flora Hewlett, AT&T, Aetna, ARCO and Stuart Foundations.)

Overview

The JOBSTART demonstration was created in 1985 as an alternative approach to common practice under the Job Training Partnership Act (hereafter JTPA) at a time when JTPA emphasized short-term services for relatively employable clients. JOBSTART provided a *longer-term* combination of basic skills education, occupational training, support services and job placement assistance to young, low-skilled school dropouts. JOBSTART was modeled on the Job Corps, but at a lower level of intensity and in a non-residential setting. JOBSTART's average stay of 6.8 months was twice that of JTPA and about the same as Job Corps.

POPULATION

JOBSTART enrolled 17-to-21-year old, economically disadvantaged school dropouts who read below the 8th grade level and were eligible for JTPA Title IIA programs or the Job Corps. The impact sample of JOBSTART youth was made up of slightly more women than men (53.6 percent); was 8.9 percent white, 44.3 percent African American, 43.6 percent Hispanic, and 3.2 percent "other," 58.7 percent left school before the 11th grade, and 47.1 percent had not worked during the year prior to random assignment.

Evidence of Effectiveness

The evaluation randomly assigned young people in each of 13 sites to either the JOBSTART experimental group or a control group. Earnings impacts were reported by site[1], for the full sample and for several subgroups. Earnings are in 1988 dollars.

- The highest earnings gains, by far, were at the Center for Employment Training (hereafter CET) in San Jose, California. (For more information on CET, see the Minority Female Single Parent Demonstration, pp. 101-104.) Experimentals earned $32,959 over a four-year period, while controls earned $26,244, a gain of $6,715.
- Other sites, with diverse program characteristics, had earnings ranging from a gain of $2,538 over four years to a loss of $6,336.

The full sample and several subgroups had modest gains (not statistically significant) in average total earnings—far less than the earnings gains at CET. Relative to the control group, experimentals' earnings gains *over four-years* were:

- full sample: $17,010 vs. $16,796, a gain of $214
- custodial mothers: $8,959 vs. $8,334, a gain of $625
- other women: $13,923 vs. $13,310, a gain of $613
- men arrested between age 16 and program entry: $22,835 vs. $20,344, a gain of $2,491
- youths who dropped out of school for educational reasons (such as poor grades, dislike of school, and discipline problems): $17,590 vs. $16,409, a gain of $1,181

"While the message from recent research is far from optimistic, the conclusion that no program has enduring effects is overly pessimistic. In JOBSTART, there were apparent earnings gains in the third and fourth years of follow-up, well after the end of program services."   **MDRC**

Some subgroups experienced modest losses (not statistically significant) in average total earnings:

- men: $23,364 vs. $23,637, an earnings loss of $273
- youths who dropped out of school for employment-related reasons (such as a desire to work) $22,022 vs. $22,840, a loss of $818
- youths who dropped out of school for other reasons: $16,877 vs. $17,249, a loss of $372

Other impacts reported for the full sample and subgroups included participation in education and training, receipt of a GED or high school diploma and arrest rates. Relative to the control group, by the end of the fourth follow-up year, experimentals had:

- received substantially more education or training
  — full sample (94 vs. 56.1 percent)
  — men (94.3 vs. 51.3 percent)
  — custodial mothers (95 vs. 59.7 percent)
  — other women (93.2 vs. 60.9 percent)
- were more likely to have earned a GED or high school diploma
  — full sample (42 vs. 28.6 percent)
  — men (42 vs. 28.3 percent)
  — custodial mothers (42 vs. 26.7 percent)
  — other women (41.6 vs. 31.3 percent)[2]

Experimentals had fewer arrests than controls in the initial year of follow-up (10.1 vs. 12.6 percent). However, 29 percent of both experimentals and controls were arrested at least once during the four year follow-up.

The cost of JOBSTART was approximately $4,500 per student/participant. MDRC: "At the end of the four-year follow-up period, JOBSTART had begun to pay off for participants. JOBSTART experimentals experienced a net gain in income of $141 per person . . . [and] small reductions in the receipt of various forms of public assistance. Women who were custodial mothers at entry into JOBSTART experienced an estimated $1,004 increase in net income . . . For other women and for men, the effect of JOBSTART on their income remained negative after four years of follow-up . . . For society, the resources devoted to JOBSTART exceeded the benefits produced by the program."

Key Components

"When the JOBSTART Demonstration began . . . there was a growing realization of the employment problems ahead for young people without a high school diploma. Already, the severe decline in the inflation-adjusted earnings of school dropouts had begun, and an increasing proportion of young dropouts were outside the mainstream economy, neither working nor participating in skill-building activities. Since that time, the debate has intensified over how to best ease the transition into the workforce for those who might otherwise be unable to move readily from adolescent to eventual self-sufficiency."
MDRC

JOBSTART operated between 1985 and 1989 in 13 sites ranging from community-based organizations to schools to Job Corps centers. In each site, 17-to-21-year-old, economically disadvantaged school dropouts with poor reading skills were offered educational, vocational and support services:

- self-paced instruction in basic academic skills (at least 200 hours)
- occupational skill training in a classroom setting combining theory and hands-on experience (at least 500 hours)
- training-related support services, including assistance with transportation and child care, counseling and, in some cases, work-readiness training, life skills training, or needs-based or incentive payments tied to program performance
- job placement assistance

Some sites provided all services, others served as brokers of services. Sites varied broadly based on: whether education and training were offered sequentially or concurrently; how much education and training were integrated; the stability of funding and program operations; and the extent to which the core JOBSTART components were implemented.

The CET site was known for providing:

- access to job-specific training right away, to participants without high school diplomas or GEDs, with no up front assessment of basic skills
- academics integrated with job-specific training
- an open-entry open-exit approach
- intensive services concentrated during a short period of time
- training in occupations in demand in the labor market
- strong job placement efforts, focused directly on the well-researched needs of the local labor market

Contributing Factors

Work provides "young people an opportunity to apply what they learn in the classroom to actual work situations, adding relevance and meaning to their training experience. It also offers a way for those with little exposure to the wold of work to become more acclimated to the work environment and learn the importance of punctuality, relationships with supervisors, and other basic aspects of the workplace."   MDRC

"[I]t is easier to improve the employment and earnings of those who do not spend much time in the world of work (for example, young mothers) than of those who are already in the labor force but fail to find and keep steady, well-paying jobs (for example, poorly skilled young men)."   MDRC

Regarding CET

MDRC cautions that it is difficult to isolate which factors of CET led to positive earnings impacts, especially as some sites with highly negative earnings impacts had similar characteristics. However, the CET site can lead to a tentative understanding of successful program structures.

A Focus on Employment

Focusing on getting participants employed as quickly as possible, CET did not require participants to complete classroom education before they could be placed in job training. In some other sites, services were sequential and classroom education had to be completed before participants could begin job training. Many participants in the sequential sites grew impatient and left the program before they completed the educational portion, thereby not receiving job training or job placement assistance.

Increase Employer Involvement to Better Link with Labor Market

MDRC: "Strengthening the link between education and training and the job market through greater employer involvement is key to the success of programs and their participants. Through such involvement, programs can determine the employment needs of the local job market and train youths to meet them. In addition, employers can provide participants with opportunities to understand more clearly how their training applies to the workplace. Early links with employers also increase the possibility that they will hire participants after the program."

Intensive Services Concentrated During a Short Period of Time

Research suggests that the more youth participated, the better their earnings. By offering education and job training concurrently, CET was able to both increase services and decrease the time needed to complete the program.

Works Best for Youth with Serious Barriers to Employment

MDRC: "The relatively high employment rates [outside the program] for youths with fewer barriers to employment are likely to produce large initial earnings losses for such participants that will be hard to compensate for later. JOBSTART earnings impacts were strongest for those less likely to be employed in the absence of the program," especially for men with a prior arrest and custodial mothers.

Address Psychological and Developmental Needs of Youth

MDRC: Many sites "expanded the scope of their work, moving beyond narrowly defined employment issues to help youths address problems of emotional development, personal safety, housing, health care, and interpersonal skills."

Alternative Educational Setting

MDRC: "JOBSTART worked better for young people who were 'pushed out' of regular school because of problems in that educational environment rather than 'pulled out' by a desire to work or pressing problems outside the school setting. Apparently JOBSTART succeeded in creating an alternative educational setting that 'felt different' from regular high school and could make a difference for young people who had serious problems in a traditional setting."

Longer-term Assistance After Placement

MDRC: "For many youths, there is a need for continued help to adjust to the demands of supervisors and the workplace, while for others new issues of child care or transportation emerge. Further, since the initial jobs of young school dropouts rarely pay well, there is a need for staff to help youths make a favorable transition from a first job to a better, second job, or to further training and education."

Study Methodology

This study used random assignment: 2,312 youth who applied were randomly assigned to either the experimental or the control group. Follow-up surveys attempted to reach all members of both groups 12, 24 and 48 months after they were randomly assigned. Analysis was based on a sample size of 1,941 for whom 48 months of follow-up data were available.

Geographic Areas

Thirteen sites: Buffalo and New York, NY; Atlanta, GA; Hartford, CT; San Jose, Monterey Park and Los Angeles, CA; Chicago, IL; Pittsburgh, PA; Dallas and Corpus Christi, TX; Denver, CO; and Phoenix, AZ.

Contact Information

Research Organization

Robert J. Ivry, Senior Vice President
Manpower Demonstration Research Corporation
Three Park Avenue
New York, New York 10016
(212) 532-3200, Fax (212) 684-0832

Funding and Monitoring Organization

David Lah, Chief, Evaluation Unit
Office of Planning and Research
Employment & Training Administration
U.S. Department of Labor, N-5637
200 Constitution Ave., NW
Washington, D.C. 20001
(202) 219-5472, Ext. 105, Fax (202) 219-5455

[1] MDRC cautions that the analysis of earning impacts across sites is less certain than that for the full sample and subgroups because (1) it is difficult to isolate the influence of any single dimension of individual programs; (2) sites served different populations and had varying labor markets; (3) the study was designed to compare experimental and control impacts within, not between, sites; and (4) small sites led to findings which were usually not statistically significant.

[2] Subgroups defined by work experience, welfare receipt, prior education, initial reading level, reason for dropping out of school, prior criminal record, and age all showed similar large positive impacts for GED receipt or obtaining a high school diploma.

A Summary of:

LEAP: Three-Year Impacts of Ohio's Welfare Initiative to Improve School Attendance Among Teenage Parents

April 1996, Manpower Demonstration Research Corporation (MDRC), (New York, NY)
by David Long, Judith M. Gueron, Robert G. Wood, Rebecca Fisher and Veronica Fellerath

(Evaluation funded by Ohio Department of Human Services, Ford Foundation, Cleveland Foundation, BP America, TreuMart Fund, George Gund Foundation, Proctor and Gamble Fund, and U.S. Department of Health and Human Services.)

Overview

Ohio's Learning, Earning, and Parenting (hereafter LEAP) program uses financial bonuses and sanctions to encourage pregnant and parenting teens on welfare to remain in or return to school.

Teens get $62 for enrollment and an additional $62 each month they attend school regularly. Teens who do not enroll in school get $62 deducted from their welfare grant each month until they comply. The sanctions and bonuses are not cumulative. Case managers evaluate each teen's status each month, put in a request for a bonus or sanction, explain rules, offer guidance, and authorize support services such as reimbursement for child care and transportation costs.

POPULATION

LEAP targeted Ohio teen mothers on welfare who had not completed high school. The evaluation focused on the experiences of teens in seven Ohio counties three years after they were determined to be eligible for LEAP.

Evidence of Effectiveness

"The findings suggest that LEAP can produce promising outcomes, particularly when it gets to teen parents while they are young and still in school."
                                          MDRC

The evaluation reported direct effects of LEAP on the rate of high school graduation, GED receipt and less direct effects on employment and welfare receipt on LEAP teens, compared to a randomly assigned control group. Compared to control group members, LEAP participants:

- graduated from high school or earned GEDs at higher rates
    (1) if they became eligible for LEAP while already in school or in a GED program (46 vs. 39 percent graduated)
    (2) if they were dropouts under 18 (13 vs. 3 percent complete school within three years of becoming eligible for LEAP)
- were more likely to be working
    (1) 33 vs. 28 percent employment rate for the group
    (2) if they became eligible for LEAP while already in school or in a GED program (39 vs. 27 percent working)

- were more likely to have left the welfare rolls (17 vs. 12 percent)

However, LEAP participants who were 18 or over and already out of school had no increase in either school completion or employment, despite significant sanctions.

Program effects varied substantially across geographic areas. In Cleveland, both high school graduations and GED receipt increased significantly. Gains in Cleveland appear linked to factors outside of the LEAP program itself. For example, Cleveland strictly enforced a state regulation that teenagers under 18 could not leave high school to prepare for the GED test. Cleveland also offered extra services, such as on-site day care, access to state's GRADS program (which instructs teen parents in home and life skills), on-site LEAP case managers and teen-focused GED programs. Finally, Cleveland had many alternative high schools with flexible hours and/or strong vocational education components that made high school completion easier and more appealing for teen welfare mothers.

LEAP cost $537 per year per teen in Cleveland. Costs for other sites were not given in this report.

Contributing Factors

Financial Incentives

LEAP demonstrated that financial incentives and penalties can affect behavior for younger teens, especially those who were enrolled in school when the program began. Younger teens subject to increases and reductions in their welfare payments based solely on whether they attended school or a GED program, finished school and entered the work force in greater numbers than control group members. However, the high sanction rates for older out-of-school youth was troubling. The out-of-school welfare mothers who were 18 or over did not respond to sanctions by returning to school and, therefore, did not make gains in school completion, employment, or getting off welfare. The cuts in their welfare benefits only had the effect of decreasing the money the mothers reported spending on necessities for their children.

Need System-wide School Reform

LEAP was welfare reform and did not affect schools. Many teens in the LEAP program saw their schools as dangerous and disorderly places, where learning is difficult, and refused to return to school despite financial incentives. Therefore, LEAP is only one part of a strategy to assist teen mothers. The findings from Cleveland suggest that a more comprehensive strategy which includes LEAP and system-wide school reform yields better outcomes.

Study Methodology

All teens in the seven counties who were determined eligible for LEAP were assigned at random to either a program group or a control group. MDRC then measured the differences in average outcomes between the two groups over time, using data from a survey administered to 913 teens (446 program teens and 467 control group teens) and from administrative records for all 4,325 members who lived in five of the largest urban school districts in the seven counties. MDRC also analyzed program operations by studying the use of bonuses and sanctions in Ohio's three largest counties (Cuyahoga, Franklin and Hamilton.) This evaluation is the fourth of five scheduled evaluations. MDRC plans to complete one additional evaluation in 1997.

Geographic Areas

The full evaluation is being conducted in 12 Ohio counties. *This* report focuses on seven counties containing about half of the LEAP caseload (Cuyahoga, Franklin, Hamilton, Lawrence, Lucas, Muskigum and Stark.)

Contact Information

Research Organization
Robert J. Ivry, Senior Vice President
Manpower Demonstration Research Corporation
Three Park Avenue
New York, NY 10016
(212) 532-3200, Fax (212) 684-0832

Minority Female Single Parent

A Summary of:

Evaluation of the Minority Female Single Parent Demonstration: Volume I Summary Report

October 1992, by John Burghardt,
Anu Rangarajan, Anne Gordon and Ellen Kisker

More Jobs and Higher Pay: How an Integrated Program Compares with Traditional Programs

1990, by John Burghardt and Anne Gordon

Evaluation of the Minority Female Single Parent Demonstration: Fifth-Year Impacts At CET

December 1993, by Amy Zambrowski,
Anne Gordon and Laura Berenson

All three evaluations by Mathematica Policy Research, Inc. (Princeton, NJ).

(The projects and all three evaluations funded by Rockefeller Foundation.)

Overview

Between 1982 and 1988, the Rockefeller Foundation funded four community-based organizations to operate employment training programs for minority single mothers, known collectively as the Minority Female Single Parent (hereafter MFSP) demonstration. Participants were offered services to address the barriers that make it difficult for poor single mothers to secure good jobs and escape their dependence on welfare. While services varied, each site selected particular occupational areas for which they prepared their trainees. At each site participants were offered:

- remediation of basic reading, math, and communications skills
- job-skills assessments
- job-skill training
- job-search training
- job-placement assistance
- child care or referrals
- counseling and other support services

The most successful of the MFSP sites was the Center for Employment Training (CET), San Jose, California (for more information on CET, see JOBSTART, pp. 93-97) which produced substantial earnings gains in a short time frame even for participants without high school diplomas or GEDs. These gains persisted, again even for dropouts, to the 30-month point. Gains persisted for some participants, but not for dropouts, to the 60-month point. CET gave participants without high school diplomas or GEDs access to job-specific training right away, with no up front assessment of basic skills (often required in job training programs).

> **POPULATION**
>
> MFSP participants were female and minorities. Of the 3,965 women participating, over two-thirds had received welfare in the year prior to applying to the program. Their average age was 28; 71 percent were African American and 25 percent Hispanic; and 56 percent were high school dropouts. Nearly two-thirds had children under 6 years of age.

Evidence of Effectiveness

"[T]reatment group members were significantly more likely to have earnings of more than \$1,200 per month . . . a few members of the [treatment] group earned more than \$2,800 per month, whereas no control group members' earnings are in this range."   Mathematica

"The return on one dollar spent by society on the CET program is \$1.23."   Mathematica

Key Components

"The open-access, integrated approach to job training appears to be a promising method for preparing low-skill workers for better jobs."
                                                   Mathematica

Contributing Factors

"Immediate, job-specific training with a strong focus on getting trainees into jobs is a more effective way to improve the earnings of single mothers than are alternative strategies that seek to improve basic skills before offering job training."
                                                   Mathematica

The three Mathematica reports summarized here describe preliminary findings at 12 months for all sites, impacts at 30 months for all sites, and impacts at 60 months only for CET. This summary covers the 60-month CET data only. After five years, compared to control group members, women who participated in CET:

- earned an average of \$95 more per month (\$667 vs. \$572)
- worked more hours (85 vs. 77 hours per month, not statistically significant)
- had better earnings gains if they had completed 12 or more years of schooling (\$824 vs. \$563)
- had little gain in earnings if they did not complete high school (\$588 vs. \$574)

The four MFSP sites varied in their strategies for delivering education and training services, assessment, and counseling; strategies and the amount of support for child-care and job placement; the scale of program operations; and approaches to service provision.

The CET site:

- gave participants without high school diplomas or GEDs access to job-specific training right away, with no up-front assessment of basic skills
- provided concurrent and integrated work and learning opportunities, i.e. remedial education was integrated directly into training for a specific job, rather than provided prior to job training or concurrently in a separate class
- an open-entry open-exit approach, i.e. participants could be placed in jobs when _they_ felt they were ready

Integrated Training Design
Mathematica: CET's "design was distinguished by two features: that women would enter job training immediately, regardless of their previous educational attainment, and that remedial education would be integrated directly into training for a specific job, rather than provided prior to job training or concurrently in a separate class."

- showed little reduction in welfare receipt
- had equal GED attainment rates while more participated in some education and training (85 vs. 59 percent)

At a cost of \$3,900 per participant, CET had a positive cost benefit for society, with net benefits of \$975 per participant over five years. Benefits to participants were more than \$2,500. However, from the government-budget perspective, costs exceeded benefits by about \$1,600 per participant because reductions in welfare benefits were small.

- provided intensive services concentrated during a short period of time
- trained in occupations in demand in the labor market
- worked closely with employers to ensure that the training curriculum met their needs and phased skill offerings in and out in response to demand
- organized training to simulate workplace conditions
- used instructors with recent experience in industry
- focused on employment and provided strong and active assistance in finding jobs after program completion.

Two other sites used a sequential approach, in which women with poor basic skills were placed initially in remedial education courses, and could enter job skill training only after having improved these skills. The fourth site provided classes in general employability, had short course duration and did not focus on preparation for a specific job.[1]

Employer and Labor Market Focus
Mathematica: CET "organized training to simulate workplace conditions, used instructors with recent experience in industry, worked closely with employers to ensure that the training curriculum met their needs, and phased skill offerings in and out in response to demand." Participants were provided active assistance in finding jobs after program completion.

"The strong findings at CET . . . necessitate examining whether programs that emphasize remedial basic education are really the best way to improve the earnings of and reduce welfare dependency among poor single mothers."

Mathematica

Full-Time and Demanding, Yet Self-Paced Curriculum

Mathematica: CET "used an open-entry and open-exit self-paced competency-based training approach, in which instructors functioned as coaches and counselors. This approach moved applicants quickly into training, avoided the necessity for academic-style testing, and allowed trainees to receive individual attention."

More is Needed for Dropouts

CET worked for dropouts to the 30-month point, but more is needed to sustain that success over the long run.

Resources and Large-Scale Operation

CET is a large program headquartered in San Jose, CA and operated in many sites and several states. It has access to a wide range of job-skill courses and sophisticated equipment which provide economies of scale.

Study Methodology

Nearly 4,000 program applicants were assigned randomly to a treatment group or a control group across the four sites. Interviews of participants at each site were conducted at 12 and 30 months. Follow-up interviews were conducted at 60 months only for the CET site.

Geographic Areas

Atlanta (GA) Urban League; Opportunities Industrialization Center, Providence, RI; Center for Employment Training (CET), San Jose, CA; Wider Opportunities for Women, Washington, DC. CET's headquarters and largest site is in San Jose. CET operates training centers in 25 sites in three western states, with the majority in California.

Contact Information

Research Organization
John Burghardt
Mathematica Policy Research, Inc.
P.O. Box 2393
Princeton, New Jersey 08543-2393
(609) 799-3535, Fax (609) 799-0005

---

[1] For a description of program operations at CET and the other three sites see Alan Hershey, *The Minority Female Single Parent Demonstration: Program Operations, A Technical Research Report*, (New York: Rockefeller Foundation, 1988).

New Chance

A Summary of:

New Chance: Interim Findings on a Comprehensive Program for Disadvantaged Young Mothers and Their Children

September 1994, Manpower Demonstration Research Corporation (MDRC), (New York, NY) by Janet C. Quint, Denise F. Polit, Hans Bos and George Cave

(Evaluation funded by U.S. Department of Labor and 22 other funders.[1])

Overview

New Chance was designed to test whether providing a comprehensive and intensive set of services to young mothers on welfare and their children—could significantly improve their employment and educational prospects, as well as their overall well-being. Services were offered in two phases, with Phase I emphasizing education-related services, and Phase II focusing mostly on employment-related services.

POPULATION

The women recruited by New Chance were highly disadvantaged. They were on average 19 years old and had their first child when they were about 17; 77 percent were members of minority groups; fewer than one in 10 had ever been married; 37 percent had dropped out of school before their first pregnancy. Few had worked full-time over a sustained period and the majority had not worked at all in the 12 months prior to enrolling in New Chance. Overall, 2,322 women were selected for the program across the 16 sites.

Evidence of Effectiveness

"[I]t is noteworthy that [New Chance participants'] poverty, use of public assistance, and educational and social disadvantages persisted. The absolute level of disadvantage of these young mothers and their children needs to be taken into account in designing programs and policies to improve thier self-sufficiency and life prospects."   **MDRC**

MDRC's interim evaluation found that, during the first 18 months of program follow-up, relative to a randomized control group, New Chance participants:

- were more likely to earn a GED by the 18-month point (43 vs. 30 percent—even among those women who became pregnant during the course of the program)
- had little difference in employment (43 vs. 45 percent had been employed by month 18)
- had comparably high rates of birth (57 vs. 53 percent becoming pregnant after the program began)
- received more services (85 vs. 60 percent participated in an education program; 33 vs. 23 percent had skills training)

- showed no difference in welfare receipt, literacy test scores or health measures

All 16 sites implemented Phase I components and almost all offered the hours for each service recommended by program guidelines. Phase II activities were more difficult to implement, and there was more variation among sites in how well the work-related components were put into place. The quality of child care at the sites was consistent with child care experts' guidelines and tended to be of higher quality than that generally provided by centers serving low-income families.

" . . . long-term follow-up is critical to determining the effectiveness of programs designed for young people, who may be better able to capitalize on what they have learned in these programs after they have gained greater maturity and their lives have become more stable." **MDRC**

Sponsoring agencies spent an average of $5,073 per program participants, excluding child care, which cost an additional $2,575 per participant.

The population targeted by New Chance is very disadvantaged. MDRC: "Over the brief period of a year and a half, the majority had stopped and started one or more programs, and over half had become pregnant; substantial minorities of sample members had stopped and started one or more jobs, had had a baby, and had changed living arrangements at least once. Given this volatility, it is too soon to know

whether the early positive impacts will eventually outweigh the negative ones, or vice versa." This interim report, documenting the first 18 months of the New Chance program, is the third in a series. The first two reports were: "New Chance: Implementing a Comprehensive Program for Disadvantaged Young Mothers and Their Children" (MDRC 1991) and "Lives of Promise, Lives of Pain: Young Mothers After New Chance" (MDRC 1994). The fourth and final report will assess the long-term effects of the program (employment and other outcomes after 42 months).

Key Components

" . . . young mothers participating in these programs have confronted many serious obstacles to advancement, some psychological in nature, others related to dysfunctional families, dangerous schools and neighborhoods, and other factors in their social, physical, and economic environments." **MDRC**

New Chance was a national demonstration project that operated between 1989 and 1992 at 16 locations in 10 states. It provided an array of services in a structured, intensive environment. Participants were scheduled to attend the program five days a week, generally from 9 a.m. until 3 p.m. The service components included:

- Education (adult basic education; GED preparation)
- Employment-related services (career exploration, pre-employment skills training, work internships,

occupational skills training, job placement assistance)
- Health and personal development (Life Skills and Opportunities curriculum, health education and health services, family planning, adult survival skills training)
- Services to enhance the development of participants' children (parenting education, child care, pediatric health services)
- Case management (the case manager works intensively, with a relatively small caseload, to encourage, advocate for, and motivate the participant)

Contributing Factors

Participant Motivation

The strongest program effects were seen in attainment of the GED. New Chance was a voluntary program. Most participants indicated at the beginning that they were very interested in earning the GED. Participants seemed less interested in or focused on employment and career prospects.

Absenteeism

MDRC: "In general, women who were initially the most disadvantaged, educationally and otherwise, tended to have fewer hours of participation. Reasons for absenteeism cited by the young women included: their own illnesses (including pregnancy-related discomforts) and those of their children, disruptions in child care arrangements, conflicting appointments, and lack of support or active discouragement from family members or boyfriends."

Need a More Intensive, Consistent Family Planning Component

MDRC: "Programs for young mothers have been notably unsuccessful in affecting young mothers' fertility behavior. Programs may have more success if family planning received ongoing, regular follow-up by program staff who feel comfortable discussing sexuality, and if an unequivocal message about postponing pregnancies is delivered continuously."

Need a Stronger Emphasis on the Employment Component

Most participants were more interested in the GED than in gaining employment skills. Because the services were offered sequentially, some participants did not get to the employment component of the program at all, but left after obtaining their GEDs. To improve employment outcomes, MDRC recommends that program staff emphasize how program activities relate to getting and keeping a job. "It is likely that job development and job placement need to be aggressive and ongoing. The rapid turnover of the young mothers who worked also suggests the need to pay more attention to job-retention skills."

Provision of Additional Services

Given the numerous problems faced by the target population, additional services focusing on mental health and substance abuse problems may help participants make the transition to self-support. Following up with counseling after participants complete Phase I may help propel them into a more independent life. Providing some outreach to "significant others"—who often have a profound influence on the participant's motivation to remain and succeed in the program—may help bolster a young women's determination to take full advantage of the New Chance offerings.

Study Methodology

MDRC used a rigorous model featuring: (1) random assignment of a large sample to either an experimental (New Chance) or control group; (2) collection of baseline information; (3) collection of extensive follow-up information; (4) exhaustive tracing efforts to minimize sample bias; and (5) data analysis through rigorous statistical procedures.

Geographic Areas

New Chance operated in 16 sites across the country: three in both California and Pennsylvania, two sites in both New York and Oregon, and one each in Colorado, Florida, Illinois, Kentucky, Michigan and Minnesota.

Contact Information

Research Organization
Robert J. Ivry, Senior Vice President
Manpower Demonstration Research Corporation
Three Park Avenue
New York, New York 10016
(212) 532-3200, Fax (212) 684-0832

[1] DeWitt Wallace-Reader's Digest Fund, Meyer Memorial Trust, Pew Charitable Trusts, Foundation for Child Development, National Commission for Employment Policy, Neighborhood Reinvestment Corporation, an Anonymous Funder, and the Ford, W.K. Kellogg, UPS, Charles Stewart Mott, Stuart, W.T. Grant, Skillman, David and Lucile Packard, AT&T, Bush, Koret, Mary Reynolds Babcock, Allstate, and Grand Metropolitan Foundations.

Project Redirection

A Summary of:

The Challenge Of Serving Teenage Mothers: Lessons from Project Redirection

October 1988, Manpower Demonstration Research Corporation (MDRC), (New York, NY)[1] by Denise F. Polit, Janet C. Quint and James A. Riccio

(Monograph funded by U.S. Departments of Labor and Health and Human Services and the Ford and William T. Grant Foundations.)

Overview

Project Redirection (hereafter PR) was a national research demonstration to test an approach to helping pregnant teens and young mothers. It sought to enhance educational, job-related, parenting and life-management skills of young pregnant or parenting women, most of whom were on welfare. Features of PR included:

- the "Community Women Component"—trained women from the community who served, for a small stipend, as mentors to 1-to-5 teenagers, for at least 5 hours per week for each teen
- individual counseling
- peer group sessions
- on-site life management and employability components
- referrals to other services, including health services and education
- child care, transportation and recreational services
- stipends for participation ($30/month with deductions for unsatisfactory attendance)

POPULATION

Participants in PR were adolescent girls age 17 or under who were: pregnant for the first time (56 percent) or mothers of young children (44 percent); receiving or eligible to receive welfare (over 70 percent) and without a high school diploma or GED (59 percent had dropped out of school, half did so before they were pregnant). In the main demonstration period, 1980 to 1982, four sites served 805 teenagers, 90 percent of whom were "ethnic minorities."

> "The Community Women Component . . . most clearly distinguished Redirection from other programs for pregnant and parenting teens."
> **MDRC**

Evidence of Effectiveness

The Manpower Demonstration Research Corporation (hereafter MDRC) evaluation measured effects of PR on participants relative to a matched comparison group using responses to interviews conducted at one, two and five years. Evaluators found the following:

- One year after program completion, PR participants had better outcomes than comparison women (not detailed in this summary).
- At the two-year point, no gains were found for the average participant. However, more participants than comparison group members who were school dropouts at enrollment had obtained a diploma or GED (20 percent vs. 11 percent) and more program teens than comparison group members who were receiving AFDC payments at enrollment were employed (16 percent vs. 10 percent).

Several positive outcomes were found for all participants five years after program enrollment.[2] At the five-year point, relative to the comparison group, PR participants:

- were more likely to be employed (34 vs. 28 percent)
- were working more hours per week on average (13 vs. 9 hours)
- had higher weekly earnings on average ($68 vs. $45) even when they had more than one child ($80 vs. $54 for 2 children, $46 vs. $24 for 3 children)

"Because women with more children tend to have lower rates of employment and higher rates of welfare dependency than women with fewer children, it was surprising that the mothers in the Redirection group had better employment and welfare outcomes than the comparison group—despite their somewhat larger family size."
MDRC

- were less likely to be living in an AFDC household (49 vs. 59 percent), even though they were more likely to be in AFDC households at the two-year point
- had more children, fewer abortions (mean numbers of pregnancies, abortions and live births were 3.1, 0.3 and 2.4 vs. 2.9, 0.5 and 2.0)
- were providing their children with a more positive home environment, as measured on the HOME scale (mean score of 44 vs. 40)
- were more likely to enroll their children in Head Start (47 vs. 34 percent)
- showed no difference in educational outcomes (percent in school/completed, percent with diploma/GED), overall household income, or birth control usage.

In addition, despite many positive outcomes, "the absolute levels of the outcomes experienced by PR participants are disheartening" and serve to underscore the severe disadvantages faced by this population of young mothers. After five years, the majority of the women still did not have diplomas or GEDs, were not working, had received AFDC in the previous year and were living in poverty.

Some subgroups of women in PR showed greater gains. Relative to similar members of the comparison group, PR participants who were receiving AFDC payments at enrollment:

- had higher weekly earnings ($76 vs. $37)
- were less likely to be in AFDC households (57 vs. 71 percent)

Relative to similar members of the comparison group, PR participants who had the lowest vocabulary scores at follow-up:

- worked more hours per week (10 vs. 5 hours)
- had higher weekly earnings ($44 vs. $20) (weekly earnings which were still very low compared to $101 per week for participants with higher vocabulary scores)

Contrasted with the children of comparison women, the children of PR participants:

- showed better cognitive skills, as measured by a test of vocabulary knowledge (scores of 86 vs. 80), but were still below the 20th percentile nationally
- exhibited fewer behavioral problems, as measured by a scale of problem behaviors based on maternal self-reports (scores of 92 vs. 105—neither score shows that children are "maladjusted")

Contributing Factors

"A leading priority . . . was to create a warm and welcoming environment that was supportive and nonjudgmental, so that teens would be encouraged to confide in others."
MDRC

On-site Services
Teens achieved more positive outcomes for program areas addressed on-site, such as parenting and employability skills development, than for off-site services, such as education. Program operators believed that on-site services were usually of higher quality and more developmentally appropriate than some of the off-site services.

Caring Adults
MDRC: "Teens may be most motivated not only to attend sessions held at the program site—where they are on familiar turf and not "hassled"—but also to incorporate what they learn in their daily lives, in efforts to please and get praise from staff members whom they trust and respect." On-site services, program staff, and the community women were seen as instrumental in creating a supportive environment for the young women. Program staff and the community women provided individualized attention and support to participants. Community women received both pre-service and in-service training.

Study Methodology

Effects were measured through interviews of participants and members of a matched comparison group. Interviews were conducted at one and two years (sample size 675) and five years (sample size 277) after participant enrollment. The five-year interview also examined outcomes for the children of the young women.

Geographic Areas

Organizations implementing PR during the evaluation phase were the Harlem YMCA, New York City; El Centro del Cardinal, Boston; Chicanos Por la Causa, Phoenix, AZ and Children's Home Society, Riverside, CA.

Contact Information

Research Organization

Robert J. Ivry, Senior Vice President
Manpower Demonstration Research Corporation
Three Park Avenue
New York, New York 10016
(212) 532-3200, Fax (212) 684-0832

---

[1] This monograph summarizes the major lessons from research on PR, drawing on the five-year impact study and on several earlier MDRC reports, including: "Building Self-Sufficiency for Teens: Final Implementation Report of Project Redirection," 1984; "Final Impacts from Project Redirection: A Program for Pregnant and Parenting Teens," 1985 and "Choices and Life Circumstances: An Ethnographic Study of Project Redirection Teens," 1983.

[2] Some positive outcomes at the five-year point were for outcomes not measured at the two-year point, such as child development (the children were too young) and most of the economic impacts (the women were too young to be likely to have had steady employment).

STRIVE

A Summary of:	**STRIVE's Results: Evaluating a Small Non-Profit Organization in East Harlem**	**Employment Training: Successful Projects Share Common Strategy**
	Fall 1993, Robert F. Wagner Graduate School of Public Service, New York University, by Juliet Ofori-Mankata and Bo-Young Won (Evaluation funded by Ford Foundation.)	(GAO/HEHS- 96-108) May 1996, United States General Accounting Office

Overview

Support Training Results in Valuable Employment (hereafter STRIVE), established in 1984, provides tools to successfully enter the job market to young adults who have experienced difficulty in securing and maintaining employment. STRIVE provides both attitudinal training and post-program support once participants are employed. STRIVE's objective, for 12 sites, is to place 2,500 individuals in jobs annually (an 80 percent placement rate for participants who complete the training program) and to ensure job retention for at least 2,000 of them (an 80 percent retention rate for those placed in jobs).

POPULATION

Open admittance to persons 18-to-30-years-old who express a need for STRIVE's services. The project targets individuals whose difficulty in obtaining employment stems primarily from poor attitudes and inappropriate behaviors. In 1994, STRIVE Central in East Harlem trained 415 individuals who were: 50 percent men, 50 percent women, 71 percent African American, 16 percent Hispanic, 34 percent receiving public assistance, 33 percent single parents, 64 percent high school graduates, 18 percent GED recipients. STRIVE programs are located in inner-city areas and often serve public assistance recipients, social service income recipients, individuals whose parents constitute the working poor, and persons with criminal records.

Evidence of Effectiveness

Researchers from NYU and the General Accounting Office provided the following information on dropout rates, job placement, and job retention.

- NYU evaluators examined two dropout rates: (1) the number of individuals who, upon registering and attending the orientation, decided to leave the program after the first day— usually because STRIVE is not the traditional employment skills development program they expected (40 percent); (2) those who leave after they are well informed about the nature of the program and

its requirements and had begun to participate (5 percent).

- GAO reports that from May 1985 through December 1994, the East Harlem STRIVE site helped 2,424 individuals secure employment. According to project officials, nearly 80 percent of those individuals maintained employment. In 1994, STRIVE Central trained 415 persons, 318 (77 percent) of whom were placed in employment (figures not independently verified.)

- NYU reports that from 1991 to 1993, on average, 82 percent of all participants had been employed for at least two years.

Additional information was gathered from interviews with three employers and survey responses from 11 employers which had consistently hired STRIVE participants:

- 63 percent had a relationship with STRIVE for an average of one to two years (relationships ranged from six months to eight years)
- 90 percent identified attitudinal qualities as the strengths of their STRIVE employees and indicated that STRIVE participants had moderate to high levels of motivation
- 55 percent indicated that STRIVE prepared its clients "well" or "very well" for positions in their organizations

- 66 percent felt that STRIVE could better assist participants through follow-up services and encouraging them to aspire to positions beyond the entry level

STRIVE is primarily privately funded, predominately through a grant from The Clark Foundation that requires a two-for-one dollar match from other sources, such as local employers. Services are free to both employers and participants. STRIVE officials noted that 90 percent of STRIVE's resources are allocated to direct services. In 1995, per capita costs were $1,500 for placement and $1,650 for follow-up services (program director's figures).

Key Components

"STRIVE's training and placement approach differs from those offered by other non-profit (public and private) agencies supported by public funds, because of its emphasis on attitudinal needs of clients. Training stresses characteristics such as punctuality, spirit of cooperation, and the ability to take constructive criticism. For the purposes of acquiring successful employment, these elements are emphasized over skills such as typing, word processing, and data entry [included in STRIVE] but not to the extent that [they] are found in other employment training initiatives."

New York University

STRIVE is one of 18 programs recognized as exemplary by the Promising and Effective Practices Network (PEPNet) in 1996. (PEPNet, a program of the National Youth Employment Coalition (NYEC), is a nationwide network of youth employment/development initiatives demonstrating high standards in the areas of: quality management, youth development, workforce development, and evidence of success. PEPNet offers organizations tools to analyze and evaluate their practices against identified effective principles and practices. Manufacturing Technology Partnership, pp. 30-33, is also a recognized PEPNet program.)

STRIVE is a privately funded organization with a ten-year history of emphasizing attitudinal training over job training. Its mission is to prepare, train, place, and support inner-city youth and young adults in long-term employment experiences and to demonstrate the impact that attitudinal training and post-placement support of clients have on their long-term employment. Both for-profit and non-profit organizations hire STRIVE participants who successfully complete the program, which is comprised of a three-week workshop, job development services, and follow-up services.

Three-week workshop:
- training intended to promote attitudinal change in:
  - punctuality

  - spirit of cooperation
  - ability to take constructive criticism
- testing in reading and mathematics
- if needed, referrals to remedial education or GED services
- moderate computer training
- exercises targeting development of verbal or written communication skills

Job development:
- individual assessment of job interests
- consultation on the prerequisite skills for careers/jobs that participants would like to pursue
- resume writing and interviewing skills

Follow-up services:
- once participants are placed in jobs, post-placement support for up to two years consisting of periodic phone calls to participants and employers to discuss experiences and assess job performance
- meetings with employers at their respective workplaces to discuss the progress of former participants
- problem resolution

STRIVE participants are employed in receptionist and clerical positions (29 percent), maintenance (10 percent), sales (12 percent), mail/shipping (12 percent), food service (7 percent), cashier (20 percent), teller (6 percent), and customer service (4 percent). Graduates have been employed by over 120 different companies in New York City.

Contributing Factors

"STRIVE encourages participants to shed the victim mentality, become self-sufficient, and acquire a solid work ethic."   GAO

Attitudinal Training Model

NYU: "Designers of the program believe that employers are willing to provide skills training for entry-level employees who have good attitudes and are willing to learn. The attitudinal model is optimal for STRIVE's client population because it provides them with the skills 'to get through the door,' and to hold the initial job."

No Better Training for Work than Work Itself

NYU: "[D]isciplined attitudinal training in a 'realistic' work environment meets the needs of both potential employers and STRIVE participants . . . The structure and content of STRIVE's attitudinal training are intended to replicate the job experience. The attitudinal model forces young adults to: confront and correct self-defeating attitudes, develop effective communication skills and the confidence to migrate through the work environment."

Individual Attention

NYU: STRIVE "is structured so that each participant focuses on their respective strengths and weaknesses. Trainers maintain on-going reports on each client. They document client behavior and skills after each session, and discuss, on a one-to-one basis, each individual's development. Training encourages clients to emphasize self-development over comparing themselves with other members of the training group."

Trusting Relationships

NYU: "The program is structured to foster a relationship of trust between trainers and participants. It is expected that this type of relationship will facilitate a level of communication between [staff and] trainees that eventually will bring about change in personal attitudes. The resulting cooperative attitude, is perceived to be a powerful tool for clients to have; and it is regarded as a meaningful trait by the employers that hire them."

Long-Term Follow-Up

NYU: "The follow-up service that STRIVE provides its clients is the unique aspect of this program. We did not identify other employment training programs that provide this service for at least two years." Researchers found that employers were not always aware of, and need to be better informed about, the follow-up services. Provision of these services can foster and maintain a high level of communication and interaction with employers, to the benefit of both participants and employers.

Study Methodology

Researchers evaluated the East Harlem STRIVE site using a diagnostic approach including collecting information about the organization's structure and purpose. They assessed the program through site visits, staff and participant interviews and surveys, including questionnaires mailed to 20 randomly selected employers of STRIVE participants.

Geographic Areas

STRIVE's principal site is East Harlem, NY. It has been replicated in Pittsburgh, PA; Chicago, IL; and Miami, FL. Other sites are being developed.

Contact Information

Research Organizations
Robert F. Wagner Graduate School of Public Service (call STRIVE for information)

Carlotta C. Joyner, Director
Education and Employment Issues
U.S. General Accounting Office
441 G Street, NW
Washington, DC 20548
(202) 512-7014, Fax (202) 512-6117
[(202) 512-6000 or info@www.gao.gov for copies]

Implementing Organization
Lorenzo D. Harrison
Deputy Executive Director/Vice President
East Harlem Employment Service/STRIVE
1820 Lexington Ave.
New York, NY 10029
(212) 360-1100, Fax (212) 360-5634

YouthBuild

A Summary of:

YouthBuild In Developmental Perspective: A Formative Evaluation of the YouthBuild Demonstration Project

September 1996, Ronald F. Ferguson of Harvard University and Philip L. Clay of the Massachusetts Institute of Technology

(Evaluation funded by DeWitt Wallace-Reader's Digest Fund, Ford Foundation, Charles Stewart Mott Foundation and Lilly Endowment.)

Overview

YouthBuild (hereafter YB) was designed to improve the lives of disconnected youth by teaching them basic life skills and employability skills through work on community housing rehabilitation projects coupled with attendance at a YouthBuild alternative high school that offered personal counseling and leadership development along with GED preparation.

POPULATION

This evaluation covered 177 participants in the second cycle of the YB demonstration who were 16-to-24-year-olds, mostly male (84 percent), lacking a high school diploma or GED (78 percent), minority (seven percent white, 71 percent African American, 15 percent Hispanic, one percent Native American, two percent Asian/Pacific Islander, and four percent "other"), unemployed, and living in high risk neighborhoods. More than half were in households receiving public assistance (55 percent). More than half reported some prior involvement in the criminal justice system (49 percent in Year One, 65 percent in Year Two).

Evidence of Effectiveness

An evaluation of the 1991-94 demonstration at the first five replication sites in diverse cities was designed to study the replicability of the comprehensive New York City YouthBuild model. One hundred seventy-seven (177) trainees at five sites participated in the second cycle of the demonstration, on which this evaluation focuses. For these sites, evaluators found:

- Although YB serves what is generally viewed as a difficult population—mostly minority males, 65 percent of whom had prior dealings with the criminal justice system and 33 percent of whom had been convicted and incarcerated for felonies—it showed favorable outcomes for 69 percent of the participants, an average attendance rate of 85 percent, and better performance than comparable programs, even those serving many fewer

"In New York, the program operated at two sites. These sites ... attracted adolescents and young adults who were mostly disconnected from schools and jobs. . . . these young people lobbied the city council for money to support the fledgling program. Their claim was that through this program they would develop both themselves and their communities."   **Ferguson and Clay**

minority adjudicated males, on two particular measures where performance could be compared:

— longer average lengths of stay (8.3 months in Year One and 6.3 months in Year Two) than comparable programs (the highest was 6.8 months for JOBSTART; other programs were at less than 6.3 months)

— a higher percentage of participants who achieved their GED (an average of 20 percent) than many comparable programs

- a 17 percent dropout rate (for reasons "that are difficult to classify as successes or failures of the program" including death, poor health, and the relocation of families)

- of those who did not drop out, 69 percent achieved positive terminations (finished the program cycle or left with the blessing of YB to go into a job or to further schooling) and 31 percent had negative terminations (expelled from or quit YB without moving into a job or a school setting that YB approved)

- 38 percent of positive terminations were for full-time employment or for "part-time employment, school or training"

- The construction training portion of the program was generally successful in producing "job ready" laborers. It was less successful in producing workers who were ready to enter apprenticeships in the construction trade.

- 66 percent of the second-year participants who were employed directly after YB went into construction-related jobs at an average wage of $7.60 per hour, and 33

percent who did not get construction jobs had an average wage of $6.80 per hour

- Graduates from YB showed improvement in positive behaviors related to: Time Management (index measures are time spent hanging out and how often they stay up past 2 a.m., keep to a schedule for sleeping and waking, hang out with friends past midnight, and hang out with friends during the day); Leadership Proclivity (index measures are current participation in community organizations or volunteer work and the likelihood that in five years that they will vote regularly, play a positive role in the community, participate in organizations, be politically active, and want to be a community leader); Caring for Children (index measures are how often they spent time with, tried to set a good example for and baby sat their child); and Ethics, Drugs and Crime (index measures are how often they drank beer or wine, followed friends into trouble, used marijuana, broke the law for money, broke a promise, drank hard liquor, used hard drugs).

Each of the YB sites was responsible for securing its own funding, in addition to some national foundation funds through YouthBuild USA. Sources of funds included private and community foundations, local government, state government, corporate charities, JTPA, and collaboration with other agencies.

Key Components

YB provides disadvantaged youth with concrete skills through a construction training program and work on community rehabilitation projects, helps them gain their GEDs or high school diplomas through classroom training in an alternative high school and fosters the development of new modes of thinking and living through counseling and leadership training. Reflecting a belief in the importance of comprehensive program design, YB required replication sites to include all of the following:

- academic remediation, including preparation for the GED, high school diploma or college

- skills training toward decent paying jobs, including construction-related jobs

- an immediate, visible role rebuilding the community that allows young people to gain respect from their families and neighbors

- personal counseling from respected role models
- positive peer support with a value system strong enough to compete with "the streets"
- leadership development and civic education
- linkages with employers
- support after graduation
- staff development, focused on adults developing a respect for youth, including involving youth in significant decision-making

Trainees were expected to participate in YB full-time for 10 to 14 months, as a member of a cohort that started together and had a common graduation, although some participants could be placed in jobs or college before the end of the program cycle if appropriate.

Contributing Factors

A Process of Personal Transformation

The researchers documented a common process by which young people could be observed to go through a personal transformation that accompanied success in the program. In-depth interviews with 67 youth traced the participants through five stages: (1) developing trust in the safety and competence of the program, (2) learning to respect the program's rules and to value guidance, (3) learning to cope with "survivor's guilt" caused by leaving the old peer group, (4) learning new strategies and mastering new skills, and (5) finally assimilating a new and positive identity that fosters a healthy life style and a sense of positive expectancy about one's future.

Fidelity to the YouthBuild Model, Strong Executive Leadership, and Time to Plan

Evaluators summed up a number of features that the strong programs had and the weak ones lacked, which included a strong commitment to the YB model and qualified and devoted executive leadership. Those programs with stable, consistent, and skillful leadership, as well as the time and resources for pre-planning and sufficient time between program cycles were the most successful.

A Suitable Construction Site

The most successful sites had a suitable construction site for training YB participants.

Freedom from Inappropriate Constraints and Adequate, Flexible Funding

Keys to program success included (1) _not_ being based in a financially weak host organization or one that did not share YouthBuild's culture or mission, (2) having adequate funds to fill staff positions or provide necessary supplemental services, such as counseling, and (3) having flexible funding rather than categorical funding with strict limitations.

Participant Selection

Successful sites had recruitment, screening and selection methods that identified motivated participants who were committed to overcoming past influences and changing their lives.

Directors and Staff Who were Dedicated to Youth's Personal Growth

In addition to being likeable and emotionally supportive, directors and staff need to be "steadfast in their insistence that youth should make the most of what YouthBuild has to offer. These are directors and staff who work steadily and competently to lead youth into developmental engagement toward personal growth, and not merely social engagement for an enjoyable experience."

Update

Information provided by Dorothy Stoneman, Director, YouthBuild USA, April 1997:

Between 1994 and 1996, 100 YB programs were established through funding from the U.S. Department of Housing and Urban Development under Title D "Hope for Youth" of the Housing and Community Development Act of 1992. These newer programs are showing the same characteristics as the original replication sites, the same factors are determining success, the same transformational process is observable among the youth, the demographics of the trainees are about the same, and the rates of success and attendance are similar. The rate of achievement of the GED or high school diploma is increasing, with

some sites approaching 100 percent achievement if the students entered with a 7th grade reading level; the average achievement of the GED in 1996 was 33 percent of all enrollees and 50 percent of all graduates for a random group of 10 sites, including a wide range of incoming reading levels.

A subset of 68 YB programs has formed the YouthBuild USA Affiliated Network and set program design and performance standards for themselves. They have established an accountability system to be implemented by YB USA, including a management information system and regular program audits performed by independent evaluators.

Study Methodology

Evaluators used both qualitative and quantitative assessments of YB, including site visits and surveys administered at base-line and during the final week of the second year of the demonstration. Surveys included indices measuring the degree to which graduates acquired the perceptions, values and behaviors that YB's components and qualities are designed to foster.

Geographic Areas

The evaluation focused on five demonstration sites: Boston, MA; Cleveland, OH; Gary, IN; San Francisco, CA and Tallahassee, FL.

Contact Information

Research Organizations
Ronald F. Ferguson
Malcolm Weiner Center for Social Policy
John F. Kennedy School of Government
Harvard University
Cambridge, MA 02138
(617) 495-1104, Fax (617) 496-9053

Philip L. Clay
Department of Urban Studies and Planning
Massachusetts Institute of Technology
77 Massachusetts Avenue, Bldg. 7-338
Cambridge, MA 02139
(617) 253-6164, Fax (617) 253-8312

Implementing Organization
Dorothy Stoneman
YouthBuild USA
58 Day Street, P.O. Box 440322
Somerville, MA 02144
(617) 623-9900, Fax (617) 623-4331

Youth Corps

A Summary of:

Evaluation of National and Community Service Programs Impacts of Service: Final Report on the Evaluation of American Conservation and Youth Service Corps

August 1996, Abt Associates (Cambridge, MA) by JoAnn Jastrzab, Julie Masker, John Blomquist and Larry Orr

(Evaluation funded by Corporation for National Service.)

Overview

The National and Community Service Act of 1990, Subtitle C, funded conservation and youth service corps to organize out-of-school youth, 18-to-25-years-old, into crews under the direction of adult staff to carry out community service projects, usually in the environment and human services. (The eight sites in the evaluation are a subset of 91 year-round programs, operating in 197 sites, funded under the National and Community Service Act in the 1993/4 grant cycle.) Corps are intended to provide long-term benefits to the public, instill a work ethic and a sense of public service in participants, and be of substantial social benefit in meeting unmet human, educational, or environmental needs (particularly needs related to poverty) in the community where volunteer service is performed. Service corps vary broadly, but generally provide temporary paid employment in service activities, about 32 hours/week and a mix of services about 8 hours/week.

Typical corps services are:

- introduction to the world of work
- job training
- job search
- basic and remedial education, including GED preparation and a combination of both contextual, "hands-on" learning and traditional classroom education
- life skills training

POPULATION

Youth corps serve approximately 22,000 youth annually. Eighty-six percent of the participants in the intensive study sites were persons of color. Most participants (70 percent) were out-of-school young adults ages 18-25. Fifty-seven percent were males. Most participants were educationally and/or economically disadvantaged: more than half (56 percent) did not have a high school diploma or GED and 70 percent reported a household income of $15,000 or less in the year prior to entry into the corps.

Evidence of Effectiveness

"The most dramatic positive impacts were on African American males."   Abt Associates

The study found that "large and mature" National and Community Service Corps produce a net monetary benefit for society. For the four larger, more established programs studied, society gained $1.04 in benefits, over and above costs, for each hour of service.

Participant impact data is based on random assignment information from four large, longer-running sites. Fifteen months after entry into the youth corps, compared to control group members, participants:

- were more likely to work for pay (99 vs. 73 percent)
- worked more hours (over 2,030 vs. 1,465 hours)
- were less likely to be arrested (12 vs. 17 percent)
- were less likely to earn a technical certificate or diploma (8 vs. 13 percent) (Abt: "Apparently, participation in the corps served as a substitute for enrollment in additional education, at least in the short run.")

The study also found significant impacts by gender and for each major ethnic group of corps participants when compared to their control group counterparts:

- African American males:
  — had higher earnings (1½ times as high, at $705 per month)
  — experienced more employment (91 vs. 62 percent)
  — were more likely to have earned an associate's degree (nearly 4 vs. 0 percent)
  — were more likely to have changes in educational aspirations (for example, nearly 66 vs. less than 40 percent indicated they would like to graduate from college)
- African American females:
  — experienced more employment (90 vs. 60 percent)
  — received an award on their job more often (nearly 35 vs. 9 percent)
  — were less likely to be unmarried and pregnant at follow-up (6 vs. 21 percent)
- Hispanic males:
  — worked more hours (2,300 hours vs. 1,450 hours)
  — received more promotions (over 33 vs. 19 percent)
- Hispanic females:
  — experienced more employment (91 vs. 53 percent)
  — were more likely to have changes in educational aspirations (nearly 66 vs. 61 percent indicated they would like to graduate from college)
  — were less likely to receive a raise at their current job (0 vs. 40 percent)
- White males:
  — were less likely to be employed at follow-up (59 vs. 90 percent)
  — had lower monthly earnings ($875 vs. $1,238)

  — scored lower on the measure of perceived control of work outcomes (8 percent lower)
- White females:
  — were more likely to have earned an associate's degree (over 25 vs. 0 percent)
  — expected to graduate from a 4-year college or attend graduate school more often (90 vs. less than 60 percent)
  — consumed fewer alcoholic beverages (3 vs. 32 percent consumed five or more alcoholic beverages in one sitting during the previous month)

Participants were highly satisfied with the corps, perceived their services as valuable to the community, considered the corps to be a positive investment of their time, would recommend the program to a friend, reported satisfaction with the corps' operating rules and staff and reported developing at least one very good personal relationship during their corps experience.

Sponsors of the service projects were highly satisfied with the quality of the service provided. Almost 80 percent of sponsors rated the quality of corps member work as "good" or "excellent." Virtually all of the sponsors (99.6 percent) would be willing to work with the corps again.

Service beneficiaries, such as elderly residents of nursing homes and visitors to public parks, attested to the value of the services provided. Nearly three-quarters of the beneficiaries perceived improvement in the quality of life resulting from program services, and over 2/3 rated the quality of services to be "good," "very good," or "excellent." Nearly all of the service projects were completed for community-based or not-for-profit organizations, government agencies, or educational institutions.

During the 14-month period covered by this report, the eight programs analyzed for community impacts contributed over one million hours of service, an average of 435 hours per participant. Program completers averaged 1,130 hours of service. Collectively, the eight sites generated services worth almost $14 million, based on estimates of the value of the services and the returns of additional education received by corpsmembers.

More detailed cost-benefit analyses were conducted for the four larger, more established corps programs. Costs were estimated at $16.62 per service hour ($6.76 for participant stipends, fringes, and benefits; $9.66 for other operation costs at the state and local level; and $.20 for administrative costs at the national level.) These four programs averaged 290 participants each and over 230,000 hours of service during the study

period, or 793 service hours per participant. This means a cost of $13,180 per participant over 14 months. The value of program output averaged $13.63 per service hour for the four larger corps programs. The cost to society was calculated as the difference between (1) local, state and national operational costs ($9.66 + $.20) plus forgone earnings of participants ($2.92) and (2) the value of program output ($13.63) and the value of returns to additional education ($.19) for a total benefit to society of $1.04 per service hour.

Contributing Factors

Paid Work
Youth in the corps were working at full-time jobs that paid above the minimum wage. The positive employment, hours worked and earnings results in the follow-up period, when compared to a control group, are largely attributed to this steady work experience in the corps.

Opportunities Within and Outside of the Corps Varied by Subgroup
Abt: "The corps appear to provide a critical source of employment and earnings for non-white participants. In contrast, white females seem to do equally well both inside and outside of the corps in terms of employment and earnings. On the other hand, high-paying employment opportunities appear to be more accessible to young white males outside the corps."

Work That No One Else Was Doing
Nearly 25 percent of sponsoring groups indicated that the work done by corps members would not have been done in their absence. Of the nearly 56 percent that said some of the work would have been done, the sponsor generally had supplies available but little or no labor resources. Even when sponsors said all of the work would have been done with or without corps members, many qualified their responses with such statements as "eventually," or "using overtime of our staff."

Economies of Scale/Greater Experience
The larger corps had an operating cost per service hour roughly half that of the smaller corps.

Study Methodology
A community impact analysis, based on site-visit and survey information, was conducted for eight youth corps programs, serving 2,382 participants. Of these eight sites, the four larger, more mature programs were included in a cost benefit analysis and a participant impact analysis, incorporating a rigorous experimental design. In these four programs, 626 applicants were randomly assigned to a treatment or control group.

Geographic Areas
The eight study sites were: Washington State Service Corps; City Volunteer Corps, New York, NY; Greater Miami Service Corps; Santa Clara District, California Conservation Corps; YouthBuild, Boston; Civic Works, Baltimore; New Jersey Youth Corps of Camden County; Wisconsin Service Corps, Milwaukee. The Washington State, New York City, Miami and California programs underwent a more intensive evaluation.

Contact Information
Research Organization
JoAnn Jastrzab, Senior Research Associate
Abt Associates, Inc.
55 Wheeler Street
Cambridge, MA 02138-1168
(617) 349-2372, Fax (617) 349-2670

Funding and Monitoring Organization
Lance Potter, Director of Evaluation
Corporation for National Service
9th Floor, 1201 New York Ave., NW
Washington, DC 20525
(202) 606-5000, Ext. 448, Fax (202) 565-2786

Section II
Building on the Community

*Initiatives with a focus on members of the community and their active roles in changing the
learning environment for youth and in improving entire communities.
Community partners offer fresh perspectives on careers, provide intensive mentoring,
build trust and respect through guidance and reassurance and may even offer direct service in participants' homes.
Students provide service to their communities while enhancing their academic, occupational and leadership skills.*

Big Brothers Big Sisters

A Summary of:

Making a Difference: An Impact Study of Big Brothers Big Sisters

November 1995, Public/Private Ventures (P/PV), (Philadelphia, PA) by Joseph P. Tierney, Jean Baldwin Grossman, with Nancy L. Resch

(Evaluation funded by the Lilly Endowment, The Commonwealth Fund, Pew Charitable Trusts and an anonymous donor.)

Overview

Big Brothers Big Sisters of America (hereafter BBBS) is a 93-year-old program whose autonomously funded local affiliates support one-to-one mentoring matches between volunteer adults and young people.

At the time of the study, BBBS maintained 75,000 active matches between adult volunteers and youths as young as 5 and as old as 18.

POPULATION

In the sample group of 959 10-to-16-year-olds who applied to BBBS programs in 1992 and 1993: over 60 percent were boys; over 55 percent were members of a minority group (71 percent of whom were African American); 95.6 percent lived with only one parent or grandparent; over 40 percent were receiving food stamps and/or cash public assistance; almost 55 percent had experienced the divorce, separation or death of a parent or guardian; more than 25 percent had experienced physical, emotional or sexual abuse.

Evidence of Effectiveness

Public/Private Ventures (hereafter P/PV) conducted baseline interviews of applicants to the eight BBBS agencies in the study and then randomly assigned the youth to treatment and control groups. After 18 months, all sample members were reinterviewed. Interviews showed that, compared to the control group, youth participating in BBBS were estimated to be:

- 46 percent less likely to initiate drug use (minority Little Brothers and minority Little Sisters were 70 percent less likely to initiate drug use)
- 27 percent less likely to initiate alcohol use (minority Little Sisters were 54 percent less likely to initiate alcohol use)
- 32 percent less likely to hit someone

Participants also reported that they:

- felt more competent about doing their schoolwork (especially minority Little Sisters and white Little Brothers)
- skipped 52 percent fewer days of school (Little Sisters skipped 84 percent fewer days)
- skipped 37 percent fewer classes
- improved 3 percent in grade point averages, a surprise finding for a non-academic intervention program (Little Sisters' GPAs improved almost 6 percent and minority Little Sisters' improved 8 percent)
- improved the quality of relationships with their parents, primarily due to increased trust (especially between white Little Brothers and their parents)
- lied to their parents 37 percent less
- improved the quality of relationships with their peers

Little effect, positive or negative, was shown on "self-concept" or on the number of: incidents of stolen or damaged property; times youth did "risky" things, fought, cheated on a test, used tobacco, were sent to the principal's office or visited a college or library; hours per week spent reading and doing homework; books read or social and cultural activities attended.

While it is difficult to separate out the annual cost of the "matched" relationship from other services of the BBBS agency, the average cost per "matched" youth across 500 agencies is less than $1,000 per year.

Key Components

"Big Brothers Big Sisters of America, [is] the oldest, best-known, and, arguably, the most sophisticated mentoring program in the United States."
                                   Public/Private Ventures

The following features aid the development and maintenance of BBBS quality matches:

- stringent guidelines for screening volunteers by professional program staff to eliminate applicants who pose a safety risk, are unlikely to keep their time commitment, or are unlikely to form positive relationships with a young person
- an orientation for volunteers to explain program requirements and rules, with some sites providing more extensive training on sexual abuse, developmental stages of youth, communication and limit-setting skills, tips on relationship-building and other issues
- a matching process which takes into account adult

volunteer, youth and parental preferences; geographical proximity of adult volunteer and youth; gender; race and religion—most matches are made within gender and staff try to make same-race matches
- supervision to support effective matches, including required monthly telephone contact by agency case managers with the adult volunteer and the youth and/or parents

The effectiveness of the matches is likely due to a substantial time commitment by both the volunteer and youth—both agree to meet two to four times per month for at least a year, with a typical meeting lasting four hours.

Contributing Factors

"Participation in a [BBBS] program reduced illegal drug activity and alcohol use, began to improve academic performance, behavior and attitudes, and improved peer and family relationships. Yet the [BBBS] approach does not target those aspects of life, nor directly address them. It simply provides a caring, adult friend."   **Public/Private Ventures**

Caring Relationships

P/PV: "Our research presents clear and encouraging evidence that caring relationships between adults and youth can be created and supported by programs, and can yield a wide range of tangible benefits" to both participants and the larger society.

Effective Standards and Support Systems

P/PV: "These findings . . . do not mean that the benefits of mentoring occur automatically. The research . . . describes the effects of mentoring in experienced, specialized local programs that adhere to well-developed quality standards. In our judgment, the standards and supports [BBBS] programs employ are critical in making the relationships work, and thus in generating the strong impacts we have reported. If such standards and supports can be duplicated, the expansion and replication of mentoring initiatives for early adolescents would appear to be a strong and sensible

investment, from which at least several million youth could benefit." In contrast to BBBS, relatively unstructured mentoring programs were not as effective.

A Developmental Approach

P/PV: "The findings in this report speak to the effectiveness of an approach to youth policy that is very different from the problem-oriented approach that is prevalent in youth programming. This more developmental approach does not target specific problems, but rather interacts flexibly with youth in a supportive manner."

Case Managers

Each match is monitored by BBBS agency case managers through required, frequent and direct contact with volunteers, participants and their parents. Case managers provide guidance and support for problems that might arise.

Study Methodology

P/PV conducted a random assignment study of 959 10-to-16-year-olds who applied to BBBS programs in 1992 and 1993. Baseline interviews of each applicant were followed by random assignment of one-half to the treatment and one-half to the control group. Twenty-two percent of treatment group members were never matched. All sample members were re-interviewed after 18 months.

Geographic Areas

P/PV chose eight of 500 local accredited BBBS agencies for this study. Criteria were a large caseload and geographic diversity. The sites were Philadelphia, PA; Rochester, NY; Minneapolis, MN; Columbus, OH; Wichita, KA; Houston and San Antonio, TX; and Phoenix, AZ.

Contact Information

Research Organization
Maxine Sherman, Communications Manager
Public/Private Ventures
One Commerce Square
Philadelphia, PA 19103
(215) 557-4400, Fax (215) 557-4469

Implementing Organization
Thomas M. McKenna
National Executive Director
Big Brothers Big Sisters of America
230 North 13th Street
Philadelphia, PA 19107-1538
(215) 567-7000, Fax (215) 567-0394

Communities in Schools

A Summary of:

The National Evaluation of Cities-In-Schools

April 1995, The Urban Institute (Washington, D.C.)
by Shelli B. Rossman and Elaine Morley

(Evaluation funded by U.S. Department of Justice, Office of Juvenile Justice and Delinquency Prevention.)

Overview

Communties In Schools, Inc. (formerly known as Cities In Schools and hereafter referred to as CIS) is a stay in school program aimed at bringing together disparate services in a coordinated, school-based effort. A key goal of CIS is to restructure service delivery by providing services in public schools in a broad variety of ways by a team of adults made up of CIS and school district staff, and, sometimes, staff repositioned from social service agencies and similar organizations.

> **POPULATION**
> Students identified by each affiliate CIS program as being "at-risk" of dropping out of school.

Evidence of Effectiveness

The Urban Institute examined CIS efforts and results over three years, from the fall of 1991 into early 1994. Researchers found that CIS programs "clearly serve the targeted population" of at-risk young people. The evaluation covered many process areas and reported on several student outcomes:

- 77 percent of students receiving CIS services in the 1989-90 school year were still in school or had graduated in 1992-93 (68.9 percent of those eligible to graduate did so)
- CIS students' cumulative dropout rate was 21 percent over three years or about 7 percent annually (the annual dropout rate nationally is 4.5 percent; for students from low income families it is 12 percent)
- of the 49 percent of students with high absenteeism before entering CIS (10 or more absences in the previous year), 68 percent improved their attendance

- of the approximately 25 percent of students with severe absenteeism before entering CIS (more than 21 days or more than 10 percent of the school year), 70 percent improved their attendance by an average of 6.6 days
- 49 percent of the students for whom academic records were available improved their GPAs
- of the 45 percent who entered CIS with GPAs of 1.99 or lower, 60 percent improved their GPAs during their first year in CIS
- of students with the most severe academic problems (with GPAs of 1.0 or below), 79 percent improved an average of one grade point
- students enrolled in CIS academies (schools-within-schools or alternative schools) demonstrated greater improvements than students in CIS sites at typical public schools

Key Components

CIS, Inc. is a non-profit organization that provides training and technical assistance to suppport the replication and operation of CIS programs. The national organization includes CIS headquarters and five regional offices under which fall autonomous state and community CIS programs. At the community level, CIS projects are generally formed through partnerships involving local government (e.g. school districts), service agencies, and local businesses, each structured as a nonprofit corporation. Size of CIS programs range from 20 to several thousand students. A CIS school site may include the following:

- case management—needs assessment, developing service delivery plans, and monitoring progress
- individual or group counseling (may be informal and carried out by "caring adults" rather than professional counselors)
- volunteer tutors and/or mentors
- a CIS class that teaches life skills (which may include employment-related topics, remedial education and tutoring)
- after school or in-school programs on conflict resolution and violence abatement, community service activities, transition to work, substance abuse prevention, and pregnancy prevention or teen parenting classes

"The CIS model is intended to bring various agencies together as a team in order to promote more effective provision of services to youth and their families." **Urban Institute**

Most CIS programs offer:

- emergency advice or referrals to non-CIS students
- programs or events in which non-CIS students can participate

Some CIS sites operate as "academies." These include the basic elements of the CIS model and are organized as "alternative schools" where students are block-scheduled with other CIS students for all or most of their classes. Characteristics that differentiate the CIS academy model may include the use of innovative teaching methods and curricula structured to meet the special needs of CIS students. Some CIS in-school programs are called "corporate academies" due to corporate sponsorship, but they do not otherwise differ from other CIS in-school programs.

Researchers also conducted case studies of 10 exemplary CIS programs. These programs were selected because they offered particularly strong examples of features such as: collaborative partnerships, strategic planning and development, effective management practices, parental involvement, and/or specific service components, such as case management, employment training, substance abuse prevention, mental health services, and crime and violence prevention.

Contributing Factors

Caring Adults

Urban Institute: "Students were particularly enamored with the warm, supportive relationships that CIS staff initiated and sustained."

More Emphasis on Jobs/Employability

Urban Institute: "In general, the students' wish list for expanding CIS services focused on the need for jobs, particularly those they perceived as being of high quality (i.e., reasonably well compensated, pleasant working environment, and respectful employer-employee relations)."

Works Best for Those Most At-Risk

Those CIS students who reported that they had the most severe problems prior to enrollment also

reported the most dramatic improvements in attitude and behavior. These reports are consistent with the improvements in attendance and GPA for students with the lowest attendance and GPAs at enrollment.

Parental Involvement

One CIS goal is to work with youth holistically by providing services to the family as well as the child. However, most ongoing parental involvement occured through telephone contact at the sites in the sample. Many sites found it difficult to engage parents.

Repositioned Staff

Staff who are repositioned to CIS from various service agencies (e.g., counselors from social service or substance abuse agencies) are key ingredients that differentiate CIS from other programs. However, few CIS programs have the diversity of repositioned staff that is needed to provide a comprehensive range of services at the school site. Sites were successful in obtaining services for students through off-site referral. CIS has not led to significant changes in the way agencies provide services.

Case Management

Case management was more fully implemented where social workers served as project directors, or where social workers were repositioned to assist with CIS, than in programs with little or no social worker involvement.

Tracking/Evaluation and Decentralization

Urban Institute: "The national organization and CIS Board have appropriately turned attention to quality control issues. A Quality and Standards Committee was established in 1993 that requires and collects standard measures of student outcomes." Autonomous state and community affiliates initially made it difficult for the national CIS to enforce data collection on student outcomes, evaluation and quality control.

Other

Other identified keys to success are: initial and on-going staff training, a commitment to top-down reform on the part of the school district; principal and faculty support; good working relationships between the CIS office and the schools with CIS projects; and the allocation of staff to coordinate and provide support for volunteers involved in tutoring and mentoring.

Study Methodology

Researchers examined: (1) the CIS national organization, focusing on training and technical assistance provided; (2) representative CIS sites to gauge student outcomes; and (3) case studies of 10 exemplary sites. Data was collected through interviews (by telephone and in-person) with headquarters staff, community and school-based staff and selected students; direct observation of training sessions; site visits; and a review of student records. Comparison data was not collected.

Geographic Areas

The evaluation is based on 21 sites: Helena/West Helena and Marianna, AR; Pinal County, AZ; Long Beach, CA; Adams County, CO; Miami PIC and Palm Beach County, FL; Griffin-Spalding, GA; Chicago, IL; High Point and Rocky Mount, NC; Metropolitan Corporate Academy, NYC; Philadelphia and Southwestern, PA; Columbia, SC; Austin, Houston and San Antonio, TX; Richmond and Greensville-Emporia, VA; and Seattle, WA.

Contact Information

Research Organization
Shelli Rossman and Elaine Morley
The Urban Institute
2100 M Street, NW
Washington, D.C. 20037
(202) 833-7200, Ext. 3775, Fax (202) 659-8985

Implementing Organization
Linda A. Britt
Communities In Schools, Inc.
1199 North Fairfax Street, Suite 300
Alexandria, VA 22314-1436
(703) 519-8999, Fax (703) 519-7213

Home Visitation by Nurses

A Summary of:	**Improving The Life-Course Development of Socially Disadvantaged Mothers: A Randomized Trial of Nurse Home Visitation**	**The Prenatal/Early Infancy Project**

by David L. Olds, Charles R. Henderson, Robert Tatelbaum and Robert Chamberlin, in *American Journal of Public Health*, November 1988, Vol. 78, No. 11

by David L. Olds, in *14 Ounces of Prevention: A Casebook for Practitioners*, 1989, American Psychological Association, (editors Richard H. Price, Emory L. Cowen, Raymond P. Lorion and Julia Ramos-McKay)

(Evaluation funded by Ford Foundation.)

Overview

The Home Visitation by Nurses project (hereafter HVN) consisted of home visits by nurses designed to prevent a wide range of maternal and child health problems associated with poverty and to encourage parents[1] to complete their education, obtain training, and make informed decisions about finding employment and bearing additional children.

POPULATION

Conducted in a semi-rural, primarily white community, this project was open to any woman bearing a first child. Women with risk factors relating to maternal and child health and parental "life-course development" were targeted. Of the 400 women enrolled, all were under 30 weeks pregnant, 89 percent were white, 85 percent met at least one of the following risk characteristics: (a) young age (less than 19 years old- 47 percent), (b) single-parent (62 percent), (c) low socio-economic status (61 percent came from families of "semi-skilled and unskilled laborers.") Twenty-three percent had all three risk characteristics.

Evidence of Effectiveness

This randomized comparison group evaluation looked at a number of factors including maternal prenatal health behaviors and infant care giving. In this summary, we focus primarily on the findings and contributing factors related to education, employment and pregnancy rates of *mothers*. Due to the small number of non-white participants, only findings for white participants were given. Compared to a randomized comparison group, the nurse-visited white women:

- who had not graduated from high school when they registered in the study, returned to school more rapidly (59 vs. 27 percent either graduated or enrolled in an educational program by their 6th month postpartum). (However, by the 10th month postpartum, the effect of the program held only for those women who had been unmarried at registration. There were no treatment differences in the proportion of women who graduated or remained in high school at the 22nd month postpartum nor for overall educational achievement at the 46th month postpartum.)

- who were poor, unmarried and older (19 years old or older) worked two and one-half times longer than their counterparts in the control group, between birth and the 22nd month post-partum and women who were poor, unmarried and younger (under 19 years old) worked more than their counterparts in the control group by the 46th month post-partum, leading to an 82 percent increase in the number of months worked by both teenagers and older women in contrast to poor, unmarried women in the control group
- had 22 percent fewer subsequent pregnancies
- who were poor and unmarried (all ages), had 42 percent fewer subsequent pregnancies and postponed the birth of second children an average of 12 months longer
- who were poor, unmarried, older women, were on public assistance 157 fewer days for 24 months postpartum (a 40 percent reduction). This effect did not, however, continue for months 24 to 48 postpartum.
- made better use of the formal services available to them; experienced greater informal social support, improved their diets more, and reduced the number of cigarettes smoked; had a 395 gram improvement in birth weight of the children of very young teenagers; had a 75 percent

reduction in pre-term delivery for smokers; had a reduction of 75 percent in verified cases of child abuse and neglect for poor, unmarried teenagers (a reduction from 19 percent to 4 percent); and had a decreased incidence of maltreatment and of emergency room visits for their children

In 1980 dollars, the program cost $3,173 per family for 2½ years of intervention. By the time the children were four years old, nurse-visited low-income families cost the government $3,313 less per family than the comparison group. When focused on low-income families, the investment in the service was recovered with a dividend of about $180 within two years after the program ended. (Costs calculated in "Studies of Prenatal and Infancy Nurse Home Visitations," David L. Olds.) The cost of home visitation may be offset by avoided foster-care placements, hospitalization, emergency-room visits, child protective services worker time, parental return to the workforce, and a reduction in the number of subsequent children.

Key Components

"These individuals [family, friends, husbands or boyfriends] were assumed to play decisive roles in determining the extent to which the women would improve their health habits, finish their educations, find work, secure appropriate child care, and address the needs of the children."   Olds

HVN was established to improve women's prenatal health habits, infant care giving skills, social support, use of community services, and educational and occupational achievements and to help women reduce unwanted additional pregnancies and their reliance on welfare. It was carried out in a small, semi-rural, very low income county of approximately 100,000 residents in the Appalachian region of New York State (Elmira, NY). The community has an abundance of health and human services, yet consistently exhibited the highest rates of reported and confirmed child abuse and neglect in the state.

In this focused prevention strategy, nurses conducted home visits from pregnancy through the first two years of the baby's life and provided:

- parent education on nutrition; health habits; regular exercise; the use of cigarettes, alcohol and drugs; fetal development; the physiology of pregnancy; preparation for labor and delivery; newborn care; infant development; and use of the health system

- encouragement to parents to complete their own education, to obtain vocational training, and to make decisions for themselves about finding employment and bearing additional children
- assistance on making child care arrangements and methods of finding jobs and interviewing
- assistance in involving family members and friends in the pregnancy, early care of the child, support of the mother, and invited participation in each home-visit
- linkages of parents and family members to other formal health and human services
- encouragement to keep prenatal visits, visit the parents' doctors, and communicate with parents' doctors regularly to clarify and reinforce physicians' recommendations in the home

The initial visit was made within seven days after enrollment. The nurses visited families once every other week throughout pregnancy for 60 to 90 minutes. Home visits continued at the following rates 0-6 weeks, weekly; 6 weeks-4 months, every 2 weeks; 4-14 months, every 3 weeks; 14-20 months, every month; and 20-24 months, every 6 weeks.

Contributing Factors

"The nurses tailored the specific content of their home visits to the individual needs of each family. For example, the nurses helped all interested women find employment but gave special consideration to those who were poor and lacked other sources of income; they discussed family planning with all families but gave extra attention to those who wanted to avoid additional pregnancies."   Olds

Home Visits

Olds: "Home visitation is a useful vehicle for the delivery of prevention services. It provides a means of reaching out to parents who distrust formal service providers or who lack self-confidence—those least likely to show up for office-based services . . . Without a major home visitation component, a significant portion of the families who most need the service will not receive it . . . A persistent, caring nurse, however, can be remarkably successful in engaging a significant portion of those who are unreachable through other means."

In-Depth Knowledge of Family Needs

Olds: "[N]urses were able to acquire a more complete understanding of those factors in the home and family that interfered with parents' efforts to cope with the pregnancy and early care of the child. By assessing the home environment, the nurses could provide more sensitive, informed services themselves and could help other service providers do the same. Because the parents in our program did not always articulate their needs clearly, it helped to have sensitive home-visiting nurses get to know them so that appropriate services could be provided."

Life-Course Development

Olds: "By helping young women find ways to continue their education, find jobs, and plan future pregnancies, the nurses helped them increase their financial resources and reduce the stresses associated with caring for several young children."

Access to and Knowledge of Services

Olds: "[B]y linking parents with other health and human services, the nurses helped reduce many of the stresses that lead to maternal depression, poor prenatal health habits, and interference with care giving," and helped connect parents to available supportive social service networks from which they would otherwise have felt isolated.

A Foundation of Respect for Parents

Olds: "[W]e wanted to avoid giving parents the message that they were incompetent or incapable of caring for their children, it was important to begin the program during pregnancy. Offering help once the baby was born might have been interpreted as an indication that we thought parents had made mistakes or were incapable of caring for their children."

Reduce Dependence on Formal Services

A possible risk in linking families with health and human services was in increasing the family's dependence on formal services. This problem was minimized by helping parents continue their education, find employment, and turn to friends and relatives for other assistance.

Service Agency Cooperation

Olds: "To elicit the cooperation of [various] service agencies, we developed a proposal to carry out the study and presented it to representatives of [service agencies]. We considered each of their concerns and resolved them as we refined the program. As the study proceeded, we informed them of the findings of the study. They in turn played a central role in seeing to it that the program was continued by the county health department after the experimental phase of the study was completed."

Update

In an unpublished paper, "Studies of Prenatal and Infancy Nurse Home Visitations," David Olds describes findings from another study of nurse visitation conducted in Memphis, TN in 1990 and 1991. The population for this study included women less than 29 weeks pregnant with their first child, was 92 percent African American, 97 percent unmarried, 65 percent 18 years old or younger, and 85 percent from households with incomes at or below the federal poverty guidelines. The 1,139 women registered were randomized for a treatment group and a comparison group (receiving transportation for prenatal care and developmental screening for the children). Services were similar to those offered in Elmira, NY with home visits taking place four weeks after registration and then once every other week throughout the pregnancy. The nurses were scheduled to visit once a week for the first six weeks postpartum, once every week from six weeks to 21 months postpartum, and then once a month from 21 to 24 months postpartum. Data was gathered through blind interviews with treatment and comparison group members. In addition to findings on prenatal conditions and care giving, after 24 months postpartum, compared to similar comparison group members, the nurse-visited women:

- had 26 percent fewer second pregnancies
- had 20 percent greater household incomes

- who had "high psychological resources" reported 29 percent less AFDC enrollment (about two months less). Olds: "This suggests that the program was able to help those women with fewer mental health symptoms, higher IQ's and more active coping styles in becoming less dependent on welfare, but was unable to do so with women with fewer psychological resources."

Preliminary cost calculations in 1992 dollars have been completed for program costs per family where the child has reached two years of age based on the time spent by the nurse (home visits, missed appointments, travel, and phone calls) training to deliver the services, actual delivery of the service (nurses' and supervisors' salaries), equipment, supplies, and other overhead. Based on these components, the program cost $6,119 per family or $2,626 per year for the 2-year, 4-month program.

Study Methodology
The Elmira, NY evaluation compared women in experimental groups with women in control groups. The sample was stratified on a number of demographic factors and then women were randomly assigned to home visits or to comparison services (transportation for health care and screening for health problems). The evaluation followed the children and families until the children were 4 years old.

Geographic Area
Elmira, New York.

Contact Information
Research Organization
David L. Olds, Professor of Pediatrics, Psychiatry, and Preventive Medicine
Director, Prevention Research Center for Family and Child Health
University of Colorado Health Sciences Center
303 East 17th Avenue, # 200
Denver, CO 80203
(303) 861-1715, Ext. 226, Fax (303) 861-2441

[1]The study refers to "parents," rather than "mothers," because about 40 percent of the women were married and a significant number of the unmarried women were living with the father of the baby.

Jobs for America's Graduates

A Summary of:

Comparisons of the March 1992 Labor Force and Employment Status of JAG Program Participants with Those of Non-Enrolled Young High School Graduates in the U.S.

March 1993, Center for Labor Market Studies, Northeastern University (Boston, MA)
by Andrew Sum and Joanna Heliotis

(Evaluation Funded by Jobs for America's Graduates.)

Jobs for America's Graduates, Inc. 1995-1996 School Year Annual Report

The Performance Outcomes of JAG School-to-Work Transition Programs, for the Class of 1994

September 1994, JAG National Network

Overview

Jobs for America's Graduates (hereafter JAG) targets students at-risk of dropping out and aims to secure quality jobs for its graduates that will lead to successful careers. The program does this by keeping students in school through graduation and giving them employability skills along the way. JAG provides nine months of in-school services and nine months of follow-up.

POPULATION

JAG targets students at-risk for failure and dropping out. Specifically, the program looks for students who are one or more years behind their grade level or who are deficient in basic skills compared to their classmates. Currently, JAG serves over 40,000 young people. In 1992, JAG participants were 50.2 percent African American, 39 percent white and 10.8 percent Hispanic and "other". Slightly over 41 percent of JAG participants were members of "poor/near poor" families.

Evidence of Effectiveness

"JAG was established to demonstrate, evaluate and then nationally replicate, a comprehensive school-to-work transition model in diverse labor markets. For the past 16 years, local and state affiliates have documented the delivery of services and outcomes for all participants using the JAG Management Information System." **JAG**

For nine months after high school graduation, from June until March each JAG affiliate prepares a monthly report tracking the status of that year's participants. The Northeastern University study used information from March 1992 placement reports for the 8,200 students in the JAG Class of 1991. The JAG class of 1991 had:

- a graduation rate of 90.5 percent

Northeastern chose to compare JAG participants to national data using (1) a subgroup of 4,081 JAG 1992 high school graduates who were not attending a college or university or serving in the military, and (2) all U.S. high school graduates under 20 years old in March of 1992 who were not attending a college or university or serving in the military. Compared to the national group, JAG participants:

"JAG participants are chosen for participation . . . because they have been identified by the selection team as being "at risk" of joblessness upon graduation. Thus the findings (compared to the hypothetical labor market) are rather promising about the likely short-term effects of JAG . . . however, these findings are no substitute for a more rigorous impact evaluation using comparison and control groups." **Northeastern**

- were more likely to be in the civilian labor force (89 vs. 83 percent)
- had a higher employment rate (68.7 vs. 65.8 percent)
- had a slightly higher unemployment rate (23 vs. 21 percent)

As JAG participants are considerably more likely than the comparison group of all U.S. graduates to be African Americans or to come from "poor/near poor" families, Northeastern calculated a _hypothetical_ set of national labor market outcomes representing the expected outcomes if the comparison group were distributed by race and family income identically to JAG participants.[1] When compared to this hypothetical labor market, JAG graduates:

- had a higher civilian labor force participation rate (88.7 percent vs. 74 percent)
- had a lower unemployment rate (22.5 percent vs. 33.1 percent)
- had a higher employment rate (68.7 percent vs. 52 percent)

An in-house analysis of combined placement data for programs operated by JAG affiliates, produced the following findings for the JAG Class of 1994 (12,055 participants) as of September of 1994:

- 86.4 percent graduated from high school
- 78.9 percent had a positive outcome status (civilian job placement, military service enlistment, college/university enrollment or enrollment in other postsecondary training or education)
- the employment rate was 58 percent,
- the full-time jobs rate was 62 percent
- the full-time placement rate (full-time jobs plus those combining school and work) was 78.1 percent
- 33.2 percent of pursued further education
- 21 percent (of JAG graduates) were neither employed nor enrolled in an education or training program

The JAG National office uses internal benchmarks to assess the performance of JAG affiliates. JAG seeks to raise the graduation rate to 90 percent, the positive outcome rate to 80 percent, the employment rate to 60 percent, the full-time jobs rate to 60 percent and the full-time placement rate (full-time jobs plus those combining school and work) to 80 percent.

JAG cost $1,100 to $1,500 per student per year.

Key Components

Among JAG's key program elements are:

- a "specialist" who works with 30-50 young people and is held strictly accountable for their progress
- reducing barriers that might keep a young person from graduating, getting a job or going on to postsecondary education and training
- involving participants in the JAG Career Association
- classroom instruction in 37 employment competencies (identified by the business community)
- bringing the business community into the process through work-based learning experiences that lead to mastery certification

- intensive marketing to employers to open up jobs that lead to careers
- at least nine months of follow-up and support after JAG graduates leave school
- computerized tracking of program operations and results

In addition, JAG runs longer programs that extend services to the lower grades, target students at-risk for dropping out as early as the 8th grade, and work to recover dropouts.

Contributing Factors

Program Emphasis is on Connecting Graduates with Quality, Full-time Jobs

The Class of 1994 performance measures were two points above the JAG standard for placing graduates in full-time jobs (60 percent full-time jobs rate). This reflects the fact that job placement after graduation is JAG's top priority.

Job Specialists are Key to Success

Job specialists are held accountable for the success of

30-50 of the most at-risk young people in the school. This person is responsible for initial recruitment to the program, helping young people to complete high school successfully, identifying jobs and helping JAG graduates obtain them, and helping JAG participants secure a raise or promotion within nine months. This personal element is critical to JAG participants' success.

Study Methodology

The Northeastern University study used information from March 1992 placement reports for the 8,200 students in the JAG Class of 1991 and compared JAG participants to national data using (1) a subgroup of 4,081 JAG high school graduates who were not attending a college or university or serving in the military, and (2) all U.S. high school graduates under 20 years old in March of 1992 who were not attending a college or university or serving in the military. In addition, evaluators compared JAG data to a hypothetical labor market with the same percentages of minority and poor youth as the JAG sample.

The September 1994 outcomes report used information from monthly placement reports for the 12,055 students in the JAG Class of 1994.

Geographic Areas

JAG operates in 550 high schools in 26 states and territories.

Contact Information

Research Organization
Andrew Sum, Director
Center for Labor Market Studies
Department of Economics
Northeastern University
360 Huntington Avenue
Boston, MA 02115
(617) 373-2242, Fax (617) 373-3640

Implementing Organization
Adrienne Smith, Director of Program Development
Jobs for America's Graduates
1729 King Street, Suite 200
Alexandria, VA 22314
(703) 684-9479, Fax (703) 684-9489

[1] Northeastern cautions that the two groups were far from perfectly matched and that they could not control for geographic area, local labor market conditions, prior work experience, high school performance and behavior.

Learn and Serve, Higher Education

A Summary of:

Evaluation of Learn and Serve America, Higher Education: First Year Report, Volume I

May 1996, Institute on Education and Training, RAND (Santa Monica, CA) by Maryann Jacobi Gray, Sandra Geschwind, Elizabeth Heneghan Ondaatje, Abby Robyn and Stephen P. Klein and Higher Education Research Institute, University of California, Los Angeles, by Linda J. Sax, Alexander W. Astin and Helen S. Astin

(Evaluation funded by Corporation for National Service.)

Overview

Learn and Serve America, Higher Education (hereafter LSAHE) is an initiative developed under the National and Community Service Act of 1990 and administered by the Corporation for National Service (hereafter CNS). It encourages postsecondary students to participate in community service while improving their academic and life skills.

POPULATION

Learn and Serve volunteers were college students. Participants were more likely than non-participants to have performed volunteer work in high school (88 percent vs. 70 percent), tutored another student, attended religious services, participated in a community action program, or been a guest in a teacher's home. Participants also had more confidence in their leadership abilities, were more likely to be women [70 percent], and were less likely than non-participants to attend college in order to make more money.

Evidence of Effectiveness

This RAND/University of California, Los Angeles (hereafter UCLA) evaluation covers LSAHE's first year (1995) funded at $9.5 million for 116 grantees. The final report will be issued later in 1997. To determine if LSAHE affected student outcomes, the UCLA half of the evaluation team administered post-program surveys to 2,309 participants and 1,141 non-participants at LSAHE institutions, assessing outcomes in the areas of civic responsibility, academic development, and life skills. For some measures,

evaluators administered pre- and post-program surveys to learn how students had changed over the course of their LSAHE service.

- On seven measures used to compare levels of civic responsibility before and after LSAHE, service participants had higher levels of civic responsibility than non-participants. The most striking differences were between students' commitment to:
  - influencing social values, which increased by 7.8 percentage points for LSAHE participants and

"LSAHE largely achieved its goals in its first year of operation. Community organizations were strongly positive about the contributions of student volunteers. Institutional support for service learning, although uneven, appears to be increasing. Further, students who participate in service show stronger gains than non-participants in academic achievement, life skills, and civic responsibility."   RAND

decreased by 2.1 percentage points for non-participants, and

— helping others in difficulty, which increased by 7.8 percentage points for LSAHE participants and 4.7 for non-participants.

- LSAHE students also scored higher than non-participants on measures relating to academic development. The greatest difference was seen in plans to prepare for graduate or professional school (14.3 points higher) and doing extra work for courses (17.1 percentage points higher).

- In all 13 categories used to measure changes in life skills, LSAHE participants had higher scores than non-participants: satisfaction with college leadership opportunities (22.9 points higher), seeing the relevance of coursework to everyday life (17 points higher), leadership ability (13.5 points higher), knowledge of different races/cultures (13.9 points higher), and acceptance of different races/cultures (13.8 points higher). Before and after tests showed that LSAHE

participants also gained more than non-participants in both social self-confidence and leadership ability.

- In a regression analysis designed to control for underlying differences between LSAHE participants and non-participants irrespective of their LSAHE service, LSAHE participation was seen to have a small positive effect on all outcome measures of civic responsibility, academic development, and life skills.

- Researchers concluded that the more time students devoted to service, the stronger the positive effects were, particularly in the areas of civic responsibility and life skills.

- Community organization staff rated student volunteers highly for effectiveness in promoting positive outcomes for recipients in the areas of education, health and human needs, public safety and environment and for their enthusiasm and interpersonal skills with youth. Staff rated LSAHE volunteers more highly than other volunteers, and regarded them as equally competent as paid staff.

Key Components

LSAHE "emphasizes the links between service and academic learning by encouraging postsecondary students to participate in community service. LSAHE strives to: (1) serve the educational, health-related, public safety, and environmental needs of communities; (2) enhance students' academic learning; and (3) build organizational support for service within higher education and community-based organizations."   RAND

CNS grants to higher education or community organizations encourage postsecondary education students to engage in community service in four priority areas: education, human needs, public safety, and the environment. The key to the LSAHE model is service-learning, defined as a method whereby participants learn and develop through active participation in organized service that: (1) meets community needs, (2) helps foster civic responsibility and (3) is integrated into the academic curriculum and educational process and incorporates structured time for students to reflect on their experience in giving service.

LSAHE funds were used to build institutional capacity for service programs, usually through integrating a service component into academic courses (70 percent), providing technical assistance (69 percent), and establishing information resources (38 percent). Seventy-five percent of the institutions responding to the Annual Accomplishments Survey set up a volunteer or service learning center on campus and offered incentives for student and faculty participation.

Contributing Factors

Community Support and Benefits

Community organization staff rated student volunteers very highly and thought that they accomplished a great deal. Community organization staff thought the positive aspects of student service outweighed any negative aspects including the fact that students often could not volunteer as many hours as community organizations would have liked because of conflicts with class or work and were not always available for an entire K-12 semester.

LSAHE Student Selection

Researchers indicate that LSAHE participants may have possessed more positive qualities in the areas of civic responsibility, academic development and life skills than other students even *before* they devoted time to LSAHE. However, the regression analysis that tried to control for such differences did find small positive impacts across all measures.

Study Methodology

The evaluation included both qualitative and quantitative methods. Evaluators used numerous data sources for this report, including surveys and site visits. To determine if LSAHE affected student outcomes, the UCLA half of the evaluation team administered post-program surveys to 2,309 participants and 1,141 non-participants at LSAHE institutions, assessing outcomes in the areas of civic responsibility, academic development, and life skills.

Geographic Areas

LSAHE grants were awarded to nationwide.

Contact Information

Research Organization
Maryann Jacobi Gray
The RAND Corporation
P.O. 2138
Santa Monica, CA 90407-2138
(310) 393-0411, Ext. 6156, Fax (310) 393-4818

Dr. Alexander Astin
The Higher Education Research Institute
University of California, Los Angeles
Graduate School of Education and
    Information Studies
3005 Moore Hall, Mail Box # 951521
Los Angeles, CA 90095-1521
(310) 825-1925, Fax (310) 206-2228

Implementing Organization
Lance Potter, Director of Evaluation
Corporation for National Service
9th Floor, 1201 New York Ave., NW
Washington, DC 20525
(202) 606-5000, Ext. 448, Fax (202) 565-2786

A Summary of:

National Evaluation of Learn and Serve America School and Community-Based Programs: Interim Report

February 1997, by Alan Melchior, Center for Human Resources, Heller Graduate School, Brandeis University (Waltham, MA) and Abt Associates (Cambridge, MA)

(Evaluation funded by Corporation for National Service.)

Overview

Learn and Serve America, School and Community-Based Programs (hereafter LS) supports school and community-based efforts to involve school-aged youth in community service and to help young people develop through involvement in service-learning. LS was established under the 1993 National and Community Service Trust Act and is the successor to the Serve-America Program (see pp. 126-128). LS is administered by the Corporation for National Service and funded through grants to states and national organizations, and through them to individual school districts, schools and community organizations. In 1994-95, the first year of the program, the Corporation awarded approximately $30 million in grants supporting over 2,000 local efforts involving over 750,000 school-aged youth.

POPULATION

Approximately 1,000 middle and high school students in well-designed, "fully-implemented," school-based service-learning programs and comparison group students were included in the evaluation. Participants included 29 percent middle school students and 71 percent high school students. Forty percent were male and 60 percent female. The group was racially and ethnically diverse (58 percent white, 17 percent African-American, 19 percent Hispanic, and 4 percent Asian, Native American or multi-cultural). Thirty-eight percent of the participants were economically disadvantaged.

Evidence of Effectiveness

The LS evaluation studied the impact of well-designed, fully-implemented service-learning programs in seven middle schools and ten high schools in nine states. The interim report details the program impacts for students who participated during the 1995-96 academic year. The final report for evaluation will examine longer-term, follow-up impacts and will be completed in early 1998. The evaluation was designed to address: (1) the impact of program participation on participants; (2) the institutional impacts; (3) the impacts LS programs have on their communities; and (4) the return (in dollar terms) on the LS investment. Data from the first year of the evaluation suggest that these programs are having a positive impact on both the program participants and the community at large.

The evaluation found positive, statistically significant impacts (at a 0.05 level or higher) for participants in

"While none of these findings suggest that service-learning by itself is an effective preventative for at-risk behavior, the data on teenage parenting in particular do suggest that service-learning can contribute to a multi-faceted intervention . . . [and] service may contribute to the effectiveness of programs targeted to reducing at-risk behaviors among school-aged youth."   Brandeis/Abt

"[S]tudents in service learning programs are more likely to be involved in volunteer service as a result of program participation, and they provide significantly more hours of service than young people who are not enrolled."   Brandeis/Abt

". . . there is a sufficient pattern of impacts to suggest that fully-implemented service-learning programs can help support civic development and improved educational achievement." Brandeis/Abt

Key Components

these well-designed, fully-implemented LS sites on a number of measures of civic and educational development. Relative to a comparison group, participants in LS:

- scored 3-5 percent higher on a measure of personal and social responsibility
- scored 3-5 percent higher on a measure of acceptance of cultural diversity
- scored 8.4 percent higher on a measure of service leadership
- scored higher on a measure of work orientation
- showed a marginally significant impact (at the 0.10 level) on teenage pregnancy
- scored higher on a measure of school engagement and showed GPA increases in English (2.55 vs. 2.48, not statistically significant), mathematics (2.31 vs. 2.05), social studies (2.66 vs. 2.47) and science (2.43 vs. 2.25) and greater aspirations to graduate from a four-year college. Positive impacts were particularly strong for middle school students, with a 16 percent difference in core GPA, a 25 percent difference in mathematics grades, and a nearly 30 percent difference in social studies grades
- were 30 percent more likely to have been involved in some form of service activity during the previous six months, and provided 2.6 times as many hours of volunteer service (an average of 100 vs. 37.5 hours of service)
- showed no statistically significant impact on a measure of personal and social development

Programs benefited a wide range of youth, including white and minority students, males and females, educationally and economically disadvantaged students. Students with previous involvement in

Service-learning combines meaningful service in the community with a formal educational curriculum and structured time for participants to reflect on their service experience. While the LS programs vary in structure and format, sites in the evaluation were selected through a purposive sampling process aimed at identifying well-established, fully implemented, school-based service-learning programs that had been in existence for more than

service also continued to benefit from involvement in a formal service-learning program.

Among program participants:

- More than 95 percent reported satisfaction with their community service experience and felt the service performed was helpful to the individuals and the community served.
- Eighty-seven percent believed that they learned a skill that would be useful in the future, and 75 percent said that they learned more than in a typical class.
- Over 90 percent felt that students should be encouraged (though not required) to participate in community service.

Among the community agencies, schools, hospitals and others agencies where students provided assistance:

- 99 percent rated their experience with the LS program to be good
- 97 percent indicated that they would pay at least minimum wage for the work being done and 96 percent reported that they would use participants from the program again
- 90 percent indicated that the LS volunteers had helped the agency improve their services to clients and the community
- 66 percent reported that the experience had increased the agency's interest in using student volunteers
- 56 percent said that participating in the program had produced new relationships with public schools, and 66 percent said that it had fostered a more positive attitude toward working with the public schools
- 82 percent reported that the LS program had helped to build a more positive attitude towards youth in the community

one year, and reported higher than average hours of service (an average of 77 hours per student), linked to regular use of written and oral reflection, and a formal course curriculum. Specific components of these evaluation sites included:

- integration of service into formal course curriculum, either as part of a core subject (for example, an English or Social Studies class) or an elective course

"The primary purpose of Learn and Serve is the involvement of school-aged youth in programs and classroom activities that link meaningful service in the community with a structured learning experience (i.e., service-learning). The goals of the program are to help young people develop as responsible citizens, improve their academic skills, and develop as individuals while helping to meet 'the unmet human, educational, environmental, and public safety needs of the United States.'"

Brandeis/Abt

- substantial hours of direct service—participants reported more than two times the median among the national sample used to select evaluation sites
- at least some hands-on, face-to-face experience with recipients for three-quarters of participants
- a combination of group and individual service assignments (60 percent of students)
- regular reflection and writing—substantial time to "process" the service experience through formal and informal group discussions, journal writing, research papers, and group presentations (76 percent of participants reported time set aside to discuss service experiences and 44 percent reported keeping a journal)
- a relatively high quality experience for the majority of program participants (over 70 percent felt they had real responsibilities, did things themselves, had a variety of tasks and made a contribution to their service site)

Contributing Factors

Greater Impacts than Serve-America Evaluation

The scope and methodology of the Serve-America and LS evaluations differed, the first examining a representative sample of programs and the second focusing on a subset of "high-quality" programs. Though findings were not directly comparable, the LS evaluation showed a stronger, more diverse set of impacts for middle school students, particularly on school grades, four measures of civic development, and three measures of academic performance. LS results are also stronger for high school students, including impacts on three measures not seen in the Serve-America evaluation: Attitudes towards Diversity, School Engagement, and Course Grades. Marginal impacts were also shown on Educational Competence, Course Failures, Educational Aspirations, and involvement in delinquent behavior.

Program Quality and Maturity

The stronger impacts of the LS evaluation suggest that higher quality and more mature programs had more positive impacts.

Study Methodology

The evaluation sites were selected from a pool of 210 middle and high school service-learning programs that had been randomly selected and contacted as part of the site selection process. This analysis is based on pre-and post-program surveys and school record data for approximately 1,000 middle and high school program participants and comparison group students from the 1995-96 school year, on-site interviews with teachers and small groups of students and telephone interviews with approximately 150 community agencies where students performed their service.

Geographic Areas

Study sites were in CA, FL, NM, NY, NC, OH, PA, TX, and WI.

Contact Information

Research Organization
Alan Melchior
Center for Human Resources
Heller Graduate School, Brandeis University
Waltham, MA 02254-9110
(617) 736-3775, Fax (617) 736-3773

Abt Associates, Inc.
55 Wheeler Street
Cambridge, MA 02138-1168
(617) 349-2372, Fax (617) 349-2670

Implementing Organization
Lance Potter, Director of Evaluation
Corporation for National Service
9th Floor, 1201 New York Ave., NY
Washington, DC 20525
(202) 606-5000, Ext. 448; Fax (202) 565-2786

New Futures

A Summary of:	**Building New Futures for At-Risk Youth: Findings from a Five-Year, Multi-Site Evaluation**	**The Path of Most Resistance: Reflections on Lessons Learned from New Futures**
	May 1995, Center for the Study of Social Policy (CSSP), (Washington, D.C.) (Initiative and evaluation funded by The Annie E. Casey Foundation.)	August 1995, The Annie E. Casey Foundation (Baltimore, MD)

Overview

In 1987, the Annie E. Casey Foundation sought to encourage a fundamental restructuring of the way communities planned, financed and delivered educational, health and other services to at-risk youth. Through grants averaging $10 million over five years to five mid-sized cities, the Foundation launched New Futures (hereafter NF)—a five-year, privately-funded, demonstration project targeted to communities with high proportions of disadvantaged families. NF was designed to improve community life by changing the prospects of at-risk youth.

POPULATION

The NF initiative was targeted at mid-size cities (populations between 100,000 and 500,000) with high concentrations of poverty, high dropout rates, high teen pregnancy rates and large minority populations (greater than 30 percent enrollment in the public schools).

Evidence of Effectiveness

"New Futures was often described as failing against benchmarks that neither the sites nor the Foundation would have used to judge the effort. Sometimes [it] was judged solely as a school reform initiative, sometimes on the basis of a single city, and sometimes on ambitious child-outcome goals long before any reasonable person would expect significant impact." **Casey Foundation**

The evaluation examined the process of establishing NF and provided some information on achievement, dropout and pregnancy rates and transitions to jobs or college for at-risk youth in the NF communities. Information was derived from an analysis in differences over time in program-collected data on youth and on pre- and post- test scores. There was no comparison group. According to this information:

- the percentage of students scoring in the lowest quartile on a reading achievement test decreased from Year One to Year Five (middle school students: 28.4 to 25.4 percent; high school students: 24.7 to 21.7 percent; 25.4 is the national average for all youth)
- dropout rates decreased from the class of 1992 to the class of 1993 (36.7 to 31.9 percent), while annual dropout

rates increased from 1987 to 1992 (middle school students: 9.3 to 10.6 percent; high school students: 14.0 to 14.4 percent, consistent with national trends)
- the proportion of middle school teens reporting they ever had sex decreased from Year One to Year Five (44 to 39 percent) and the proportion of teens using birth control increased from Year One to Year Five (36 to 61 percent), however the percentage of teens who were pregnant or parenting increased from Year One to Year Five (middle school students: 2 to 6 percent; high school students: 7 to 11 percent)
- the number of high school seniors accepted for college or who had a full-time job lined up by the spring of their senior year did not increase

Key Components

"Some observers suggest that the obstacles faced by a change effort like New Futures, such as reaching a consensus among diverse youth-serving agencies or creating new funding and service agreements, are insurmountable. In our view, such skepticism is unwarranted. Although New Futures was indeed fraught with these and other difficulties . . . Even when these efforts fall short of their greatest ambitions, they can help guide a community's long-term planning for youth development and ultimately produce real change in the lives of young people."   Casey Foundation

The development of new governance bodies at the local level was proposed to oversee a range of NF interventions including:

- after-school programs
- special academic programs for students who were behind their peers
- clustering teams of students and teachers to create a "school-within-a-school" feeling
- teen health centers (either in schools or in the community)
- career education centers

While the programs and interventions offered in the NF cities varied widely, three key structural components were common to all:

- **A Collaborative**. NF cities were required to establish collaborative initiatives that would fundamentally alter the way services are delivered to youth. Each of the target cities developed a collaborative representing the various sectors of the community, including social service agencies and schools. Collaboratives were incorporated as non-profit corporations.
- **Service Integration**. The underlying premise of NF was that the fragmented human service systems had to be integrated and streamlined so that at-risk youth and their families could have their needs—housing, economic, education, mental health, and social service—met at one central location or through one central contact.
- **Case Manager Systems**. About 20 case managers worked with individual youth and their families in each city, helping them gain access to services and acting as mentors for personal and family problems. Case managers were located in middle and high schools where each carried a caseload of 25-35 students. Case managers also assisted the collaboratives by providing direct information about student needs and problems in obtaining necessary services.

Contributing Factors

"These collaboratives were to have the authority to pool funding and programs in order to allow categorical institutions and staff to cross boundaries, blend their work, or, at the very least, coordinate better."   Casey Foundation

Systemic Change

Casey Foundation: "After a lot of incomplete success and some plain failure, we remain absolutely convinced that system change . . . is the only promising, practical, and logical avenue for attempting to bring about reduced hardship and improved outcomes for the millions of poor children and families in this country . . ." The Casey Foundation's recommendations to itself on funding and managing an ambitious, comprehensive systemic reform initiative included expanding the planning period, allow for rethinking and course adjustments, realizing that broad-scale initiatives are not for every community if communities are not ready or willing to take them on, and that broad-scale initiatives should not focus on just one or two outcomes, such as school achievement and high school graduation rates, as proxies for broader measures of child well-being.

Provide Time to Work Together

Casey Foundation: "[B]roadly representative collaborative decision-making bodies will always need significant time to work together" especially to overcome communication gaps created by the historical isolation of participants from one another across racial, class, and cultural lines and due to the regular day-to-day responsibilities of school administrators, mayor's staff, social service personnel, and neighborhood center staff in addition to working on New Futures.

Involve All Stakeholders Early

Casey Foundation: "[A] truly diverse array of local stakeholders must be involved early, and . . . this expectation must be communicated as early and as clearly and consistently as possible."

Make Roles Clear

Casey Foundation: "First and foremost is the importance of clear roles, frank and respectful communications, and well-defined partnerships that are clear about goals, strategies, processes and outcomes."

Support Local Leadership

Casey Foundation: "Because system change ultimately requires the political reassignment of local public dollars and public functions, it absolutely demands local ownership . . . The role of the Foundation and other outside catalysts should be one of a limited partner—not an owner . . . local ownership and leadership cannot be replaced successfully by any amount of Foundation staff work or technical assistance." Sites should be helped to design evaluations and select technical assistance resources.

Social-Capital and Economic-Development Initiatives

Casey Foundation: "[I]n some low-income communities, service-system and institutional-change initiatives, by themselves, cannot transform poor educational, social, and health outcomes for vulnerable children and families. Because of this lesson, the Foundation's change strategies now include social-capital and economic-development initiatives that target entire low-income neighborhoods."

Pregnancy and Parenting Rates

Pregnancy and parenting rates may be rising even in the face of declining rates of sexual activity and increased use of contraceptives because more young women who do become pregnant are choosing to give birth.

Study Methodology

Evaluation was incorporated in the NF initiative from the beginning. As part of their grant contracts, the five target communities agreed to implement school-based information systems tracking data on the school experiences, pregnancy/parenting rates, and post-graduation plans of all public school students. A qualitative evaluation and individual profiles of youth and their families were also conducted.

Geographic Areas

NF was implemented in five cities: Dayton, OH; Lawrence, MA; Little Rock, AR; Pittsburgh, PA; and Savannah, GA. After Year Two Lawrence, MA was replaced by Bridgeport, CT.

Contact Information

Research Organization
Tom Joe, Director
Center for the Study of Social Policy
1250 Eye Street, NW
Washington, DC 20005
(202) 371-1565, Fax (202) 371-1472

Implementing Organization
Miriam Shark, Senior Associate
Annie E. Casey Foundation
701 St. Paul Street
Baltimore, MD 21202
(410) 547-6600, Fax (410) 223-2927

Quantum Opportunities

A Summary of:	**Evaluation of the Quantum Opportunities Program (QOP): Did the Program Work?**	**Quantum Opportunities Program: A Brief on the QOP Pilot Program**
	June 1994, by Andrew Hahn, with Tom Leavitt and Paul Aaron (Evaluation funded by the Ford Foundation.)	September 1995, Both studies conducted by Center for Human Resources, Heller Graduate School, Brandeis University (Waltham, MA)

Overview

The Quantum Opportunities Program (hereafter QOP) was a year round, multi-year, comprehensive service program for disadvantaged youth (all from families receiving food stamps and public assistance) launched in five communities in 1989. Twenty-five disadvantaged students in each community were randomly selected to enter the program beginning in ninth grade and continuing through four years of high school.

QOP was operated by community-based organizations in the five communities served (Opportunities Industrial Centers in four sites; Learning Enterprise in Milwaukee). QOP was focused around education activities (tutoring, homework assistance, computer-assisted instruction) and development activities (life and family skills,

planning for the future including postsecondary education and jobs). Community service was also stressed. Community agencies provided service after school on their premises and, in some cases, in school settings (where the schools provided time and space). Young people were provided with caring adult mentors who stuck with them over four years, no mater what.

> **POPULATION**
>
> QOP students were selected randomly from families receiving public assistance in each of the five project cities. Eighty-six percent were ethnic minorities and only 9 percent lived with both parents.

Evidence of Effectiveness

Brandeis researchers evaluated four QOP sites. Relative to a control group, QOP students:

- graduated from high school more often (63 vs. 42 percent)
- dropped out of school less often (23 vs. 50 percent)
- went on to postsecondary education more often (42 vs. 16 percent)
- attended a 4-year college more often (18 vs. 5 percent)
- attended a 2-year institution more often (19 vs. 9 percent)
- became teen parents less often (24 vs. 38 percent)
- more often: took part in a community project in the six months following QOP (21 vs. 12 percent); were volunteer tutors, counselors or mentors, (28 vs. 8 percent) and gave time to non-profit, charitable, school

or community groups (41 vs. 11 percent, only statistically significant at the Philadelphia site)

The effects of QOP increased over time, as measured at the end of each high school year. After the first year, there were no significant differences seen between the QOP and control groups in the 11 academic and functional skill areas measured. After two years, scores of QOP participants were higher in all 11 areas, and the difference was statistically significant in five areas. By the time QOP students and control sample were leaving high school in 1993, QOP student group scores in all 11 areas were much higher than control student scores, and the differences were statistically significant in every area.

"In contrast to most youth programs in the 'add-on' or 'second-chance' tradition, QOP was designed to encourage long-term involvement through an array of services. Meaningful relationships with adults would be encouraged without fear of having bonds abruptly severed when the programs ended."
                                    Brandeis University

There was wide variation among the program sites. One of the five original sites, Milwaukee, was dropped from the evaluation after problems with implementation and follow-up. Of the remaining four, Philadelphia had the most significant outcomes. For example, the rate of 4-year college attendance was nearly three times higher than the rate in San Antonio, five times higher than Oklahoma City, and eight times higher than Saginaw. Researchers noted that at the Philadelphia site, staff developed and

maintained strong bonds with the QOP students, and were able to forge a cohesive group identity.

The Ford Foundation forward funded QOP at $1.3 million for four years. The evaluation's cost/benefit analysis showed that QOP cost $10,600 per participant over the *four* year period and that $3.68 was gained for every dollar spent if QOP college students earned a degree. Even if only one-third of QOP college students ultimately received degrees, the benefit-cost ratio was $3.04 for every dollar spent.

Key Components

QOP also featured financial incentives for participants and staff. Students received small stipends for participating in program activities (starting at $1 per program hour, and rising to $1.33)

and bonuses for completing activities ($100 for every 100 program hours). They also received a matching amount in an account that could be used only for post-program activities, such as college and training.

Contributing Factors

Caring Adults

Brandeis: "If young people are connected with caring adults for sustained periods of time, year-round, positive results do emerge." Program administrators and staff, as well as teachers and mentors, took an active interest in the welfare of the QOP students, encouraging them, visiting them, following up and doing everything they could to keep them in the program. "Once in QOP, always in QOP" was the unofficial motto, and most program counselors took it to heart.

Sense of Community

The project sites were small, with only 25 students in each. Students were able to bond with each other and with adults in the program, particularly at the Philadelphia site.

Multiple Services Encompassing All Aspects of Youths' Lives

The QOP program was designed to address the many challenges and obstacles that disadvantaged youth face. QOP focused on developing basic skills (academic and functional) for future success, strengthening life and social skills to make better choices and operate more effectively with families

and peers, broadening horizons through cultural trips and other experiences, and taking pride in the community through active service.

Quality Staff

Results from the most effective project site—Philadelphia—show what can be accomplished with a dedicated, quality staff. Brandeis: "The differences, for example, between San Antonio and Philadelphia cannot be attributed to the neighborhood setting, the characteristics of participants, or to the program model. What distinguishes these sites is the degree of buy-in from the host organizations and the commitment of staff at all levels."

Financial Incentives As Part of a Comprehensive Program

While financial incentives were important to some students, and helped with family expenses, it appeared that they were not the decisive factor in QOP participation. When they are part of a comprehensive, well-developed program, financial incentives can be effective in maintaining student interest in and attendance at program events. However, they do not appear to operate effectively in the absence of a strong program featuring much personal contact with staff.

"Simply put, when a quantum opportunity was offered, young people from public assistance backgrounds—African American males, females, whites, Asians, others—took it! They joined the programs and many stayed with the programs or the staff associated with the initiatives, for long periods."
                                    Brandeis University

Financial Resources

The Ford Foundation funded the QOP program upfront, making it possible to plan for and deliver a host of services over an extended period of time. Both staff and students knew the resources were there to carry through on their commitments.

Study Methodology

In 1989, program designers randomly assigned 50 disadvantaged students in each of the five sites to either a program or a control group. Researchers compared the progress of the two groups with periodic questionnaires and basic skills tests.

Geographic Areas

The pilot project took place in five communities: Philadelphia, PA; Saginaw, MI; Oklahoma City, OK; San Antonio, TX; and Milwaukee, WI.

Contact Information

Research Organization

Andrew Hahn
Center for Human Resources
Heller Graduate School, Brandeis University
Waltham, MA 02254-9110
(617) 736-3774, Fax (617) 736-3851

Implementing Organization

C. Benjamin Lattimore
Opportunities Industrialization
    Centers of America, Inc.
1415 Broad Street
Philadelphia, PA 19122
(215) 236-4500, Ext. 251, Fax (215) 236-7480

Serve-America

A Summary of:

National Evaluation of Serve-America: Final Report

October 1995, by Alan Melchior of Center for
Human Resources, Heller Graduate School,
Brandeis University (Waltham, MA) and
by Larry Orr, Abt Associates (Cambridge, MA)

(Evaluation funded by Corporation for National Service.)

Overview

Serve-America (hereafter SA) was established by the
National and Community Service Act of 1990 to
involve school-aged youth in community service
through school and community-based activities. [SA
was succeeded by Learn and Serve America, School
and Community-Based Programs (see pp. 117-119).]
Sponsors hoped that through service-learning young
people would become more aware of their
communities, develop civic responsibility, build self-
esteem and self-confidence and improve their critical
thinking and academic skills.

> **POPULATION**
>
> About 434,000 school-aged youth (K-12) and
> 95,000 nonparticipant volunteers were involved in
> SA in 1993-1994. Roughly equal percentages of
> males and females participated, and the group
> was ethnically diverse (65 percent white and 28
> percent African American or Hispanic). Twenty-
> one percent of the participants were economically
> disadvantaged.

Evidence of Effectiveness

Researchers examined the impact of SA on the
student participants, the institutions involved and
their communities. The statistically significant results
included:

- Relative to a comparison group, high school students in
  SA:
  — had 20 percent fewer absences
  — scored six percent higher in communication skills
  — scored 5.3 percent higher in work orientation
  — scored 5.3 percent higher on a measure of personal
    and social responsibility
  — were 13 percent more likely to give volunteer
    service, and were involved in a greater number of
    volunteer activities
  — gave 300 percent more hours of volunteer service
  — were 20 percent more likely to expect to be involved
    in future service activities
  — were 22 percent more likely to expect to serve as a
    counselor, mentor, or tutor in the future

- Relative to a comparison group, middle school students
  in SA:
  — had 35 percent fewer absences
  — did more homework (e.g., 12 percent of SA students
    spent 11 or more hours per week on homework,
    compared to two percent of comparison group
    students)
  — performed 90 percent more hours of service

In addition, researchers surveyed students and
community agency staff on the quality of the service
experience and the services provided. Eighty-five
percent of high school participants and 66 percent of
middle school students said they had learned a skill
that would be useful in the future, and 96 percent of
high school participants and over 75 percent of
middle school students believed the services they
performed were helpful to the community and to the
individuals served. Host agencies rated the quality of

"The primary goal of Serve-America was to involve young people in community service as a means of building their understanding of their communities, their sense of social responsibility, and their commitment to community involvement—to help build an 'ethic of civic responsibility' among young people."   Abt/Brandeis

Key Components

Contributing Factors

"Given the early point in its development, the Serve-America program has demonstrated a significant number of impacts on program participants, institutions, and the communities in which it operated. The program has been widely implemented and is affecting large numbers of youth across the country."   Abt/Brandeis

the work performed by participants very highly—an average of 9.7 on a 10 point scale. Ninety-four percent said they would sponsor participants again. Finally, the programs produced about $3 in direct benefits for every program dollar spent (not including the value

A key feature of SA is its emphasis on local program design. For this reason, programs were quite diverse and varied in scope (e.g., school-wide, district-wide, single classroom), age and grade level targeted, and program setting (e.g., urban, suburban, rural). About 70 percent of the programs were school-based and 23 percent were run by community-based agencies. The rest were run by adult volunteers or were targeted at fostering school/community partnerships.

Program Impact
SA had a clear, positive impact on middle and high school students, mainly in the areas of civic and social responsibility. Aside from better attendance and (for middle school students) more time spent on homework, program participation had no impact on the students' academic performance, although evaluators note that increased "time on task" is considered essential to learning.

Program Quality
Simply putting students in any type of service program is not likely to have a significant impact on student perceptions of themselves or their community. According to the report, " . . . the quality of the program experience—in terms of degree of responsibility, the presence of challenging tasks, the opportunity to make decisions, time for reflection, etc.—appears to be the clearest program factor in

of the program for the participants themselves, or indirect community benefits).

Each participant costs SA $37 per year. When other federal and matching funds are included, the cost is $90 per participant per year.

Researchers identified three major program strategies within this mix:

- 41 percent were volunteer service programs without a formal, structured curriculum
- 40 percent integrated service-learning into a regular academic course such as English or mathematics
- 13 percent developed an additional service-learning course that featured research, discussion, writing on community issues and service in the community
- 6 percent used a mixture of the strategies above

explaining differences in participant impacts among different programs."

Community Benefits
Although SA's priorities placed the impact on the community as secondary to the impact on the student, researchers noted that community organizations were impressed with the student volunteers and rated their work highly. Even though the volunteers were relatively young, they were able to make significant contributions to the community.

Middle School Students
SA for middle school students was often less intensive (in terms of direct service hours) than the programs for high school students and tended to be more integrated with the academic program. As a result, fewer positive outcomes were seen for middle school students and it was difficult to separate out the specific impact of the program.

Study Methodology

Researchers collected data over an 18 month period (June 1993-December 1994) at thirteen study sites. They administered participant and comparison groups surveys; reviewed school records; and conducted interviews with program staff, students, school administrators, service site representatives, parents and others.

Geographic Areas

SA was implemented across the United States, but Abt/Brandeis based most of the research findings on a representative subset of 13 programs—4 in CO, 3 in MA, 3 in OH, and 3 in SC.

Contact Information

Research Organization
Larry Orr
Abt Associates, Inc.
4800 Montgomery Lane, Suite 600
Bethesda, MD 20814
(301) 913-0520, Fax (301) 652-3635

Alan Melchior
Center for Human Resources
Heller Graduate School, Brandeis University
Waltham, MA 02254-9110
(617) 736-3775, Fax (617) 736-3773

Implementing Organization
Lance Potter, Director of Evaluation
Corporation for National Service
9th Floor, 1201 New York Ave., NW
Washington, DC 20525
(202) 606-5000, Ext. 448, Fax (202) 565-2786

YOU and Youth Fair Chance

A Summary of:

Improving Chances and Opportunities: The Accomplishments and Lessons From a National Community-Focused Youth Services Initiative

February 1997, Academy for Educational Development (New York, NY) (Chapter 6, "Youth Outcomes") by Margaret Terry Orr and Cheri Fancsali

A Positive Force: The First Two Years of Youth Fair Chance

December 1996, Mathematica Policy Research, Inc. (Princeton, NJ) by Walter Corson, Mark Dynarski, Joshua Haimson and Linda Rosenberg

(Evaluations funded by the Employment and Training Administration, U.S. Department of Labor.)

Overview

Youth Opportunities Unlimited (hereafter YOU) and Youth Fair Chance (hereafter YFC) are two related Department of Labor (hereafter DOL)-funded youth demonstration projects designed to improve life opportunities for all youth in certain targeted areas by providing a comprehensive array of youth services in a coordinated and concentrated strategy. The initiatives targeted high-poverty neighborhoods by encouraging links among education, employment, social services, juvenile justice, recreation programs and other community-based activities. They also established new, community-based governance strategies designed to impact the community as a whole, not just a small number of participating youth.

The AED outcome evaluation listed above focused only on the YOU initiative.[1] The YOU demonstration began with funding for seven sites in FY 1990-91; four more sites were added in FY 1992-93, bringing the total sites to 11. Preliminary results from all 11 of the YOU sites formed the basis for a second wave of youth-focused DOL initiatives called Youth Fair Chance (YFC), 17 of which were funded in FY 1995-96. Furthermore, as a result of recommendations from

POPULATION

(Population information is for YOU sites, from the AED evaluation.) YOU [and YFC] were designed to serve all youth in an area designated as high-poverty, thus there are no eligibility requirements other than residence in the target area [and age]. The 11 YOU target-area communities had an average population of 22,338 in 1990. Targeted [YOU] communities had approximately 1,700 to 6,200 youth between the ages of ten and 19—900 to 3,500 of whom were between the ages of 15 and 19. Compared to the U.S. average, YOU communities had higher rates of : poverty (60 vs. 10 percent), children living in poverty (80 vs. 20 percent); public assistance (three to six times higher than the national average, twice as high as for African-American and Latino households nationally); adolescent births (in 1992, ten- to- 24 percent vs. the national average of six-to-ten percent for minority adolescents); juvenile arrests (as much as three times the national average); school dropout; poor school performance; and lower median family incomes ($15,427 vs. $37,579).

the preliminary AED YOU evaluation, DOL provided funding for a national technical assistance (TA) contract team to support the 17 YFC sites.[2] A final Mathematica outcome evaluation will be published at the conclusion of the YFC initiative.

Evidence of Effectiveness for YOU

"The improved youth outcomes were better (sometimes substantially) in most sites than the changes occurring citywide and nationally, suggesting that these gains are not random chance, but real improvements in youth behaviors that resulted from the demonstration."   AED

YOU program impacts were measured by improvements in education, adolescent parenthood and juvenile delinquency. Over the course of the YOU demonstration, many of the 11 target sites showed improvements in reducing the severity of their various youth problems. The particular services used, e.g., intensive efforts to counteract school failure, were strongly correlated with subsequent improvements in each community's youth problems. In sites where services were targeted and intensive, impacts included:

- reduced numbers of live births to adolescent women (in 8 of the 11 sites)
- reduced incidence of juvenile arrests (in three of the original seven sites, arrests of young men decreased by up to 22 percent, in two of the additional four sites, slight reductions were noted)
- reduced dropout rates among high school youth (in six of the 11 sites including five of the original seven sites; five sites had worsening dropout rates, including three of the four add-on sites)

Key Components for YOU

YOU was designed to develop innovative approaches for addressing the needs of youth by creating a range of opportunities for youth to complete their education, prepare for employment and postsecondary education, and obtain assistance with personal problems. To meet these goals, YOU:

- emphasized positive youth development and did not focus solely on youth deficits

- made services accessible to all youth in the target area, not just those who met certain requirements
- did not require participating programs to track narrowly defined outcomes, but encouraged them to focus on and develop (1) broadly defined outcomes; (2) individual youth more holistically, including their general preparedness for productive, independent adult lives; and (3) integrated youth services sustained by a range providers

Evidence of Effectiveness for YFC

Mathematica completed (December 1996) an interim process evaluation of YFC with the outcome evaluation still to be written. Therefore, at this time any comparison with the earlier YOU program outcomes would be premature.

Key Components for YFC

In addition to the key components of the YOU initiative listed above, the 1993 legislation also resulted in several changes to the YOU model which have been key to YFC success so far. They include:

- Expanding the definition of youth from 15-19 (YOU) to 14-30 (YFC), which has enabled young adults in targeted communities to become eligible for services for the first time
- Structuring YFC primarily for school-to-work transition services and training; this was not a part of the original YOU design. The complexity of implementing school-to-work programs makes it too early to determine whether

or not the YFC model can successfully assist in improving service to all youth in-and-out-of-school.
- Providing sustained technical assistance at government cost to all YFC communities; a support that also was not available to YOU sites.

Other components of YFC described in the evaluation are:

- YFC's collaborative structure has been key to its ability to access services that could address a wide range of needs. Giving the community a role in influencing program direction has been an important and useful feature of the YFC model.

- A community-based learning center which provides education, training, employment and support services (particularly case management) for youth and young adults who live in the target areas. The fact that all youth in the community are eligible for services eliminates the potential stigma of participation and makes enrollment easier.

- The YFC sites have invited the YOU sites to join ranks with them in establishing a National Network to obtain both public and private funds to sustain and enlarge their youth-serving programs after federal grant funds are expended.

Contributing Factors

YOU (according to AED)

Targeted and Intensive Services

The availability and intensity of dropout prevention, alternative schools and other educational support services appear to correlate positively with the improvements at the 11 YOU sites. Reductions in adolescent birthrates were consistent with target efforts in three of the four sites that developed extensive services aimed at preventing adolescent pregnancy, supporting adolescent parents through health-related and adolescent parenting services. The fourth YOU site offered the most intensive prevention and parenting services, but the full scope of these services was not underway until Year Four and, therefore, had not been in operation long enough for the AED evaluation report to quantify impact. Sites that had significantly invested in sports and recreational activities and in making a community center available for youth produced reductions in juvenile arrests between 1990 and 1994. Conversely, the worsening of this problem in five sites is highly correlated with the lack of extensive services in four of the five.

Caring Adults and Other Factors

Primary benefits identified by youth served through the various YOU initiatives included: relationships with caring and supportive adults; exposure to educational, job skills training and career opportunities; flexible class schedules; and the motivation and means to turn away from negative influences and behaviors and to channel energies in positive directions.

YFC (according to Mathematica)

Case Management

Mathematica: "Case managers were a vital part of YFC. For many participants, their relationships with the case managers was the main YFC intervention. Many youths came to YFC centers burdened by personal problems or crises and relied heavily on their case manager's support. Case managers assessed clients' needs, developed service plans, identified and accessed appropriate services, and monitored the fit between the clients' needs and the services they were receiving."

A Flexible Approach

Mathematica: "Flexibility to meet the needs of local youths is at the heart of YFC programs." Evaluators indicated that while young people living in high poverty areas have many similar problems, no uniform national program can address the varying needs of local communities. YFC attempts to target programs and services at a community's most critical needs. "Programs may need to find child care for one youth, arrange for an eye exam for another, or obtain bus passes for another. One community may have a troubling gang problem; another may not have a gang problem, but may need to address a lack of employment opportunities."

Community Involvement

Community proved to be essential in the learning center component of YFC. Community members are familiar with the particular problems of youth in the area and serve as advocates for increased funding and participation in the absence of continued federal support.

"[M]any residents of [high-poverty] communities want to create partnerships with governments, businesses, schools, churches, and community-based organizations to create better prospects for their young people. They want to counter the negative forces of the streets that drag young people down with positive forces to help them up. One of these positive forces is the Youth Fair Chance (YFC) program."
                                        Mathematica

A Service Package

A key aspect of YFC is linking youth services and streamlining access to various programs. While the Learning Centers were able to co-locate education and employment services, the YFC areas were too small to truly streamline access by successfully reworking program rules.

Technical Assistance

According to the Mathematica interim evaluation, TA would contribute greatly to the YFC program's effectiveness.

Study Methodology

Youth Opportunities Unlimited (YOU) AED compared outcomes in target-area communities to national and citywide averages and changes over time on three primary indicators of improved youth problems (numbers of live births to adolescent women, annual school dropout rates, and incidence of juvenile arrests). The study also used youth case studies. Because of time lags in the collection and reporting of public information on key youth behaviors, only outcomes were available for the seven original sites (primarily Year Four) and only initial outcomes were available for the four new sites (primarily Year Two).

Youth Fair Chance (YFC) Mathematica conducted a mid-course process evaluation of the 17 YFC sites. The end-of-project outcome evaluation will use comparison communities to determine the changes in institutions and youth served by YFC relative to changes in similar communities not served by YFC.

Geographic Areas

The 11 YOU sites: Atlanta, GA; Baltimore, MD; Boston, MA; Columbus, OH; Denver, CO; Fresno, San Diego and Los Angeles, CA; Philadelphia and Pittsburgh, PA; and Quitman and Tunica Counties, MS.

The 17 YFC sites: Baltimore, MD; The Bronx, NY; Cleveland, OH; Cochise County, AZ; Denver, CO; Edinburg and Fort Worth, TX; Fresno and Los Angeles (2), CA; Hazard, KY; Indianapolis, IN; Memphis, TN; New Haven, CT; Racine,WI; Seattle, WA; and Tahlequah, OK.

No two sites either within or between YOU and YFC cover the same census tract areas, although in several instances they are within the same metropolitan area boundaries.

Contact Information

Research Organizations
[Youth Opportunities Unlimited (YOU)]
Academy for Educational Development
100 Fifth Avenue
New York, NY 10011
(212) 243-1110, Fax (212) 627-0407

Evaluator for AED:
Margaret Terry Orr, Associate Professor
Teachers College, Columbia University
525 W. 120th Street, Box 106
New York, New York 10027
(212) 678-3000/3728, Fax (212) 678-4048

[Youth Fair Chance (YFC)]
Walter Corson, Project Director
Mathematica Policy Research, Inc.
P.O. Box 2393
Princeton, New Jersey 08543-2393
(609) 799-3535, Fax (609) 799-0005

YFC Technical Assistance
Ann S. Meltzer, Project Director
KRA Corporation
1010 Wayne Avenue, Suite 850
Silver Spring, MD 20910
(301) 495-1591, Fax (301) 495-2919

**Funding and Monitoring Organization
(YOU and YFC)**
Beverly Bachemin, Project Officer
Office of Planning and Research
Employment & Training Administration
U.S. Department of Labor, N-5637
200 Constitution Ave., NW
Washington, D.C. 20210
(202) 219-5677, Ext. 153, Fax (202) 219-5455

[1] In 1993, Youth Opportunities Unlimited (YOU) was formally renamed Youth Fair Chance (YFC). To avoid confusing this discussion of YOU and YFC which were separate initiatives, separately funded, with different designs and proposed outcomes and separate evaluations, this summary refers to the initial 11 sites as YOU, while the second wave of 17 grants is referred to as YFC .

[2] For more information on technical assistance for the YOU and YFC initiatives please see: Margaret Terry Orr and Manuel Guitierrez, *Building Communities for New Tomorrows: A Handbook for Youth Fair Chance*, (New York: Academy for Educational Development, 1993), and KRA Corporation with Brandeis University, Abt Associates, and Institute for Educational Leadership, *Youth Fair Chance Technical Assistance Report: Toward a Community-Wide Learning System*, (Silver Spring, MD: KRA Corporation, 1996).

Section III
Increasing Retention and Postsecondary Access

Initiatives which work to retain students in middle schools, high schools and college and on making postsecondary education an option through life skills instruction, career awareness, intensive case management, counseling, financial aid, and referrals to a broad range of services.

Career Beginnings

A Summary of:

Career Beginnings Impact Evaluation: Findings from a Program for Disadvantaged High School Students

October 1990, Manpower Demonstration
Research Corporation (MDRC), (New York, NY)
by George Cave and Janet Quint

(Evaluation funded by The Commonwealth Fund and John D. and Catherine T. MacArthur Foundation.)

Overview

Career Beginnings (hereafter CB), started by Brandeis University's Center for Human Resources in 1986 and now managed by School & Main (a Boston-based organization which works to improve education, career opportunities, and transitions to high school, college, or postsecondary training and careers for youth), "identifies high school students with college potential who, because of average grades and economically and/or educationally disadvantaged family backgrounds, might otherwise be unlikely to attend college." Through a combination of educational and employment services, it helps them enroll in college or find better jobs than they would ordinarily attain. CB integrates four types of support: career exploration and action plan development, educational enrichment, mentoring, and employment.

POPULATION

Participants in the seven diverse Career Beginnings sites were high school juniors who had substantially exceeded minimal academic requirements, ranked in the middle of their class academically, and demonstrated personal motivation and commitment beyond just school activities (for example, by working part-time or participating in school or community activities). By design, at least 50 percent of participants at each site were economically disadvantaged, at least 80 percent were from families where neither parent had a college degree, and at least 45 percent were male.

Evidence of Effectiveness

Between 1987 and 1988, seven sites were part of a control/experimental group Manpower Demonstration Research Corporation (hereafter MDRC) evaluation to study the effects of CB. The following statistically significant data show that compared to the control group, CB participants:

- had a 9.7 percent increase in the rate of college attendance in the post-high school year (53.2 percent vs. 48.5 percent for controls)

- more often started college "on schedule" in the Fall semester [the differential in college attendance was about 6 percentage points in September, October and November, and although it narrowed, persisted at a statistically significant level through May (47.9 vs. 43.4 percent)]

- had similar high retention rates in college, at least during their first year (90 percent in four-year colleges in the first year, 81 percent in two-year colleges in the first year)

- worked less and earned less—an outcome expected due to time spent enrolled in college rather than working

Key Components

Features common to all CB sites include:

- collaboration among a local college or university, public secondary schools and the business community
- jobs during the summer between the student's junior and senior year
- monthly workshops and classes throughout the student's 15 months of involvement, on a range of career development competencies and topics (financial aid, test preparation, job readiness, etc.)
- counseling to help students make educational and career choices
- adult mentors from the business and professional community who serve as role models and meet with youths one-on-one to help them plan for the future

Contributing Factors

Providing a Service "Package"

In areas without extensive community services, CB provides guidance and referrals to scarce services. In communities where young people already have a wide array of services available to them, CB coordinates local partnership efforts and structures existing services into a more efficient and effective delivery system.

A Systematic Approach to Implementation

MDRC: "Sites that were judged to have implemented the program most effectively produced the largest impacts, while sites judged the least successful at implementation had the smallest impacts." Initially, CB allowed for a great deal of flexibility, which led to considerable variation among sites. The study concluded that "program implementation matters" and "suggests the value of a more prescriptive approach." Staffing was one area where MDRC recommended "including minimum requirements to ensure that programs have the personnel necessary to give a new program the attention it needs." Insufficient numbers of staff also proved a problem.

Update

The MDRC study covers the second year of the CB pilot, 1987-1988. Upon conclusion of the pilot, 18 communities continued their CB efforts and 15 new communities initiated the next generation of the model. Information on these 33 CB sites after 1990, and through 1997, has been provided by William Bloomfield of School & Main. Of the more than 15,000 participants (largely B/C grade average, first generation in college, at-risk):

- 95 percent graduated from high school
- 71 percent went on to college compared to 37 percent of students in the same demographic group nationally who went to college

In addition to the factors contributing to CB's results in its early years, current results and staying power over the long term are attributed to:

Effective Implementation

CB worked to find the appropriate balance between broad flexibility and common goals, objectives and design. While sites have great flexibility in how they deliver services to students, years of experience have led to critical programmatic elements which are uniformly high in quality and geared to achieve measurable outcomes. The integration of good student services to achieve the "synergy" that makes them more effective, as well as the local leadership "glue" needed to hold effective community partnerships together, requires an explicit focus on management and operations.

Broad-Based and Productive Partnerships

In order to be truly systemic, CB seeks to engage a broad base of local stakeholders (principals, superintendents, business partners, post-secondary education staff, local government, etc.) and gives them active leadership, management and implementation roles and responsibilities, a key to creating a vigorous public-private partnership. As a result, CB has "less of a programmatic and more of a community development character," which increases support for education reform and improves school-to-career system-building.

Study Methodology

The evaluation examined program impacts in seven of the 24 CB sites operating in 1987-88, the second year of the program. Each site recruited approximately 200 juniors who met the CB eligibility criteria from a number of local high schools. A total of 1,574 students were randomly assigned in equal numbers to experimental and control groups. The report is based on the experiences of 1,233 youths who responded to two follow-up interviews conducted one and two years after the random assignment. The were no systematic differences at the outset between experimental and control group members.

Geographic Areas

The seven CB sites covered in the evaluation were: The Bronx, NY (Bronx Community College); Gary, IN (Indiana University Northwest); Indianapolis, IN (Butler University); Jacksonville, FL (Jacksonville University); Rochester, NY (University of Rochester); Santa Ana, CA (Rancho Santiago Community College); and Youngstown, OH (Youngstown State University).

Contact Information

Research Organization
Robert J. Ivry, Senior Vice President
Manpower Demonstration Research Corporation
Three Park Avenue
New York, New York 10016
(212) 532-3200, Fax (212) 684-0832

Implementing Organization
William M. Bloomfield, Executive Director
School & Main
750 Washington Street, NEMC Box 328
Boston, MA 02011
(617) 636-9151, Fax (617) 636-9158

CollegeBound

140

A Summary of:

A New Field Emerges: College Access Programs

June 1995, Center for Human Resources, Heller Graduate School, Brandeis University (Waltham, MA) by Lawrence Neil Bailis, Andrew Hahn, Paul Aaron, Jennifer Nahas and Tom Leavitt

(Evaluation funded by Baltimore Community and Ford Foundations.)

Overview

College access programs are based on the assumption that the best way to help disadvantaged youth improve their lives is to ensure that they graduate from high school and go on to pursue a four-year degree. "Last-dollar" scholar programs have financial assistance for college as a defining characteristic (scholarships help students pay for any remaining costs of college after financial aid has been received) and also provide a four-year support structure to get students to seriously consider college, apply to college, apply for financial aid and actually attend college. Brandeis researchers studied seven college access programs, including Baltimore's CollegeBound program (hereafter BCB) which is the primary subject of this summary.

"The Baltimore CollegeBound evaluation described in this report provides the best empirical evidence thus far that a college access program can have a demonstrable impact on college attendance for some types of students at some types of high schools."
                                        Brandeis University

POPULATION

The five programs for which the evaluators had population numbers enrolled more than 76,600 high school students (35 percent of the high school students in the districts served by these programs). The programs served 34,378 seniors, 80 percent of the seniors in their districts. The majority of scholarship recipients were female. Race and ethnicity patterns varied: 87 percent of students in BCB and 54 percent in the Columbus program were African American. In Cleveland, African Americans and whites were about evenly split. In Boston, Asians made up the largest group of recipients, followed closely by African Americans. Hispanics also received 15 percent of the scholarship awards in Boston and 13 percent in Broward County, FL.

Evidence of Effectiveness

Brandeis researchers evaluated BCB through a qualitative effort involving interviews and focus groups and a quantitative effort to assemble and analyze data on the college attendance status of more than 400 former Baltimore high school seniors one year after their scheduled graduation from high school and additional data on their high school performances (including their grades and attendance rates). Analysis of data from BCB showed:

- relative to comparable Baltimore students, BCB's last dollar scholars who attended the University of Maryland between 1989 and 1993 had a lower dropout rate (17 vs. 47 percent)

- none of BCB's last dollar scholars who entered Morgan State since 1990 had dropped out of college in the first three years, while between 16 and 31 of every 100 Baltimore City high school graduates attending college had dropped out

- improved odds of attending a four-year college, with specific odds depending on type of high school, student achievement and number of services received through BCB

To measure retention, evaluators looked at second-year scholarship renewal in Baltimore, Boston and Columbus. Of students who had received freshman year scholarships:

- in BCB, 45 percent of students were missing documentation for renewal
- in Boston, a high of 97 percent renewed in 1980 and a low of 85 percent renewed in 1990
- in Columbus, a high of 56 percent renewed in 1988 and a low of 17 percent renewed in 1989

Scholarships could be renewed if students and their counselors knew to submit and submitted the necessary documentation. In many cases scholarships were lost in the second year due to a lack of paperwork, thus affecting retention.

CollegeBound cost just over $600 per participant.

Key Components

BCB supports include:

- for 9th and 10th graders, in-class presentations to motivate students to consider college as an option
- for 11th graders, counseling on an individual basis that helps with: college applications, applying for financial aid, the SAT or other achievement tests and applying to several different colleges

Money to pay for college is provided only to those students whose financial aid package does not cover their college tuition: it pays the difference between the financial aid and the full college tuition.

Contributing Factors

The Money

The Brandeis University evaluators found for the BCB that it is the prospect of the scholarship as much as the scholarship itself that affects student enrollment and retention in post-secondary education. Motivating youth to seriously consider college, learn about different schools, apply for admission and financial aid is greatly facilitated by the promise of funds. Students get discouraged quickly if they believe that they will never get enough financial aid to make all their efforts worthwhile. The actual amount of college tuition paid for by college access programs is limited to tuition not covered through other forms of financial aid. (See I Have a Dream, pp. 186-188).

Intensive, Individualized Counseling

To be successful, last-dollar college access programs have to provide more than just the money. The Brandeis study tracked students into college. In BCB, "[S]tudents who received counseling at neighborhood schools were considerably more likely to attend college and continue through to the end of

their freshman year than those neighborhood school students who did not engage in these CollegeBound activities."

Poor Implementation Hurts

Many scholars in the college access programs evaluated did not submit documents for a second-year scholarship renewal because they did not know they could and/or because the college financial aid staff were not aware of the requirements. This suggests that college access staff in high schools must make a special effort to maintain communication with both scholarship students and college financial aid staff.

Flexibility to Adapt to Community Needs

Brandeis: ". . . ultimately, college access programs need to be tailored to the unique circumstances in each locality, including the current strengths and weaknesses of the local school system, the availability of resources to support college access programming and the unique opportunities that may be present as a result of talented individuals with the commitment necessary to fulfill the vision."

Study Methodology

Brandeis researchers conducted a literature review on college access programs in six sites, assembled summary statistics on basic program measures in the six sites plus BCB. Brandeis researchers also evaluated BCB through a qualitative effort involving interviews and focus groups and a quantitative effort to assemble and analyze data on the college attendance status of more than 400 former Baltimore high school seniors one year after their scheduled graduation from high school and additional data on their high school performances (including their grades and attendance rates).

Geographic Areas

Boston, MA; Broward County and Dade County, FL; Cleveland and Columbus, OH; Philadelphia, PA and Baltimore, MD.

Contact Information

Research Organization
Andrew Hahn
Center for Human Resources
Heller Graduate School
Brandeis University
Waltham, MA 02254-9110
(617) 736-3770, Fax (617) 736-3773

FUTURES 2000

A Summary of:

FUTURES 2000:
Three-Year Highlights

August 1996, Center for Human Resources,
Heller Graduate School, Brandeis University
(Waltham, MA) by Lawrence Neil Bailis and
Stephen Monroe Tomczak

(Evaluation part of FUTURES 2000 grant funded by DeWitt Wallace-Reader's
Digest Fund.)

Overview

FUTURES 2000 (hereafter F2000), managed by School
& Main (a Boston-based organization which works to
improve education, career opportunities, and
transitions to high school, college, or postsecondary
training and careers for youth), promotes systemic
changes in middle school classrooms through
"curriculum enhancers" and "classroom innovation
projects," coupled with a school district/community-
wide systemic approach and intensive staff
development.

POPULATION

More than 5,400 students and 400 teachers and
administrators took part in F2000 during a three-
year demonstration period in three school districts
(a fourth district was added later). Each district
had below average student performance and a
majority of students below the poverty level. *All*
students and teachers in each grade were
involved, beginning with seventh graders in the
first year and adding eighth and sixth graders in
the next two years. School & Main asserts that
taking a systemic approach is the best way "to
contribute to the overall educational improvement
of low-income and at-risk students within a given
school district."

Evidence of Effectiveness

F2000 achieved the following results as reported by
teachers, students, and parents/family members.

Of teachers in the school:

- 29 percent reported improved attendance
- 45 percent reported increased class participation
- 47 percent reported that student interest/enthusiasm for
  learning had increased
- 35 percent (up from 23 percent over a three-year period)
  reported more enthusiasm for teaching
- 53 percent reported that F2000 has contributed to
  ongoing curriculum changes in their schools
- 62 percent (up from 31 percent over a three-year period)
  reported that future career and education options are
  well-covered in their classrooms

Teachers using F2000:

- 90 to 95 percent reported that the amount of learning in
  their classroom increased
- 87 to 91 percent reported that student
  interest/enthusiasm for learning has increased

Students:

- 74 percent (up from 37 percent over a three-year period)
  judged their classes to be interesting. (However, there
  was a clear decline in the proportion of students who felt
  that their teachers seemed to care about them and a
  slight decline in the proportion of students who thought
  their classes were helping them to understand the job
  market and higher education issues.)

- 76 percent of graduating eighth graders were able to identify three or more potential career choices they would like to explore in high school

Parents/family members:

- 35 percent (up from 21 percent over a three-year period) reported that teachers had often discussed career and educational issues with their children
- 40 percent, up from 25 percent, reported that they are meeting more frequently with their children's teachers

One goal of School & Main for F2000 was institutionalization, including: (1) infusion of career-oriented content and instruction into the regular school day (as of 1994-1995, more than 400 middle school teachers in the three school districts had received F2000 training, 92 percent of teachers said they had come into contact with F2000 staff, and 80 percent said they understood the FUTURES concept well); and (2) continuation after the grant period (although the three-year demonstration period ended in 1995, F2000 continues, with permanent coordinators, in all three participating districts).

Key Components

F2000 "aims to help students to make the transition from middle school with confidence, academic competence, and with their career dreams intact."
School & Main

F2000 was "a national middle school career and educational awareness demonstration" which ran from 1992 to 1995 with demonstration grant funding from the DeWitt Wallace-Reader's Digest Fund. It "intended to provide communities with a unique opportunity to test the notion—at full scale—that middle school students with early career and educational awareness can improve their academic performance, reduce school failure, and increase college and career interest." F2000 aimed to make education come alive, promote student initiative and excitement, model the cooperative learning approach, and bring students out into the community and the community into classrooms. Other goals included increasing attendance, classroom participation and parental involvement. The major elements of F2000 included:

- **Curriculum Enhancers.** Teachers in F2000 re-examined their curriculum, created new lesson plans, and built in connections to careers and real world skills. Teachers developed these "curriculum enhancers" on their own or with teams of other teachers, students, and business and community representatives. The enhancers were not intended to change the core curriculum, but to help identify improved techniques and resources. Enhancers range from a one-class-period activity to a full-semester's lesson plan and include setting up an on-going teen court, designing a dream house, working with a graphic artist to produce brochures, and learning about journalism from a local reporter.
- **Classroom Innovation Projects.** "Classroom innovation projects" serve to relate classroom activities to the external world. They are designed and implemented entirely by students. Students apply for grants ranging from $25 to $500 for the projects. Winning proposals vary by community but all include a detailed budget and evidence of academic relevance and career exposure. Teachers act as facilitators or coaches only, and provide encouragement and support. Projects included creating a community history by interviewing citizens who spent time in Japanese internment camps (Grants, New Mexico) and creating a manual on marine biology (Portland, Maine).

Contributing Factors

School/Community Partnership
School & Main staff, school district administrators, teachers, school staff, and community partners worked together to set goals—including institutional change, professional development, and related capacity-building activities—and develop approaches to achieve them. Groups came to a common understanding that F2000 was not a "program" but a new way of looking at "school," and that they all were responsible for infusing career themes into the traditional academic curriculum on a continuing basis.

Standards and Support Systems
"The FUTURES 2000 model calls for assigning district-level day-to-day responsibility for planning

"Teachers develop 'curriculum enhancers' on the spot. The teachers—often working in groups—take a piece of curriculum and then look at what career it relates to, how it corresponds to the future challenges their students will face, and then figure out how to give it some practical application. . . . By enriching the curriculum in this way, teachers make school far more compelling, relevant, and fun for students, while learning new methods themselves."

School & Main

and implementation to coordinators, whose positions are funded by both the school districts and School & Main during the pilot phase when grant funds are available. Three years of implementing FUTURES 2000 has demonstrated that effective coordinators are the key to successfully implementing FUTURES, and that support from high level district and building administrators is the key to the ability of the initiative to penetrate into individual classrooms."

Broad-Based Professional Development

School & Main's capacity-building efforts go beyond working only with those teachers most responsive to new ideas or only to teachers in core subject areas. Rather, they include a wide-range of school staff: building managers, special education teachers,

speech therapists, counselors, librarians, other instructional staff, janitors and secretaries—many of whom were never before asked to participate in any special school project or reform initiative. School & Main provides multi day introductory professional development sessions—where participants are not handed a packaged curriculum, but use their ingenuity to create their own enhancements. It also provides numerous formal training sessions throughout the year and ongoing coaching to individual staff. Focussed professional development, rather than requiring "seat time," is considered by School & Main to be a critical catalyst to classroom engagement.

Study Methodology

The formal evaluation of F2000 used in-person interviews, the results of School & Main monitoring visits and surveys, and quantitative and qualitative data included in semi-annual reports from participating school districts to School & Main. Evaluation goals were to examine the extent to which the overall objectives were being achieved and provide useful feedback for continued refinement of the model and the ways it was being implemented.

Geographic Areas

F2000 was piloted in four diverse school districts: Junction City, KS; Portland, ME; Grants/Cibola County, NM; and Worcester, MA.

Contact Information

Research Organization
Lawrence Neil Bailis
Center for Human Resources
Heller Graduate School
Brandeis University
Waltham, MA 02254-9110
(617) 736-3770, Fax (617) 736-3773

Implementing Organization
William M. Bloomfield
Executive Director
School & Main
750 Washington Street
NEMC Box 328
Boston, MA 02011
(617) 636-9151, Fax (617) 636-9158

Higher Ground

A Summary of:

The National Higher Ground Initiative

June 1996, School & Main (Boston, MA), Center for Human Resources, Heller Graduate School, Brandeis University (Waltham, MA) by Lawrence Neil Bailis, Brad Rose and Dennis Learner

(Evaluation funded by an anonymous funder.)

Overview

Higher Ground (hereafter HG) was launched by School & Main (a Boston-based organization which works to improve education, career opportunities, and transitions to high school, college, or postsecondary training and careers for youth) in 1990 as a national pilot project, building upon School & Main's first national initiative, Career Beginnings (see pp. 137-139). While Career Beginnings was designed to help low-income and under-achieving high school students enroll in college, HG experimented with strategies to help low-income and minority students stay in college and graduate.

POPULATION

Higher Ground reaches more than 800 low-income and minority students at eight colleges and universities in six states. In 1991, 91 percent of participants were non-white and 80 percent were receiving financial aid. Fifty-one percent of participants came from families in which neither parent had attended college and 59 percent had less than a B average in high school. More than a third were former participants in School & Main's Career Beginnings initiative.

Evidence of Effectiveness

Compared to other students at the participating colleges, HG students increased their retention rate by 15 percent. This increase took place during the first two years of college, when most students drop out.

Key Components

"The four-year HG demonstration has shown that it is possible for colleges to develop packages of service and intra-campus partnerships that result in measurable increases in retention of at-risk students. HG students are more likely to stay in school than similar students who are not involved in the initiative."   School & Main

Strategies to help students stay in college and graduate initially included:

- a series of sequenced activities, including specific steps for college freshmen, sophomores, juniors and seniors, grouped under four broad categories

  (1) summer activities, including orientation, academic enrichment, and internships
  (2) academic activities
  (3) career activities, including career exploration, part-time employment, career-path planning, and "community-career connections"
  (4) mentoring

- coalition building "among the different college constituencies that are needed to develop and implement programming to meet the needs of minority and other at-risk undergraduates"
- the development and maintenance of supportive one-on-one relationships between incoming students and caring adults (including older students serving as peer mentors, HG and/or college staff members)

Contributing Factors

"The variety of components increases the odds that students will find someone that they can relate to during their college experience."   School & Main

"A range of services increases the likelihood that each student's most pressing needs will be met when they need to be met."   School & Main

Caring Relationships Between Adults and Youth

School & Main: "It's an explicit goal of HG that all students make meaningful connections with staff and faculty . . . and (move from) positions of isolation and uncertainty into relationships of trust and support. . . . The personal relationships that HG facilitates function as a safety net, a resource on which the students can fall back when the almost inevitable academic, interpersonal, or other crises spring up over the course of an undergraduate education."

A Developmental Approach & Flexibility

School & Main: "It is difficult—if not impossible—to learn lessons from a demonstration unless there is a certain degree of uniformity imposed across sites. But it is unclear how one can implement a uniform model when flexibility and customization represent core elements of the model. The many differences among colleges meant that colleges needed to be granted flexibility in designing specific activities that fit into the broad HG categories and that met high performance standards." For example, HG activities were eventually adapted from a sequenced set of activities for freshmen through seniors to a range of developmental services to address different needs of students, especially those students taking more than four years to complete college.

Providing a Service "Package"

School & Main: "Higher Ground is a set of strategies, not a program." To get around the competing goals of uniformity and flexibility, "One option might be to package the results of demonstrations such as HG as a menu, i.e., list options/suggestions that could be used to promote improved retention, and then have intermediaries such as School & Main assist individual colleges to pick and choose from items on the menu to develop a package of the most effective ways to promote retention at that school."

A Systemic Approach

These sets of strategies help HG to integrate its services into "an overall effort to make the university a better place for all students to live and learn. . . . The key to long run success is building coalitions of constituencies within colleges that can bring about and institutionalize changes in the way that colleges carry out their basic mission."

Broad-Based Professional Development

School & Main employs professional development to "help project directors, coordinators, and other college officials to go beyond the mentality that sees change efforts as discrete, time-limited projects." These individuals need to be willing to change the status quo, rechannel resources in non-traditional directions, review their roles and responsibilities, and possibly change their job descriptions. Success in implementing HG was ascribed to "working with college officials as active facilitators—not promoters—of a model and acting in a way that is respectful of the objectives adopted by college officials and the steps that they have already taken to achieve them."

Study Methodology

Eight colleges and universities in six states initiated projects based on School & Main's HG model. This evaluation focuses on seven HG projects during the second, third and fourth years of the initiative. Five research techniques were used: analysis of internal monitoring reports; analysis of information on all students who participated and the members of a comparison group; interviews with School & Main staff; on-site interviews/focus groups with HG staff, students, institutional and community partners; and a college retention program analysis based on literature review and site visits.

Geographic Areas

The seven HG projects covered in the evaluation are: California State University at Bakersfield, The Hartford Higher Education Consortium (CT), Indiana University Northwest, Rancho Santiago College (CA), The University of Tennessee of Chattanooga, Columbia College (IL), and California State University at Los Angeles.

Contact Information

Research Organization
Lawrence Neil Bailis
Center for Human Resources
Heller Graduate School
Brandeis University
Waltham, MA 02254-9110
(617) 736-3770, Fax (617) 736-3773

Implementing Organization
William M. Bloomfield
Executive Director
School & Main
750 Washington Street
NEMC Box 328
Boston, MA 02011
(617) 636-9151, Fax (617) 636-9158

I Have a Dream

A Summary of:

I Have a Dream in Washington, D.C.

Winter 1991, Public/Private Ventures (P/PV), (Philadelphia, PA) by Catherine Higgins, Kathryn Furano, Catharine Toso and Alvia Y. Branch

(Evaluation funded by John D. and Catherine T. MacArthur Foundation.)

Overview

Among tuition guarantee programs, Eugene Lang's "I Have a Dream" (hereafter IHAD) program is the best known. It started based on the belief that the cost of college tuition is the most severe barrier to educational attainment for disadvantaged youth. However, Lang soon realized that personal support was also needed. Thus, today IHAD combines personal financial commitment with individual support services to encourage at-risk youth to remain in school and attend college.

POPULATION

The study focused on students from three schools—two in Washington, DC and one in Prince George's County, MD. Sixty junior high schoolers constitute a "Dreamer" class. They are selected randomly from among a pool of disadvantaged youth (as determined by school lunch eligibility). Most are minority youth from low-income neighborhoods.

Evidence of Effectiveness

Findings from the initial implementation of IHAD at three junior high schools in the Greater Washington, DC area include:

- IHAD successfully targeted and reached very disadvantaged youth.
- Although one-third of the "Dreamers" in the DC schools reported they had repeated at least one grade, all were still in school at the time of the evaluation.
- Dreamers are impressed by the size of the financial commitment made by the sponsors, and seem to take a more positive attitude toward education when they understand the level of support sponsors are prepared to undertake.
- Dreamers in the evaluation schools strove to maintain high standards of behavior and academic performance, and helped other Dreamers when they perceived that they were falling behind in school or not living up to standards.
- Some support services, such as tutoring, are provided unevenly across programs and within schools.

IHAD costs $1,500 per student per year (in 1991 dollars).

Key Components

"With their substantial financial resources, sponsorship programs like IHAD have the potential to become major players in the social policy arena." 　　　**Public/Private Ventures**

The IHAD model is very informal and the structure is largely dependent on the individual sponsors. However, some IHAD components appear to be consistent across the programs. In all programs, groups of 60 Dreamers are randomly selected as they enter sixth or seventh grade from a pool of eligible disadvantaged youth. An individual or group of sponsors each guarantees college tuition funding. To redeem the tuition guarantee, Dreamers must enroll at a postsecondary institution within two years after graduating from high school. The sponsors also:

- fund support services, such as tutoring, summer programs, and field trips
- take an active, personal interest in the Dreamers (Project coordinators take on significant personal responsibility for the Dreamers, including, for example, "representing the family of a Dreamer at an out-of-state judicial hearing . . . [and] bringing to school a Dreamer thrown out of his house by his mother.")
- hire a project coordinator who takes on a mentoring/case management role with the Dreamers from initial enrollment in junior high until they graduate from high school

Contributing Factors

"IHAD's unique contribution may be exclusive to the private sector: an association with a wealthy and even famous benefactor . . . Publicly funded interventions can probably never deliver this sense of a special connection, or elicit the high expectations that youth—and some school officials—attribute to sponsors."

Public/Private Ventures

Early Intervention
P/PV: " . . . the timing of the IHAD intervention seems to be educationally and developmentally propitious. Because IHAD targets youth at a comparatively early age, it has the potential to address academic and social problems before they jeopardize school enrollment."

Caring Adults
Even though the sponsors are somewhat removed from the students, their support is critical to Dreamers' perceptions that someone cares about them. The fact that an individual—not an agency—has made a serious financial commitment on their behalf makes a large impression on IHAD youth. Project coordinators provide an even closer example that adults care about their welfare. Finally, community mentors add an additional layer of adult support to which the students respond positively.

Role of the Project Coordinator
Personal intervention by the Project Coordinator helps reinforce daily the commitment to education. P/PV: "Project coordinators advocate for Dreamers within a school and leverage additional resources, such as tutoring, trips or concrete assistance during emergencies. They can and do drive youth to school, thus improving attendance, and bring in parents for teacher consultations, thus increasing parental involvement."

High Expectations
Even though Dreamers are rarely dropped from the program, students selected for participation seemed very aware that they were expected to achieve. Interviews with 14 Dreamers revealed their belief that they needed to try hard in school and maintain higher behavioral standards than their peers.

Implementation
Evaluators attributed uneven support services to IHAD's informal structure and the relative autonomy enjoyed by the sponsors. P/PV: "The inconsistency of services is probably inevitable within the present Foundation structure. Sponsors enjoy complete autonomy in their selection of which services to provide and at what frequency."

Study Methodology
The one-year study included interviews with IHAD Foundation staff, sponsors, coordinators, principals and adult mentors; site visits; school records for Dreamers and non-Dreamers in the same grade; and interviews with 14 Dreamers.

Geographic Areas
Three schools: two in Washington, DC and one in Prince George's County, MD.

Contact Information
Research Organization
Maxine Sherman, Communications Manager
Public/Private Ventures
2005 Market Street, Suite 900
Philadelphia, PA 19103
(215) 557-4400, Fax (215) 557-4469

Implementing Organization
Chris White, Chairman
I Have a Dream Foundation
2501 M Street, Suite 515
Washington, D.C. 20037
(202) 775-5800, Fax (202) 775-8549

Maryland's Tomorrow

A Summary of:

Maryland's Tomorrow High School Program Outcome Evaluation: Cohorts I, II, and III

February 1995, Maryland State Department of Education, Division of Planning, Results, and Information Management

(Evaluation conducted and funded by Maryland State Department of Education.)

Maryland's Tomorrow: Lessons Learned

July 1996, Institute for Policy Studies, The Johns Hopkins University, by Marion Pines, Laura Noffke and Ann von Lossberg

(Descriptive report funded by Maryland State Department of Education.)

Overview

The Maryland's Tomorrow high school program (hereafter MT) is a large-scale, state-wide dropout prevention effort operating in 75 high schools across Maryland. Central goals of MT are dropout prevention and improved passing rates on the Maryland Functional Tests (hereafter MFT) for students who are more at-risk than the general school population. MT services begin the summer before 9th grade and continue year-round for five years, including summers and transition services for the year following graduation.

POPULATION

Ninth through 12th grade students in the State of Maryland who are "at-risk of dropping out of high school" (who are one year behind in mathematics or reading and/or were retained in grade at-least one year prior to 9th grade). MT serves approximately 7,500 students annually. In 1992-1993, MT students were 41.6 percent Caucasian, 54.5 percent African American, 3.9 percent Hispanic, American Indian and Asian/Pacific Islander, 57.7 percent male, and 42.3 percent female. (Demographics have remained roughly constant since 1992.)

Evidence of Effectiveness

The 1995 comparison group evaluation of MT by the Maryland State Department of Education examined the largest 27 of the 75 MT programs and found:

- MT students had higher graduation rates and lower dropout rates than comparison group students in more than half of the programs studied.
- In the first three cohorts, there was a 27 percent decline in the number of dropouts. These three cohorts produced 1,393 graduates. According to the comparison groups' performances, if MT services had not been provided, only 1,242 would have graduated.
- Performance on the Maryland Functional Tests improved in each of the three cohorts. The third cohort of MT students outperformed comparison students in 100 percent of the 27 evaluated schools. The percentage of MT

participants passing all the Maryland Functional Tests also increased for each of three cohorts (Cohort I: 78 vs. 62 percent of comparison students; Cohort II: 86 percent; Cohort III: 97 percent). Test scores also went up as MT participants progressed from the 9th to 11th grades.
- 9th and 10th grade GPAs were higher for MT participants than comparison group students in a majority of schools in all three cohorts. In Cohorts I and II, however, 11th and 12th grade GPAs were lower for MT participants than for comparison group students in over half of the schools.

MT programs are held strictly accountable through a Performance Management System that sets expectations for annual improvements in MFT pass rates, dropout rates, attendance, and credits earned. Annual performance outcomes are measured and an annual "report card" is issued for each of 75 programs indicating three years of trend data. MT student performance in each program is compared to all students in the school that hosts that MT program.

Based on annual MT performance data statewide:

* The school dropout rate of MT participants went down each year over a four-year period from a high of 6.52 percent in 1992-93 to 4.70 percent in 1995-96. (This brings the dropout rate for MT's at-risk participants close to the state dropout rate of 4.58 percent for all students).

MT costs approximately $1,200 per student per year of state and Job Training Partnership Act (hereafter JTPA) education set-aside funds. MT is funded primarily by the State of Maryland, with a commitment of close to $10 million a year, augmented by JTPA "8 percent funds" and local contributions. The funds go directly from the Maryland State Department of Education to the 12 Service Delivery Areas/Private Industry Councils which develop partnerships with the local school districts for program implementation.

Key Components

"Dropout intervention works in Maryland. Hundreds of Maryland's Tomorrow graduates who were previously slated for failure have come to lead productive lives beyond their greatest expectations."   Institute for Policy Studies

MT has moved from serving 100 summer students in one city (in 1985) to a year-round, state-wide dropout prevention/intervention strategy serving approximately 7,500 annually, for a period of five years. Students are involved in MT from the summer before entering ninth grade to the year following graduation from high school. MT programs serve from a few to over 300 students annually in each of 75 schools, in all 24 state jurisdictions. Some counties have small programs in every school and others have large programs in only a few of their schools.

Each MT program includes:

* case management, counseling and continued high level support

* intensive academic instruction during the summer and school year
* career guidance and exploration (career counseling and transition services for *five* years)
* summer activities, including subsidized and private employment, community service, college camps, trips, workshops, and creative arts competitions
* personal development
* skills development
* peer support
* adult mentors

Some of the most intensive MT programs operate as "school-within-a-school"-type programs with small MT classes and flexible schedules. Other sites may provide pull-out services, and many sites make use of home visits and intensive parent involvement.

Contributing Factors

"The single most important component of success found across three Maryland's Tomorrow programs (selected for in-depth analysis) was consistent, caring adults. . . . Consistency . . . is critical. At-risk students do not need to become attached to someone, only to have that person slip out of his life. This chaotic pattern too often mirrors the past and can be debilitating to the students."
                         Institute for Policy Studies

Caring Adults

MT serves as a "safe haven" for students through caring staff who take a special interest in each student. This is especially important for 9th graders, who often feel fearful and isolated in a new school. These caring adults hold MT students responsible for their actions through a strict attendance and grade monitoring system to make sure students stay in school and on-track for graduation. Personalized follow-up, sometimes highly individualized and intensive, extends for a year after graduation.

Long-term, Continuous Services

MT works with students for five years, from the summer before 9th grade until a year after high school graduation. Summer services ensure year-round contact.

Sound Implementation

MT program implementors are provided with a combination of flexibility (through self-assessment and technical assistance) and accountability (through the Performance Management System) which allows for quality implementation. The cooperation of faculty, administrators, and parents also contributes to sound implementation.

Study Methodology

The Maryland State Department of Education evaluation compared academic achievement and dropout outcomes for the first three cohorts of students in MT ('88/89, '89/90, '90/91) in 27 schools to a comparable group of students in the same schools. MT students were tracked from ninth grade through high school graduation. Data on comparison groups at each school were gathered from school records. Data on MT participants were provided by the MT MIS system managed by the Institute for Policy Studies at Johns Hopkins and the Maryland Department of Labor, Licensing and Regulations.

Geographic Areas

There are MT programs in 75 high schools across the State of Maryland, with a program in each of the 24 state jurisdictions.

Contact Information

Research/Implementing Organizations
Marion Pines, Senior Fellow
Institute for Policy Studies
The Johns Hopkins University
Wyman Park Building/3400 N. Charles Street
Baltimore, MD 21218-2696
(410) 516-7169, Fax (410) 516-4775

Irene Hechler, Branch Chief
Family Involvement and Dropout Intervention Branch, Maryland State Department of Education
200 W. Baltimore Street
Baltimore, MD 21201
(410) 767-0620, Fax (410) 333-8148

Sponsor-A-Scholar

A Summary of:

An Evaluation of the Impacts of the Sponsor-A-Scholar Program On Student Performance Final Report to The Commonwealth Fund

December 1996, Institute for Research on Higher Education (IRHE), University of Pennsylvania (Philadelphia, PA) by Amy W. Johnson

(Evaluation funded by The Commonwealth Fund.)

Overview

Philadelphia's Sponsor-A-Scholar (hereafter SAS) program is built on the idea that a relationship with a caring adult can spur disadvantaged youth to achieve in high school and continue on to postsecondary education. The program matches at-risk youth with mentors who stay with them five years—from ninth grade through the freshman college year. SAS also provides financial assistance to help students pay for college.

POPULATION

Thirty to forty students from Philadelphia public schools are served by SAS each year. Participants are nominated for the program by school staff in the 8th or 9th grade. They must be economically disadvantaged (based on qualification for the federal school lunch program) and at a middle level of academic achievement (Bs and Cs). They should also exhibit motivation to participate in the program and an interest in going on to college. Staff generally consider whether students would be able to attend college in the absence of SAS.

Evidence of Effectiveness

This 1996 analysis found that, relative to a comparison group, the 180 SAS students in the study:

- were nearly three times more likely to attend college the first year after high school
- had higher Grade Point Averages (GPAs) in 10th grade (an average of 78.8 vs. 77) and in 11th grade (an average of 78.1 vs. 76.2) and similar GPAs in the 12th grade
- participated in more college preparation activities, such as SAT prep courses, investigating financial aid opportunities or visiting a college campus (on average,

SAS students participated in one and a half more activities out of a possible seven)
- who had low GPAs and high rates of absenteeism in the 9th grade did better than the comparison group across a number of outcome measures, as did SAS students with minimal family support
- did not have a greater sense of self-esteem

Evaluators also found that:

- The rate of absenteeism in 9th grade was a strong predictor of future academic performance for both SAS and non-SAS students.

• The more personal contact a student has with his or her mentor, the better he or she does on a number of outcome measures. A mentor's age, race, or location of home did not make a significant difference in student performance.

SAS costs $1,485 per student per year in program operational costs (in 1996 dollars).

Key Components

Philadelphia Futures is the major educational program of the Greater Philadelphia Urban Coalition, a non-profit supported by the city of Philadelphia, corporate donors, The Commonwealth Fund and other private donations. Like Baltimore's CollegeBound and I Have a Dream (pp. 140-142, 149-150), SAS provides financial assistance for college and an intensive support structure to students. SAS services are delivered to students primarily at their schools on a one-to-one or small group basis. At least once a year, SAS participants from one class (i.e. the class of '95) from all high schools meet as a group. SAS features:

• $6,000 (provided by the mentor, mentor's business, a group of businesses or a group of individuals) throughout the period of college attendance to cover student essentials like books and travel money (these funds are not included when colleges calculate financial need; each student receives all $6,000 regardless of the gap between financial aid and tuition costs)
• a mentor relationship lasting five years, with mentors who see students at least monthly and keep in frequent phone contact between visits, monitor their student's

academic progress by reviewing the report card, help with financial aid and college applications, stay in contact with program staff, participate in program activities, develop a long-term relationship based on mutual respect and trust and build communication with the student's family
• a "class coordinator" for each year who monitors the mentor-student relationship, reviews nominations and selects students for the program, holds meetings for students, reviews students' academic progress and plans for summer activities, and works with school personnel to ensure that students are on a college prep track
• an "academic support coordinator" who arranges for and monitors tutoring assignments, SAT prep courses and workshops on study skills, arranges trips to colleges and sets up workshops on financial aid, college selection, college applications and related topics
• summer enrichment possibilities: summer jobs, workshops on study skills and SAT prep, academic programs at a local prep school, classes at a local community college and travel to a foreign country through the Experiment in International Living
• opportunities for students and their mentors to attend local cultural and sports events

"Many young adults are growing up and leaving the education system earlier than their capabilities warrant . . . For some, this is a result of isolation from the caring and consistent adult relationships that research has shown to be a common factor among many who do achieve success, despite disadvantaged circumstances." **IRHE**

Contributing Factors

The Quality of the Mentoring Relationship
IRHE: "Because the quality of the relationship between mentor and student—not simply the fact of a relationship—seems critical to student performance, agencies that run mentoring programs should pay close attention to the selection, training, and monitoring processes that involve mentors. . . ."

Intensive Intervention
Philadelphia Futures has altered its approach over time to support a small, but intensive and long-term mentoring program rather than a less intensive tutoring program that could reach a larger number of students, but which might be less effective. In the

early years, SAS served about 60 students a year. Students came from nearly all of Philadelphia's 34 high schools. SAS has since decided to work with 30 to 40 youth per year, with youth concentrated in just 10-12 high schools.

More than the Mentoring: Program Support Activities
IRHE: "Program supports, in addition to mentoring, seem vital. Mentoring alone cannot provide everything to at-risk high school students, if the goal is to improve their academic performance and preparation for higher education." Program supports, beyond the scholarships and mentoring were the

". . . the encouragement and guidance provided by a mentor or mentor-like figure, their sustained involvement, and proactive assistance with the college selection and application processes are key ingredients—along with financial assistance—in the success of social programs that aim to help individuals rise from poverty and get a college degree." **IRHE**

class coordinator, academic support coordinator, summer enrichment program and attending cultural events.

A Focus on High-Level Academic Skills

IRHE: "The implication of the lack of impact on students' measured self-esteem is that this outcome ought not to be the focus of mentors' efforts. While the lack of impact may be a function of a blunt measurement instrument that is not detecting significant changes in this area, the evidence suggests that programs and mentors alike ought to focus their efforts instead on high-level academic skills."

Rigorous Courses and Outside Activities

GPA gains in 12th grade may have been limited by two factors: 1) SAS students took more difficult courses than non-SAS students (significantly more SAS students were enrolled in two difficult courses— Elementary Functions and Physics); and 2) SAS students tended to participate in outside enrichment activities, which may have negatively affected their grades. (Also, as SAS evolved, students received more support services. Since the first cohort had the least services, their GPA gains were less, thereby bringing down the overall average GPA gains.)

Access to Information

SAS students participated in significantly more college preparation activities because they had access to information that non-SAS students lacked. The evaluator suggests that the city might consider strengthening its counseling and advising services to extend the types of benefits received by SAS participants to more non-participants.

Students with Fewest Resources Are Helped the Most

Those students with low GPAs and high absences in the 9th grade, as well as those with minimal family support, benefited the most from the SAS program. Students attending schools with high dropout rates, or comprehensive high schools, also benefited greatly from SAS. This suggests that the program should target its resources at those most in need for the greatest impact.

Flexible Staff

Program staff continually monitored their work and made changes as necessary.

Study Methodology

This evaluation studied 434 students (180 in the treatment group and the rest in a comparison group) from the Philadelphia public high school classes of 1994, 1995, 1996, and 1997. Researchers analyzed student, mentor and guidance counselor surveys, high school transcripts, school district information on the characteristics of the high schools attended and Philadelphia Futures' program records. Regression analysis was used to determine program impact.

Geographic Areas

SAS services have reached students who have been enrolled in all 34 of Philadelphia's public high schools.

Contact Information

Research Organization
Amy Johnson
Institute for Research on Higher Education
University of Pennsylvania
4200 Pine Street, 5A
Philadelphia, PA 19104-4090
(215) 898-4585, Fax (215) 898-9876

Implementing Organization
Marciene Mattleman, Executive Director
Philadelphia Futures
230 South Broad St., 7th Floor
Philadelphia, PA 19102

Student Support Services

A Summary of:

National Study Of Student Support Services: Third Year Longitudinal Study Results and Program Implementation Study Update

1997, Westat, Inc. (Rockville, MD)
by Bradford Chaney, Lana Muraskin,
Margaret Cahalan and Rebecca Rak

(Evaluation funded by U.S. Department of Education.)

Overview

Student Support Services (hereafter SSS) is designed to help disadvantaged students stay in college and graduate by offering academic counseling and peer tutoring. One of the federal TRIO programs, it is funded under Title IV of the Higher Education Act of 1965 to help students overcome class, social, academic and cultural barriers to higher education. [Four other TRIO programs work with low-income and first-generation students at different stages of the educational pipeline. Talent Search Centers and Educational Opportunity Centers provide less intensive college information services to young people and adults respectively. Upward Bound is designed to increase opportunities for disadvantaged youth to attend college (see pp. 160-162). The Ronald E. McNair Post-baccalaureate Achievement Program prepares low-income and first-generation college students for doctoral programs.]

POPULATION

Currently over 700 SSS projects serve 165,000 disadvantaged college students as measured by income (family incomes under 150 percent of the poverty line) and/or parents' educational status (neither parent has graduated from college), or who are disabled. In 1994, 66 percent of SSS participants at the study sites were female and 54 percent were members of minority groups.

Evidence of Effectiveness

SSS showed a small but positive and statistically significant effect for the following measures. Relative to a matched comparison group, SSS students:

- increased their GPAs by a mean of 0.11 over three years (to 2.44)
- increased credits earned by a mean of 1.25 in the first year, 0.79 in the second year, 0.71 in the third year, and 2.25 in the three years combined

- stayed at the same institution at a 7 percent higher rate in the second year (i.e., from 60 percent to 67 percent), and a 9 percent higher rate in the third year (i.e., from 40 percent to 49 percent). SSS students stayed for a third year at any higher education institution at a 3 percent higher rate (i.e., from 74 percent to 77 percent).

Students who participated the most experienced the greatest improvement. However, nearly 30 percent of

Without intervention from programs such as TRIO, "Students from high-income households enroll, persist, and graduate at much higher rates than students from low-income families . . . Enrollment and graduation rates are also impacted by the educational attainment level of the head of the student's household."   Westat

the students had low levels of participation (five or fewer hours of services in their freshman year).

SSS targeted the most disadvantaged students. Compared to the total undergraduate population, SSS participants were older and more likely to be members of a minority group (54 vs. 25 percent),

have had lower levels of academic achievement before college and have dependent children.

The average cost per participant in 1995 dollars was $867. (The cost per student has decreased over time, from $1,123 in 1970 to $744 in 1995, both measured in 1990 dollars).

Key Components

SSS provides academic counseling and other support services to disadvantaged students to help them stay in college and graduate. The actual package of services offered vary by institution. Services provided include: peer tutoring, counseling/academic advising, special cultural events, workshops and academic courses designed specifically for SSS

students. Some programs are designed as "home-base" programs which assist students in securing needed services from a variety of campus offices. Others are either single-service or full-service programs.

Contributing Factors

Services Addressing Multiple Student Needs

SSS programs that addressed a wide range of students' needs—both academic and non-academic—saw the most positive outcomes, as did programs that integrated SSS with other available services. Researchers found that peer tutoring, cultural events, workshops and academic courses designed specifically for SSS participants were particularly effective.

Sense of Community

Indirect services, such as attendance at cultural events, had a positive effect on student outcomes, reinforcing the idea that a sense of belonging is as important to succeeding in college as more concrete academic assistance. This sense of belonging was reinforced by workshops and courses for SSS students only, which had a positive impact on retention.

Peer Tutoring was the Service that was Most Consistently Effective

Peer tutoring was associated with statistically significant positive effects on retention, credits earned and GPA. Researchers suggest that peer tutoring addressed both academic and non-academic needs. Westat: "It may be that the peer tutors also acted as role models—especially in those cases where past SSS participants served as peer tutors—and thus helped to reinforce that SSS students could succeed and even provide help to other SSS students in the future."

The More Students Participated, the More They Benefited

There was a linear relationship between the level and intensity of student participation in SSS services and positive outcomes. The benefit for individual students depended both on whether they received those services that were most clearly related to positive outcomes, and on the number of hours of those services that they received.

"In essence, the levels of exposure to services, along with the types of services received, are important determinants of positive project effects. Depending on the amount of funding available, the program may need to choose between having a small effect on a large number of students or a larger effect on fewer students."   Westat

Study Methodology

Researchers compared the college retention rate, grades, and credits of program participants against those of a statistically matched comparison group of college students who were not participants. Data sources included a longitudinal survey of these 5,800 participant and comparison students over three years, service records, project performance reports, surveys of project directors and site visits.

Geographic Areas

SSS operates in postsecondary institutions throughout the United States, particularly in larger schools (over 20,000 enrolled). About 34 percent of all freshmen attended institutions with SSS projects.

Contact Information

Research Organization
Bradford Chaney, Senior Analyst
Westat, Inc.
1650 Research Blvd.
Rockville, MD 20850
(301) 251-1500, Fax (301) 294-2040

Funding and Monitoring Organization
David Goodwin
Planning and Evaluation Service
U.S. Department of Education
Office of the Under Secretary
600 Independence Avenue, SW, Room 4131
Washington, D.C. 20202-8240
(202) 401-0263, Fax (202) 401-5943

Upward Bound

A Summary of:

The Short Term Impact of Upward Bound: an Interim Report

February 1997, by David Myers and Allen Schrim

A 1990's View of Upward Bound: Programs Offered, Students Served, and Operational Issues

February 1997, by Mary T. Moore
Both studies by Mathematica Policy Research, Inc.
(Washington, DC Office)

(Both evaluations funded by U.S. Department of Education.)

Overview

Upward Bound (hereafter UB) is a federal initiative designed to increase opportunities for disadvantaged youth to attend college. UB provides academic courses, tutoring, and counseling during the school year and an intensive, college-oriented summer program. One of the federal TRIO programs, it is funded under Title IV of the Higher Education Act of 1965 to help students overcome class, social, academic and cultural barriers to higher education. [Four other TRIO programs work with low-income and first-generation students at different stages of the educational pipeline. Talent Search and Educational Opportunity Centers provide less intensive college information services to young people and adults respectively. Student Support Services (see pp. 157-159) supports retention and graduation of low-income, first-generation and disabled students in college. The Ronald E. McNair Post-baccalaureate Achievement Program prepares low-income and first-generation college students for doctoral programs.]

POPULATION

More than 600 UB projects serve 42,000 disadvantaged students as measured by income (family incomes at under 150 percent of the poverty line) or by parents' educational status (neither parent has graduated from college). Nearly three-fifths of the participants are African American, one-fifth are white, and one-eighth are Latino; 59 percent are female.

Evidence of Effectiveness

The U.S. Department of Education commissioned a six-year experimental study of program impacts, of which this report is the initial phase. This report focuses on the first few years of high school and assesses short-term impacts. It found the following statistically significant impacts:

- During their first year of participation, UB students earned:
  - about one more high school credit (in Carnegie units) than control group members
  - more credits than control group members in science (0.18), mathematics (0.16), English (0.26), foreign languages (0.13) and social studies (0.22)

  - more credits than control group members in vocational education and remedial mathematics courses
- UB students who had *lower* initial educational expectations (did not expect to complete a four-year degree) earned substantially more credits than similar control group members, surpassing the number of credits more than similar control group members that UB students with *higher* initial educational expectations (expected to complete at least a four-year degree) earned:
  - 0.6 vs. 0.1 more credits in mathematics
  - 0.8 vs. 0.1 more credits in English and Social Studies

— 3.1 vs. 0.5 more credits across all academic subjects.
- UB students who were Hispanic gained more than 2 credits, compared to gains of less than 0.5 credits for African American and white students.

UB course content appears to be academically serious:

- the majority of the projects prescribe either a foundation set of courses (reading, writing, Algebra I and II), or mathematics/science courses (precalculus, calculus and science in addition to the foundation courses)
- 50 percent of the projects offer more than 17 academic courses in the summer and 10 during the regular school year
- more than two-thirds of the projects focus on college-prep or enrichment programs

Nevertheless, a large percentage of UB students leave in the first year. About 32 percent of those who

entered the program before the summer of 1993 had left by the end of the 1993-1994 academic year. Projecting from the experience of all students in the study, Mathematica concluded that 37 percent of UB participants will leave within the first year.

Although both the program and control groups experienced a decline in their educational expectations over the course of the study, the decline was much steeper for the control group. Similarly, the educational expectations that control group parents had for their children declined at a sharper rate than did the expectations of UB parents.

The average federal cost per student in 1996 was $3,800 (in 1996 dollars).

Key Components

"Despite increases in overall levels of college attendance, a considerable gap remains between the postsecondary participation and completion rates of disadvantaged students and those of their more advantaged peers. Upward Bound is one of the main components of the federal government's enduring commitment to reduce this gap."
Mathematica

Most students enter UB in their freshman or sophomore years. They participate in weekly activities during the school year and an intensive summer program designed to simulate college. The projects are usually hosted by two- or four-year colleges, although some are hosted by community-based organizations and high schools. UB is focused on academic preparation through enhancing the high

school curriculum (often through offering academic courses in addition to those taken at high school) and emulating a college-level experience. Most projects provide a large range of support services, including tutoring, counseling, planning for financial aid, career planning, cultural awareness programs, and stipends. UB projects tend to focus their efforts on the student—not the school system or the family.

Contributing Factors

"... our initial look does suggest that larger impacts may be possible if Upward Bound projects were better able to hold students in the program, particularly students with low initial expectations ... One approach for retaining these students is to place more direct emphasis on raising expectations of lower-aspiration students so that they see the possibilities available to them if they remain in school for a longer period. Another mechanism for retaining participants may be the provision of employment opportunities during the summer and school year."
Mathematica

Employment Considerations

In some cases, students declined to enter a UB program or left during the first year for reasons related to employment. If there were more opportunities to gain work experience or workplace skills through the program, the retention rate might be higher. An earlier study—"The National Evaluation of UB: Grantee Survey Report," September 1995, Nancy Fasciano and Jon Jacobson (Mathematica), submitted to US Department of Education—showed that the retention rate was higher in programs that offered year-round work experience than in those with less than a full-year work component.

Students with Lower Expectations Left UB in Greater Numbers

Students who were not planning to complete a college degree were more likely to leave the program in the first year.

Race/Ethnicity Is a Factor in Students' Leaving

Asian students were only one-third as likely as African American students to leave UB, and Native American students only half as likely to leave as African American students. These two groups were also more likely to participate initially than African American students.

Early Intervention Improves Participation
UB recruited students in the 8th, 9th, 10th and 11th grades. Researchers found that students targeted by recruitment efforts in the upper grades were less likely to participate in UB when given the opportunity to do so.

Study Methodology
From a representative sample of 67 UB projects, 2,800 eligible applicants were randomly assigned to either UB or a control group. Researchers compared the two groups by analyzing data from a longitudinal student survey, high school transcripts, service records, surveys of the project director and the high schools from which students were recruited, site visits and program records.

Geographic Areas
UB programs are in communities nationwide.

Contact Information
Research Organization
David E. Myers
Mathematica Policy Research, Inc.
(Washington, DC Office)
600 Maryland Ave., SW
Washington, DC 20024
(202) 484-9220, Fax (202) 863-1763

Implementing Organization
David Goodwin
Planning and Evaluation Service
U.S. Department of Education
Office of the Under Secretary
600 Independence Avenue, SW, Room 4131
Washington, D.C. 20202-8240
(202) 401-0263, Fax (202) 401-5943

WAVE in Schools

A Summary of:

WAVE in Schools
Evaluation: Final Report

July 1996, Department of School and Community
Services, Academy for Educational Development
(AED) by Margaret Terry Orr

(Evaluation funded by Charles Stewart Mott Foundation.)

Overview

Work, Achievement, Values and *Education* (hereafter
WAVE) in schools provides a variety of curriculum
components aimed at preventing young people from
dropping out of school. It consists of four year-long
courses designed to be taught sequentially, but
flexible enough to be implemented in whole or in
part by a school, and targeted to different grade
levels/populations.

POPULATION

By the 1993-94 school year, WAVE In Schools had
been implemented in more than 200 locations and
served 25,000 students in 29 states. WAVE In
Schools serves students age 12 through 19 in
7-12th grade. WAVE In Schools is directed at
students identified as being at-risk for dropping
out of high school for academic, behavioral, or
family and personal reasons. Most participants
were in the 9th or 10th grade. More than ½ of the
students who participated in the program were
African American, almost ⅓ were Latino, and
about ⅙ were white, Asian or "Other." There were
roughly equal numbers of males and females in
the program. The majority of participants were
from economically disadvantaged households and
families with poor records of school success.

Evidence of Effectiveness

Based on pre- and post-program surveys of students,
evaluators determined that WAVE In Schools led to
the following statistically significant outcomes in
school performance, and self-perception:

- the average GPA of WAVE In Schools students rose from
  2.0 to 2.1
- here was an improvement in students' feelings that the
  quality of their lives was directly related to their own
  actions, from 17.8 on a 28-point scale measuring "locus
  of control" to 18.6 after program completion
- there was an improvement in feelings of self-esteem
  (from a mean of 27.9 on a 40-point scale to a mean of 29.3)
- there was a rise in student reports that they were

assigned three or fewer hours of homework per night (69
vs. 75 percent)

WAVE In Schools seemed to have no effect on several
student outcomes. The level of course completion
remained about the same, with an average of 78-79
percent of courses completed. There were few
suspensions both before and after implementation of
WAVE In Schools. When evaluators measured other
school-related attitudes, such as satisfaction,
enjoyment in coming to school, and a sense of
belonging in the school community, they found little
or no difference before and after participation in
WAVE In Schools.

Almost all students receiving the WAVE In Schools curriculum were found to have at least one risk factor (for example: eligible to receive free or reduced-price lunch, mother did not complete high school, from a single-parent household or living independently, English was their second language, over-age for grade). Eighty percent had at least two risk factors and 64 percent had 3 or more risk factors. Wondering if student outcomes varied by how many risk factors for dropping out students had and whether the schools were implementing a portion or all of WAVE In Schools, the evaluators broke the WAVE In Schools student population into four groups (where "high-risk" indicates 3 or more risk factors and "low-risk" indicates only one or two risk factors):

- High-risk students at high-implementation schools (40 percent)
- High-risk students at low-implementation schools (18 percent)
- Low-risk students at low-implementation schools (26 percent)
- Low-risk students at high implementation schools (8 percent)

For all groups of WAVE In Schools students, absences actually went up slightly, from 19.1 to 21.2 percent. However, when broken down by subgroup, high implementation sites serving low-risk students showed a marked decrease in student absences from 16.9 to 11 percent.

Key Components

The idea is "to strengthen the personal and school-related problem solving skills of youth, and to help them focus on developing career plans and employment preparation skills."   AED

WAVE In Schools is a school-based intervention program targeted at high school students deemed at-risk of dropping out. WAVE In Schools is intended to provide students with the following:

- interpersonal skills
- communication skills
- employability skills
- study skills
- leadership skills
- life skills

- time and money management skills
- constructive linkages to their community resources and business sectors

WAVE In Schools provides teacher training through their annual Professional Development Institute, a National Youth Professionals' Institute (featuring round table discussions and informal networking), a pre-service orientation training for new teachers, and on-going technical assistance.

Contributing Factors

"A program of this nature can work well for students with only a few of the qualities that put them at-risk of dropping out, and is likely to be beneficial as part of a more comprehensive effort if serving more high-risk youth."   AED

One Component of a Comprehensive Dropout Prevention Program

AED: "The WAVE In Schools program was designed to serve a wide variety of at-risk students: those doing poorly academically; those who have behavioral problems; and those facing personal or family problems that hinder their school completion. Its design is flexible enough for the program to be incorporated into more comprehensive dropout prevention programs and to be made widely available to all high school students, regardless of their risk status, as a means of preparing students for high school or for transitioning to post-high school

employment." While the full WAVE In Schools curriculum decreased school absences of youth with fewer factors putting them at risk of dropping out (with one or two risk factors), those with the greatest number of risk factors for dropping out have a number of interlocking problems that require ongoing, intensive support both in and out of school.

Implementation

WAVE In Schools was implemented differentially across schools where it seemed most useful to administrators and teachers addressing broader educational concerns than just drop-out prevention,

"WAVE is, by design, different things to different people. Implementors can choose a variety of options. The study found some schools using it as dropout prevention, some as an esteem building/life skills program and still others used it to build a school-to-work system. This makes it very difficult to evaluate given a single set of measures."   Larry Brown, President, WAVE, Inc.

including high school transition, career preparation and conflict resolution. For example, some schools used parts of the curriculum as an orientation for 9th graders and others used the entire curriculum as occupational education courses in School-to-Career

initiatives. According to the author, since WAVE often was used to help ensure success for all students rather than to prevent a particular group of students from dropping out, it is not surprising that strong outcomes were not found for dropout prevention.

Study Methodology

The WAVE In Schools evaluation included 760 students, aged 14-19 in grades 9-12, at 18 schools in 14 states. Researchers administered pre- and post-program surveys to five case study WAVE In Schools sites selected for their geographic diversity, population density and type of school. One class of students was surveyed from each of 13 broad sample schools. Surveys and interviews were conducted with teachers and principals from all schools studied.

Geographic Areas

The evaluation included five case study sites—Memphis, TN; Manchester, NJ; San Antonio, TX; Chicago, IL and Zanesville, OH—and thirteen broad sample schools in: Sutter County, CA; Washington, DC; Waukegan, IL; Union Hill and Patterson, NJ; McConnelsville, OH; Knoxville, TN and two each in Memphis, TN; New York, NY and San Antonio, TX. In 1995-96, there were approximately 215 sites with active WAVE, Inc. contracts plus many implementing WAVE concepts without having contracts.

Contact Information

Research Organization
Academy for Educational Development
100 Fifth Avenue
New York, NY 10011
(212) 243-1110, Fax (212) 627-0407

Evaluator for AED:
Margaret Terry Orr, Associate Professor
Teachers College, Columbia University
525 W. 120th Street, Box 106
New York, New York 10027
(212) 678-3000/3728, Fax (212) 678-4048

Implementing Organization
Larry Brown, President
WAVE, Inc.
501 School Street, SW, Suite 600
Washington, D.C. 20024-2005
(800) 274-2005, Fax (202) 488-7595

Implications for Youth Policy and Practice

Robert J. Ivry

Why Some Programs Shine: Elements contributing to successful youth outcomes:

- A focus on "key job-readiness skills"—basic mathematics, problem-solving, reading at higher levels, working effectively in groups, oral and written communication skills, and computer literacy.

- The centrality of paid work and internships as a motivator and venue for learning job readiness skills and gaining access to employers.

- Intensive, hands-on experiential occupational training in areas of labor market growth, supported by active employer involvement.

- Continuity of contact with caring adults—teachers, employers, community members, others.

- Financial incentives and recognition of achievement.

- Post-placement support and leadership development.

Why the Best-Laid Plans Go Awry: Factors associated with less successful programs and outcomes:

- Single-component interventions addressing only one dimension of a young person's developmental needs.

- Short-term or low-intensity interventions.

- Focus narrowly on remediating deficiencies rather than building on strengths.

- Overlook the importance of family, peers, and community in providing the supports and positive reinforcement to sustain forward progress in the program and outside it.

- Legislative and regulatory barriers.

- Insufficient investment in building infrastructure and staff capacity to support youth programs.

Policy Tools for Building Skill Levels and Increasing Opportunities for Young People

- Local leadership should invest in system-building to create a youth opportunities infrastructure, building bridges among the various systems in which youth are involved — education, employment, welfare, community service, recreation and juvenile justice—in order to create a more comprehensive and efficient youth services delivery system.

- State and local leadership should combine existing resources more creatively, including funds from public education (i.e., average daily attendance (ADA) payments), welfare/social service block grants and the juvenile justice system.

- A training fund should be developed to enhance the capacity of organizations serving youth and to provide professional development opportunities for youth workers.

- Governmental legislation and regulations should serve as enablers, maximizing the effectiveness of successful program approaches and supporting efforts to combine them for greater impact.

- The public and private sectors should continue investing in the expansion of the existing knowledge base about how youth acquire skills, access jobs, remain employed and build careers. Promising approaches need to be tested at scale and implemented more broadly. These efforts should include post-placement education and training opportunities leading to better jobs and higher wages.

Robert J. Ivry is Senior Vice President, Manpower Demonstration Research Corporation, New York City.

Bibliography of Evaluations

Academy for Educational Development. *1990. Employment and Educational Experiences of Academy of Finance Graduates: Final Report.* New York, NY: Academy for Educational Development.

Bailis, Lawrence Neil, Andrew Hahn, Paul Aaron, Jennifer Nahas and Tom Leavitt. 1995. *A New Field Emerges: College Access Programs.* Waltham, MA: Brandeis University, Heller Graduate School, Center for Human Resources.

Bailis, Lawrence Neil, Brad Rose and Dennis Learner. 1996. *The National Higher Ground Initiative.* Waltham, MA: Brandeis University, Heller Graduate School, Center for Human Resources.

Bailis, Lawrence Neil and Stephen Monroe Tomczak. 1996. *Futures 2000: Three Year Highlights.* Waltham, MA: Brandeis University, Heller Graduate School, Center for Human Resources.

Bottoms, Gene and Pat Mikos. 1995. *Seven Most Improved High Schools That Work Sites Raise Achievement in Reading, Mathematics, and Science: High Schools That Work, a Report on Improving Student Learning.* Atlanta, GA: Southern Regional Education Board.

Bottoms, Gene, Alice Presson and Mary Johnson. 1992. *Making High Schools Work: Through Integration of Academic and Vocational Education.* Atlanta, GA: Southern Regional Education Board.

Branch, Alvia, Sally Liederman and Thomas J. Smith. 1987. *Youth Conservation and Service Corps: Findings from a National Assessment.* Philadelphia, PA: Public/Private Ventures.

Burghardt, John and Anne Gordon. 1990. *More Jobs and Higher Pay: How an Integrated Program Compares with Traditional Programs.* Princeton, NJ: Mathematica Policy Research.

Burghardt, John, Anu Rangarajan, Anne Gordon and Ellen Kisker. 1992. *Evaluation of the Minority Female Single Parent Demonstration: Volume I Summary Report.* Princeton, NJ: Mathematica Policy Research.

Campbell, Patricia B., et al. 1997. *Working the System: Inner City Students Succeeding in Science, an Evaluation of the Gateway to Higher Education Program.* New York, NY: Education Development Center, Inc.

Cave, George, Hans Bos, Fred Doolittle and Cyril Toussaint. 1993. *JOBSTART: Final Report on a Program for School Dropouts.* New York, NY: Manpower Demonstration Research Corporation.

Cave, George and Janet Quint. 1990. *Career Beginnings Impact Evaluation: Findings from a Program for Disadvantaged High School Students.* New York, NY: Manpower Demonstration Research Corporation.

Center for Human Resources. 1995. *Quantum Opportunities Program: a Brief on the QOP Pilot Program.* Waltham, MA: Brandeis University, Heller Graduate School, Center for Human Resources.

Center for the Study of Social Policy. 1995. *Building New Futures for At-risk Youth: Findings from a Five-year, Multi-site Evaluation.* Washington, DC: Center for the Study of Social Policy.

Chaney, Bradford, Lana Muraskin, Margaret Cahalan and Rebecca Rak. 1997. *National Study of Student Support Services: Third Year Longitudinal Study Results and Program Implementation Study Update.* Rockville, MD: Westat, Inc.

Corson, Walter, Mark Dynarski, Joshua Haimson and Linda Rosenberg. 1996. *A Positive Force: the First Two Years of Youth Fair Chance.* 1996. Princeton, NJ: Mathematica Policy Research.

D'Amico, Ronald, Katherine Dickinson, Deborah Kogan, Maria Remboulis and Hanh Cao Yo (SPR) and Susan P. Curnan, Christopher Kingsley and Jennifer Nahas (Brandeis). 1995. *Evaluation of the Educational Component of the Summer Youth Employment and Training Program: Interim Report.* Menlo Park, CA: Social Policy Research Associates; Waltham, MA: Brandeis University, Heller Graduate School, Center for Human Resources.

Dynarski, Mark and Robert Wood. 1997. *Helping At-risk Youths: Results from the Alternative Schools Demonstration Program.* Princeton, NJ: Mathematica Policy Research.

Felner, Robert D. and Angela M. Adan. 1989. "The School Transitional Environment Program." In *14 Ounces of Prevention: A Casebook for Practitioners,* edited by Richard H. Price, Emory L. Cowen, Raymond P. Lorion, and Julia Ramos-McKay. Washington, DC: American Psychological Association.

Ferguson, Ronald F. (Harvard) and Philip L. Clay (MIT). 1996. *Youthbuild in Development Perspective: A Formative Evaluation of the Youthbuild Demonstration Project.* Boston, MA: Harvard University; Boston, MA: Massachusetts Institute of Technology.

Gray, Maryann Jacobi, Sandra Geschwind, Elizabeth Heneghan Ondaatje, Abby Robyn and Stephen P. Klein (RAND) and Linda J. Sax, Alexander W. Astin and Helen S. Astin (UCLA). 1996. *Evaluation of Learn and Serve America, Higher Education: First Year Report, Volume I.* Santa Monica, CA: RAND, Institute on Education and Training; Los Angeles, CA: University of California.

Grossman, Jean Baldwin and Cynthia L. Sipe. 1992. *Summer Training and Education Program (STEP): Report on Long-term Impacts.* Philadelphia, PA: Public/Private Ventures.

Hahn, Andrew, Paul Aaron and Roblyn Anderson. 1996. *An External Evaluation of Real: Rural Entrepreneurship Through Action Learning.* Waltham, MA: Brandeis University, Heller Graduate School, Center for Human Resources.

Hahn, Andrew, with Tom Leavitt and Paul Aaron. 1994. *Evaluation of the Quantum Opportunities Program (QOP): Did the Program Work?* Waltham, MA: Brandeis University, Heller Graduate School, Center for Human Resources.

Haywood, Becky Jon (RTI) and G. Kasten Tallmadge (AIR). 1995. *Strategies for Keeping Kids in School: Evaluation of Dropout Prevention and Re-entry Projects in Vocational Education, Final Report.* Research Triangle Park, NC: Research Triangle Institute; Palo Alto, CA: American Institutes for Research.

Hershey, Alan. 1988. *The Minority Female Single Parent Demonstration: Program Operations, A Technical Research Report.* New York, NY: Rockefeller Foundation.

Hershey, Alan, Paula Hudis, Marsha Silverberg and Joshua Haimson. 1997. *Partners in Progress: Early Steps In Creating School-to-Work Systems.* Princeton, NJ: Mathematica Policy Research.

Higgins, Catherine, Kathryn Furano, Catharine Toso and Alvia Y. Branch. 1991. *I Have a Dream in Washington, DC.* Philadelphia: Public/Private Ventures.

Hollenbeck, Kevin. 1996. *An Evaluation of the Manufacturing Technology Partnership (MTP) Program.* Kalamazoo, MI: W.E. Upjohn Institute for Employment Research.

Jastrzab, JoAnn, Julie Masker, John Blomquist and Larry Orr. 1996. *Evaluation of National and Community Service Programs Impacts of Service: Final Report on the Evaluation of American Conservation and Youth Service Corps.* Cambridge, MA: Abt Associates, Inc.

Job Corps. 1996. *Job Corps Annual Report: Program Year 1995 (July 1, 1995- June 30, 1996).* Washington, DC: U.S. Department of Labor, Employment and Training Administration, Job Corps.

Jobs for America's Graduates, Inc. 1994. *The Performance Outcomes of JAG School-to-Work Transition Program for the Class of 1994.* Alexandria, VA: Jobs for America's Graduates, Inc.

Jobs for America's Graduates, Inc. 1996. *Jobs for America's Graduates, Inc. 1995-1996 School Year Annual Report.* Alexandria, VA: Jobs for America's Graduates, Inc.

Johnson, Amy W. 1996. *An Evaluation of the Impacts of the Sponsor-a-Scholar Program on Student Performance Final Report to The Commonwealth Fund.* Philadelphia: University of Pennsylvania, Institute for Research on Higher Education.

Kemple, James J. and Joann Leah Rock. 1996. *Career Academies: Early Implementation Lessons from a 10-site Evaluation.* New York, NY: Manpower Demonstration Research Corporation.

Kopp, Hilary, Susan Goldberger and Dionisia Morales. 1994. *The Evolution of a Youth Apprenticeship Model: A Second Year Evaluation of Boston's Protech.* Boston, MA: Jobs for the Future.

Kopp, Hilary and Richard Kazis, with Andrew Churchill. 1995. *Promising Practices: A Study of Ten School-to-Career Programs.* Boston, MA: Jobs for the Future.

LaPoint, Velma, Will Jordan, James M. McPartland and Donna Penn Towns. 1996. *The Talent Development High School: Essential Components.* Baltimore, MD: Johns Hopkins University, Center for Research on the Education of Students Placed at Risk (CRESPAR).

Long, David, Judith M. Gueron, Robert G. Wood, Rebecca Fisher and Veronica Fellerath. 1996. *LEAP: Three-year Impacts of Ohio's Welfare Initiative to Improve School Attendance among Teenage Parents.* New York, NY: Manpower Demonstration Research Corporation.

Mallar, Charles, Stuart Kerachsky, Craig Thornton and David Long. 1982. *Evaluation of the Economic Impact of the Job Corps Program: Third Follow-up Report.* Princeton, NJ: Mathematica Policy Research.

Maryland State Department of Education. 1995. *Maryland's Tomorrow High School Program Outcome Evaluation: Cohorts I, II, and III.* Baltimore, MD: Maryland State Department of Education, Division of Planning, Results, and Information Management.

McPartland, James M., Nettie Legters, Will Jordan and Edward L. McDill. 1996. *The Talent Development High School: Early Evidence of Impact on School Climate, Attendance, and Student Promotion.* Baltimore, MD: Johns Hopkins University, Center for Research on the Education of Students Placed at Risk (CRESPAR).

Melchior, Alan. 1997. *National Evaluation of Learn and Serve America School and Community-Based Programs: Interim Report.* Waltham, MA: Brandeis University, Heller Graduate School, Center for Human Resources; Cambridge, MA: Abt Associates, Inc.

Meyers, David and Allen Schrim. 1997. *The Short Term Impact of Upward Bound: an Interim Report.* Washington, DC: Mathematica Policy Research.

Moore, Mary T. 1997. *A 1990's View of Upward Bound: Programs Offered, Students Served, and Operational Issues.* Washington, DC: Mathematica Policy Research.

Olds, David L. 1989. "The Prenatal/Early Infancy Project." In *14 Ounces of Prevention: A Casebook for Practitioners,* edited by Richard H. Price, Emory L. Cowen, Raymond P. Lorion, and Julia Ramos-McKay. Washington, DC: American Psychological Association.

Olds, David L., Charles R. Henderson, Robert Tatelbaum and Robert Chamberlin. "Improving the Life-Course Development of Socially Disadvantaged Mothers: A Randomized Trial of Nurse Home Visitation." *American Journal of Public Health,* vol. 78 (November 1988).

Orr, Larry (Abt) and Alan Melchior (Waltham, MA: Center for Human Resources, Heller Graduate School, Brandeis University). 1995. *National Evaluation of Serve-America (Subtitle B1).* Cambridge, MA: Abt Associates, Inc.

Orr, Margaret Terry. 1996. *WAVE in Schools Evaluation: Final Report.* New York, NY: Academy for Educational Development, Department of School and Community Services.

Orr, Margaret Terry. 1995. *Wisconsin Youth Apprenticeship Program in Printing: Evaluation 1993-1995,* Findings in Brief and Executive Summary. Boston, MA: Jobs for the Future.

Orr, Margaret Terry and Cheri Fanscali, with Carolyn Springer. 1995. *Academy of Travel and Tourism: 1993-1994 Evaluation Report.* New York, NY: Academy for Educational Development.

Orr, Margaret Terry, Norm Fruchter, Earl Thomas and Lynne White. 1987. *An Evaluation of the Academy of Finance: Impact and Effectiveness.* New York, NY: Academy for Educational Development.

Ofori-Mankat, Juliet and Bo-young Won. 1993. *STRIVE's Results: Evaluating a Small Non-profit Organization in East Harlem.* New York, NY: New York University, Robert F. Wagner Graduate School of Public Service.

Pines, Marion, Laura Noffke and Ann von Lossberg. 1996. *Maryland's Tomorrow: Lessons Learned.* Baltimore, MD: Johns Hopkins University, Institute for Policy Studies.

Polit, Denise F., Janet C. Quint and James A. Riccio. 1988. *The Challenge of Serving Teenage Mothers: Lessons from Project Redirection.* New York, NY: Manpower Demonstration Research Corporation.

Quint, Janet C., Denise F. Polit, Hans Bos and George Cave. 1994. *New Chance: Interim Findings on a Comprehensive Program for Disadvantaged Young Mothers and Their Children.* New York, NY: Manpower Demonstration Research Corporation.

Rossi, Robert J. 1996. *Evaluation of Projects Funded by the School Dropout Demonstration Assistance Program, Final Evaluation Report.* Palo Alto, CA: American Institutes for Research.

Rossman, Shelli B. and Elaine Morley. 1995. *The National Evaluation of Cities-in-Schools.* Washington, DC: Urban Institute.

Silverberg, Marsha, with Jeanette Bergeron, Joshua Haimson and Charles Nagatoshi. 1996. *Facing the Challenge of Change: Experiences and Lessons of the School-to-Work/Youth Apprenticeship Demonstration, Final Report.* Princeton, NJ: Mathematica Policy Research.

Stern, David, Charles Dayton, Il-Woo Paik and Alan Weisberg of the University of California, Berkeley. "Benefits and Costs of Dropout Prevention in a High School Program Combining Academic and Vocational Education: Third-year Results from Replications of the California Peninsula Academies." *Educational Evaluation and Policy Analysis* 11 (4): 405-416 (1989).

Stern, David, Marilyn Raby and Charles Dayton. 1992. "Evaluating the Academies." In *Career Academies: Partnerships for Reconstructing American High Schools.* San Francisco, CA: Jossey-Bass Publishers, 56-71.

Sum, Andrew and Joanna Heliotis. 1993. *Comparisons of the March 1992 Labor Force and Employment Status of JAG Program Participants with Those of Non-enrolled Young High School Graduates in the U.S.* Boston, MA: Northeastern University, Center for Labor Market Studies.

Tierney, Joseph, P. and Jean Baldwin Grossman, with Nancy L. Resch. 1995. *Making a Difference: An Impact Study of Big Brothers Big Sisters.* Philadelphia, PA: Public/Private Ventures.

Walker, Gary and Frances Vilella-Velez. 1992. *Anatomy of a Demonstration: The Summer Training and Education Program (STEP) from Pilot Through Replication and Postprogram Impacts.* Philadelphia, PA: Public/Private Ventures.

Westat, Inc. 1994. *The 1993 Summer Youth Employment and Training Program: Study of the JTPA Title IIB Program During the Summer of 1993, Final Report.* Rockville, MD: Westat, Inc.

Wolf, Wendy C., Sally Leiderman and Richard Voith. 1987. *The California Conservation Corps: An Analysis of Short-term Impacts on Participants.* Philadelphia, PA: Public/Private Ventures.

Zambrowski, Amy, Anne Gordon and Laura Berenson. 1993. *Evaluation of the Minority Female Single Parent Demonstration: Fifth-year Impacts at CET.* Princeton, NJ: Mathematica Policy Research.

American Youth Policy Forum Publications

Some Things DO Make a Difference for Youth: A Compendium of Evaluations of Youth Programs and Practices   **192 pages. $10 prepaid.**

This handy, user-friendly guide summarizes 69 evaluations, studies and reports of youth interventions involving mentoring, employment and training, education and youth development for policymakers and program practitioners as they craft strategies affecting services and support for our nation s youth, particularly disadvantaged young people. What works and why?

Youth Work, Youth Development and the Transition from Schooling to Employment in England: Impressions from a Study Mission   **72 pages. $5 prepaid.**

by Glenda Partee
Observations of an 18-member U.S. delegation of federal and state policy aides, researchers, program practitioners and representatives of non-profit youth-serving national organizations about policies and practices in England to reform the education system, support youth work and the delivery of services, and prepare young people for the workplace.

Preparing Youth for the Information Age: A Federal Role for the 21st Century   **64 pages. $5 prepaid.**

by Patricia W. McNeil
The author argues for high expectations for all students, offers a compelling vision of a high school redesigned for success and outlines strategies to support youth in their learning. Offers insights into developing state and local consensus on results, improving accountability at the state and local level and improving school quality.

Revitalizing High Schools: What the School-to-Career Movement Can Contribute   **38 pages. $5 prepaid.**

by Susan Goldberger and Richard Kazis
The authors argue that school-to-career must be an integral part of any high school reform strategy if it is to achieve scale and be of maximum benefit to young people, employers, and educators.
(Co-published with Jobs for the Future and National Association of Secondary School Principals.)

Opening Career Paths for Youth: What Can Be Done? Who Can Do It?   **16 pages. $2 prepaid.**

by Stephen F. and Mary Agnes Hamilton
The creators of Cornell University's Youth Apprenticeship Demonstration Project share practical lessons in implementing essential components of school-to-career programs. Down-to-earth!

School-to-Work: A Larger Vision   **24 pages. $2 prepaid.**

by Samuel Halperin
Lively discussion of the federal school-to-career legislation, what school-to-work is not, and what it could be when viewed as a systemic, comprehensive, community-wide effort.

Prevention or Pork? A Hard-Headed Look at Youth-Oriented Anti-Crime Programs **48 pages. $5 prepaid.**

by Richard A. Mendel
Surveys what is known about the effectiveness of youth crime prevention programs. What works and what does not? Readable and helpful in preparing for crime prevention funding.

The American School-to-Career Movement: A Background Paper for Policymakers   **28 pages. $5 prepaid.**

by Richard A. Mendel
Interviews and analysis of current efforts to link schooling and the world of employment; essential tasks to be addressed by each of the social partners in the community.

Dollars and Sense: Diverse Perspectives on Block Grants and the Personal Responsibility Act   **80 pages. $5 prepaid.**

Eleven authors offer a wide spectrum of opinion on improving our country's efforts to promote needed support for America's children and families, particularly as affected by welfare reform.
(Co-published with The Finance Project and the Institute for Educational Leadership.)

Contract With America's Youth: Toward a National Youth Development Agenda   **64 pages. $5 prepaid.**

Twenty-five authors ask what must be done to promote healthy youth development, build supportive communities and reform and link youth services.
(Co-published with Center for Youth Development and the National Assembly.)

Building a System to Connect School and Employment   **90 pages. $5 prepaid.**

Wisdom and practical guidance on system-building from educators, practitioners, researchers, policy makers, labor leaders, business organizations and federal and state government officials.
(Co-published with the Council of Chief State School Officers.)

Improving the Transition from School to Work in the United States   **40 pages. $5 prepaid.**

   by Richard Kazis, with a Memorandum on the Youth Transition by Paul Barton
Detailed analysis of the transition of American youth from school to employment. Offers strategies for improving career preparation and recommendations for federal policy.
(Co-published with Jobs for the Future.)

Youth Apprenticeship in America: Guidelines for Building an Effective System   **90 pages. $5 prepaid.**

   Discussion of educational theory and practical application by six experts at the forefront of research *and* practice on the front lines in implementing youth apprenticeship. Outlines specific approaches and lessons learned from experience in the U.S. and abroad.

<u>*Video*</u>: *School-to-Careers: Connecting Youth to the Future*   **16 minutes. $10 prepaid.**

   Presents the education and workforce challenge facing America; exciting examples of school-to-careers efforts across the country; the essential elements of the School-to-Work Opportunities Act; and lively perspectives of educators, employers and students.
(Co-produced with Jobs for the Future.)

Children, Families and Communities: Early Lessons From a New Approach to Social Services   **48 pages. $5 prepaid**.

   by Joan Wynn, Sheila M. Merry, and Patricia G. Berg
Offers both a big-picture analysis of comprehensive, community-based initiatives and a more focused look through the lens of one major initiative in eight Chicago neighborhoods.

Thinking Collaboratively: Questions and Answers to Help Policymakers Improve Children's Services   **32 pages. $3 prepaid.**

   by Charles Bruner
Ten questions and answers range from understanding what problems collaboration can solve, to knowing when it's working. Includes checklists to help policy makers increase the likelihood that local collaboratives will serve as catalysts for reform.

Serving Children and Families Effectively: How the Past Can Chart the Future   **24 pages. $3 prepaid.**

   by Peter B. Edelman and Beryl A. Radin
Over the past 30 years, thinking about how to structure and improve human services has been clouded by myth and rhetoric. The authors explore this inheritance and revisit numerous service and access models of the '60s and '70s to develop a better perspective for the '90s.

✂ - **ORDER FORM (Cut Out or Photocopy)** -

Name _____

Address_____

City _____State _____Zip _____

QUANTITY		PRICE	AMOUNT	QUANTITY		PRICE	AMOUNT
____	Some Things *DO* Make a Difference for Youth	$10.00	____	____	Contract with America's Youth	$ 5.00	____
____	Youth Work, Youth Development in England	$ 5.00	____	____	Building a System to Connect School and Employment	$ 5.00	____
____	Preparing Youth for the Information Age	$ 5.00	____	____	Improving the Transition from School to Work	$ 5.00	____
____	Revitalizing High Schools	$ 5.00	____	____	Youth Apprenticeship in America	$ 5.00	____
____	Opening Career Paths for Youth	$ 2.00	____	____	School-to-Careers Video	$10.00	____
____	School-to-Work: A Larger Vision	$ 2.00	____	____	Children, Families and Communities	$ 5.00	____
____	American School-to-Career Movement	$ 5.00	____	____	Thinking Collaboratively	$ 3.00	____
____	Dollars and Sense	$ 5.00	____	____	Serving Children and Families Effectively	$ 3.00	____
____	Prevention or Pork? Youth-Oriented Anti-Crime Programs	$ 5.00	____				
						TOTAL $	____

PREPAID ORDERS ONLY, PLEASE. Send orders to: **AMERICAN YOUTH POLICY FORUM**
1001 Connecticut Avenue NW, Suite 719, Washington, DC 20036-5541 (Federal ID 13-162-4021).
Call Lucille Easson at (202) 775-9731 for rates on bulk orders.